KNOW IT ALL!
KNOW EVERYTHING!

igloo

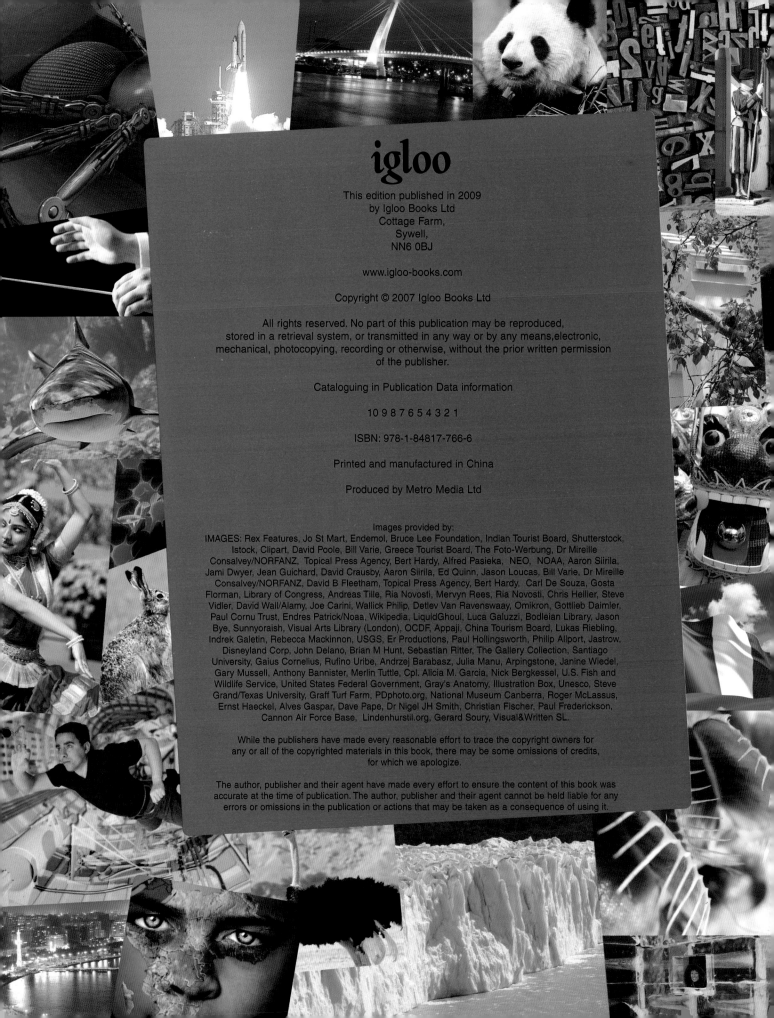

igloo

This edition published in 2009
by Igloo Books Ltd
Cottage Farm,
Sywell,
NN6 0BJ

www.igloo-books.com

Cataloguing in Publication Data information

10 9 8 7 6 5 4 3 2 1

ISBN: 978-1-84817-766-6

Printed and manufactured in China

Produced by Metro Media Ltd

Images provided by:
IMAGES: Rex Features, Jo St Mart, Endemol, Bruce Lee Foundation, Indian Tourist Board, Shutterstock,
Istock, Clipart, David Poole, Bill Varie, Greece Tourist Board, The Foto-Werbung, Dr Mireille
Consalvey/NORFANZ, Topical Press Agency, Bert Hardy, Alfred Pasieka, NEO, NOAA, Aaron Siirila,
Jami Dwyer, Jean Guichard, David Crausby, Aaron Siirila, Ed Quinn, Jason Loucas, Bill Varie, Dr Mireille
Consalvey/NORFANZ, David B Fleetham, Topical Press Agency, Bert Hardy, Carl De Souza, Gosta
Florman, Library of Congress, Andreas Tille, Ria Novosti, Mervyn Rees, Ria Novosti, Chris Hellier, Steve
Vidler, David Wall/Alamy, Joe Carini, Wallick Philip, Detlev Van Ravenswaay, Omikron, Gottlieb Daimler,
Paul Cornu Trust, Endres Patrick/Noaa, Wikipedia, LiquidGhoul, Luca Galuzzi, Bodleian Library, Jason
Bye, Sunnyoraish, Visual Arts Library (London), OCDF, Appaji, China Tourism Board, Lukas Riebling,
Indrek Galetin, Rebecca Mackinnon, USGS, Er Productions, Paul Hollingsworth, Philip Allport, Jastrow,
Disneyland Corp, John Delano, Brian M Hunt, Sebastian Ritter, The Gallery Collection, Santiago
University, Gaius Cornelius, Rufino Uribe, Andrzej Barabasz, Julia Manu, Arpingstone, Janine Wiedel,
Gary Mussell, Anthony Bannister, Merlin Tuttle, Cpl. Alicia M. Garcia, Nick Bergkessel, U.S. Fish and
Wildlife Service, United States Federal Government, Gray's Anatomy, Illustration Box, Unesco, Steve
Grand/Texas University, Graff Turf Farm, PDphoto.org, National Museum Canberra, Roger McLassus,
Ernst Haeckel, Alves Gaspar, Dave Pape, Dr Nigel JH Smith, Christian Fischer, Paul Frederickson,
Cannon Air Force Base, Lindenhurstil.org, Gerard Soury, Visual&Written SL.

Become A Know-It-All

Have you suddenly found yourself with a burning desire to know how many tons of rock fall to earth from outer space in the average year? Maybe it bugs you thinking about who would run the fire service if all the firemen went on strike? Perhaps you lie awake at night wondering what you'd be afraid of if you suffered from bathophobia, heliophobia, gymnophobia or hoplophobia?

Well, now you can have fun finding out the answers to these and all the other burning questions that have made you think, 'Where can I find the answer to that question?' In *Know It All, Know Everything,* that's where. It's the ultimate fun-packed source for, well, knowing it all. Contained within these pages, you'll find countless fascinating facts, trivia and knowledge on a mind-bogglingly variety of subjects, ranging from jobs to frogs to North America to Asia to outer space to mountains to transport to rocks to ancient Egypt to... you get the picture.

So sit back, relax, and get stuck in – either by going from cover to cover, or by dipping in and out whenever you feel like it. However you read this book, you're sure to come away from it with a head packed with fantastic facts – and you will have become a know-it-all too.

HISTORY

ARTS, INFO AND ENTERTAINMENT

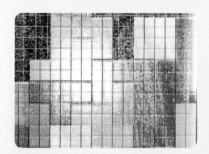

NATURAL WORLD

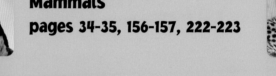

PEOPLE

PLACES

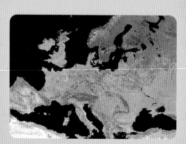

SCIENCE AND TECHNOLOGY

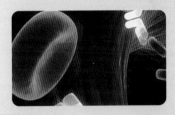

SOLAR SYSTEM/PLANET EARTH

YOUR BODY

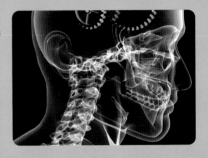

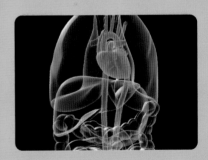

LOST MONEY
The adventure series *Lost*, filmed in Hawaii, is the most expensive ever television series. The two-part pilot episode cost between $10 and $14 million/£5 and £7 million, while subsequent episodes cost between $2.5 and $2.8 million/£1.2 and £1.4 million each. This is roughly double the cost of most hour-long TV series.

THE SECOND COUNTRY TO BROADCAST TV IN COLOR WAS CUBA, IN 1958

YOU WON'T BELIEVE IT BUT...
The TV-based Emmy Awards was named after part of an early television camera – nicknamed 'immy', and called the 'image orthicon tube'.

CHILDREN'S CHOICE
The longest running children's TV program is *Blue Peter*, a magazine show produced by the BBC. The first series was broadcast on October 16th, 1958. It was shown weekly until 1995, when it started being shown three times a week. During that time, it has had over 30 presenters.

TREKKIE FEVER
Many TV series have spun off other TV shows, but *Star Trek* holds the record for spinning off feature films. Ten films were made about its characters between 1979 and 2002. Six further TV series were also made, but only one of these was about the original set of characters.

BIG BROTHER IS WATCHING YOU
The reality series *Big Brother* has been a success worldwide, with more than nineteen countries making their own versions. The original Big Brother house was built by 75 workmen using 12.4mi/20km of cables, 57 mirrors, 33 cameras and 50 microphones.

ROBERT ADLER INVENTED THE WIRELESS TV REMOTE CONTROL– AND CALLED IT THE 'SPACE COMMAND'

GOOD FORTUNE
The game show *Wheel of Fortune* is the most widely syndicated television program in the world. The original idea has been sold to a record number of other countries – which then made their own version. It was first seen in America in 1975 – and by 1991, 54 countries had developed their own versions.

ADDING VARIETY TO VISION
The first US color broadcast – the first in the world – was a variety show called *Premiere* in 1951. But color broadcasts could not be seen on black and white TV sets, so only some viewers saw *Premiere* in its full glory. More than ten years later, TV switched to permanent color broadcasting.

ON A LOOP
In 1951, the comedy series *I Love Lucy* was the first television series to be filmed, rather than performed live. This was a change for actor-comedians, but the audience had at least one distinct advantage – episodes could be shown over and over again, so they didn't have to catch performances first time round.

THE COMEDY SERIES *FRASIER* HAS WON 37 EMMYS – MORE THAN ANY OTHER TV SHOW

TV SHOW HEAVEN
You used to just watch TV shows on TV sets, but thanks to new technology you can watch shows on your computer, cellphone or iPod. In October 2005, Apple launched the first online TV show shop, via its iTunes site. Within a year, the site was selling over a million downloads per week.

YOU WON'T BELIEVE IT BUT...
Lots of old TV series have been re-made as films – including *Starsky and Hutch*, *Miami Vice*, *The Dukes of Hazzard* and *Charlie's Angels*.

SCOOBY DOO – WHERE ARE YOU?
The original version of the hugely popular *Scooby Doo* series was rejected by TV bosses because it was too scary. At this stage, Scooby didn't have a name and was just a sidekick. But to make the program less scary they named him Scooby Doo and made him the comic star. The series sold immediately.

CRIME IN THE SUNSHINE
A 2007 study showed that glossy police series *CSI: Miami* is the world's most popular TV show. The drama about forensic police investigating crimes in sunny Florida appeared in the top ten viewing charts of the most countries worldwide – it even beat the original CSI series, from which it was spun off.

THE FIRST CAR TO BE ADVERTISED ON TELEVISION WAS A CHEVROLET, ON JUNE 9TH, 1946

YOU WON'T BELIEVE IT BUT...
The most Emmy-nominated TV series is the hospital drama *ER* – it has been nominated for a ___ 120 Emmys.

WHERE'S THE ALLIGATOR?
The 1957 US comedy series *Leave It To Beaver* broke a TV taboo when it featured a lavatory in one episode. Up to this date, TV channels had refused to show a lavatory. The groundbreaking episode involved the title character trying to hide his pet alligator in a toilet tank.

THAT'S EGGS-TREMELY UNUSUAL

Most mammals give birth to live offspring but a few lay eggs. They are known as monotremes and all five monotreme species – four varieties of the 'spiny anteater', and the platypus – live in Australia and New Guinea.

IN AUSTRALIAN SLANG, A MALE KANGAROO IS CALLED A 'BOOMER'

THE ODDEST ANIMAL EVER?

The platypus is so strange that many experts thought it was a clever model when dead specimens of the creature were first discovered in the 18th century. Platypuses have small poison spikes on their ankles that they use for defense. They are not deadly to humans but will cause agonizing pain.

MOTHER'S MILK

Wallabies breed so quickly that mother wallabies often have a baby – known as a 'Joey' – in their pouch at the same time as looking after another youngster which is only a matter of weeks older. They do this by producing different kinds of milk from different teats: one for baby and a richer milk for older offspring.

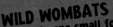

WILD WOMBATS

Wombats are small four-legged Australian marsupials. They are generally peaceful but can be fierce if attacked, and have been known to kill dingoes, or wild dogs. They can run at 25mph/40kph, but only if they need to. Generally though, they like to take it easy.

YOU WON'T BELIEVE IT BUT...

A new-born kangaroo is only the size of a pea.

IT SOUNDS A BIT HARRY POTTER, BUT A BABY MONOTREME IS KNOWN AS A PUGGLE

YOU WON'T BELIEVE IT BUT...

Young wallabies often try to climb back into their mother's pouch even though they're too old – the mother has to fight them off!

MIND THAT MOLE

The marsupial mole is a very strange Australian animal. It is completely blind, covered in pale hair and tunnels underground. Cunningly, the mole's pouch faces backwards, so it doesn't fill with sand and soil when it's burrowing.

ROOS RULE

By far the most common species of marsupial is the kangaroo, a plant-eating creature found mostly in Australia. Unlike most mammals, kangaroos walk on two legs. They are great movers, with fantastically long feet that mean they can bounce along at great speed without getting out of breath.

KOALAS HAVE FINGERPRINTS – IT'S VERY HARD TO TELL THEM APART FROM OURS

WOMBATS CAN TAKE UP TO 14 DAYS TO DIGEST THEIR DINNER

YOU WON'T BELIEVE IT BUT...
Koalas rarely drink water as they get what they need from their favorite food – eucalyptus leaves.

WHAT'S IN YOUR POCKET?
Marsupials are mammals that give birth to very immature young that then crawl into a 'pocket' in their mother's body where they live until old enough to fend for themselves. Marsupials aren't very common – only some 260 species exist – and they are only found in the Americas, Australia, New Guinea and neighboring islands.

RED JUMPER
The Red Kangaroo can grow as tall as a man and is the biggest of the roo family. It gets its name from the color of its fur, which matches the orange-red rock of the outback. Red Kangaroos can jump up to 33ft/10m in one leap.

YOU WON'T BELIEVE IT BUT...
Infant kangaroos are born into their mother's pouch and stay there for several months.

MINI MARSUPIAL
Among the smallest marsupials are the ningauis, animals that look like mice, only with very pointy snouts. They live in Australia's deserts and hunt insects and worms. They are tiny – only about 2.3in/6cm long – the length of an adult's little finger. They were only discovered in 1975.

SMELLY DEVIL
The black-furred Tasmanian Devil is a meat-eating marsupial about the size of a small dog, but far stronger. Mainly a scavenger, it feeds on whatever is available, including dead wallabies and sheep. Like skunks, they emit a horrible stink if they feel threatened.

PLAYING POSSUM
Opossums are marsupials found in the Americas, Australia, New Guinea and neighboring islands. About the size of a house cat, they are omnivorous – eating both plants and meat. They are famous for 'playing possum' – pretending to be dead to deter predators.

MORE LEAVES ANYONE?
The koala is not actually a bear but a marsupial. It's native to Australia and is one of the laziest animals – it sleeps for up to 20 hours every day. In the few hours it is awake, it eats eucalyptus leaves – the only food it likes.

THERE ARE 289 SPECIES OF OCTOPUS

DON'T CLAM UP
The Giant Clam is the largest of the 'bivalve mollusks' – invertebrates that live in shells that open like a mouth. Some people are afraid of them, claiming they can even kill. Nonsense – even if you were trapped in its 'mouth', you could easily get free.

YOU WON'T BELIEVE IT BUT...
Death from the bite of a Funnel Web Spider can be quick. Without an antidote to fight the poison, it may occur within a matter of a few days or even hours.

HEAVYWEIGHT CHAMPION
The heaviest crustacean ever caught weighed a whopping 44lbs 6oz/20.1kg. The huge lobster was a staggering 3ft 6in/1m long. The clawed fiend was caught off the coast of Nova Scotia, Canada, way back in 1977.

OYSTERS AND PEAS
The Pea Crab is the smallest crab in the world, with females measuring around 0.86in/22mm in length. Males are half that size. They live inside the shells of mussels and oysters and are known as 'oyster crabs'.

ROLLING UNDER THE MOSS
The Armadillo Bug is just one of the many names for the wood louse, one of the few crustaceans to live on land, inhabiting dark, damp places – like under mossy stones. As their nickname suggests, they can roll into a ball when threatened.

YOU WON'T BELIEVE IT BUT...
Head lice can be treated with special shampoo – however, as the years have gone by, the lice are getting stronger and there is a worry they will become immune altogether.

FOSSILS OF CRABS EVEN LARGER THAN THE JAPANESE SPIDER CRAB HAVE BEEN FOUND

PET SPIDER
The Japanese Spider Crab is the largest crustacean. It lives in the seas around Japan and has long spindly legs which, when laid flat, can measure over 10ft/3m – the same length as a giraffe's neck. They are peaceful animals and are often kept as pets in large tanks.

HOW BRAINY IS THE OCTOPUS?
Octopuses are quite smart. Scientists have tested them by putting octopuses in a maze – underwater, of course. They found the octopus has a great memory, long and short term.

YOU WON'T BELIEVE IT BUT...
The American Lobster was considered inedible and was only caught to use as fertilizer on crops. Today, it is a popular meal.

A KRAKEN MONSTER
Sailors tell tales of a sea monster called the Kraken which we now know as the Giant Squid. The largest invertebrate in the world, it grows to 45ft/14m. They live so deep in the ocean - 3,000ft/900m beneath the surface - that the first one was only captured on film as recently as 2004.

CUTTLEFISH CAMOUFLAGE
Cuttlefish are closely related to the squid and are best known for the remarkable way their skin constantly changes color. They can use this to camouflage themselves but also, scientists think, to communicate with each other.

YOU WON'T BELIEVE IT BUT...
There are 3,500 types of cockroach, which is thought to be the oldest living species, having been around for 450 million years.

NO STINK INK
Octopuses can squirt ink if they are threatened. This clouds the water, hiding the octopus from its enemy and enabling it to escape. It also dulls the smell of water for predators, making it particularly difficult for hunters like sharks.

KEEL HAUL
Barnacles are crustaceans that attach themselves to the keel, or underside, of ships. Sailors used to be punished by 'keelhauling'. They were tied to a rope, dropped into the sea and pulled across the keel of the ship. The barnacle shells would tear open the sailor's skin.

KRILL ARE BRILL
These tiny crustaceans are among the most important animals in the ocean because many other species depend on them for food, including whale sharks, manta rays, seals, dolphins and the biggest living creature of all – the Blue Whale. They are even eaten by people in Japan.

TIME FOR CONCH?
If you're in the Caribbean and you see 'conch' on the menu, make sure you know what time of year it is. While very tasty in a stew, this huge marine mollusk is an endangered species and so can only be eaten for six months of every year, from November to April, in order to allow it to reproduce.

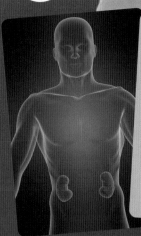

WANT TO SWAP?
The first transplant of an organ from one person to another took place in 1954, when Ronald Herrick donated one of his kidneys to his identical twin brother, Richard. Since then, doctors have learned how to transplant all the major organs. They've even managed to transplant hands.

ON THE BOIL
Louis Pasteur (1822-1895) was a French scientist whose research into germs still keeps us safe today. He discovered that heating a bottle of bad wine killed the germs inside. This is why we still drink pasteurized milk – the germs have been removed using his technique.

PAIN-KILLING DRUGS DON'T ACTUALLY STOP PAIN – THEY JUST STOP YOU FEELING IT

YOU WON'T BELIEVE IT BUT...
Penicillin, a medicine used to help fight bacteria, was discovered by accident in 1928 when Scotsman Alexander Fleming let a sample go moldy.

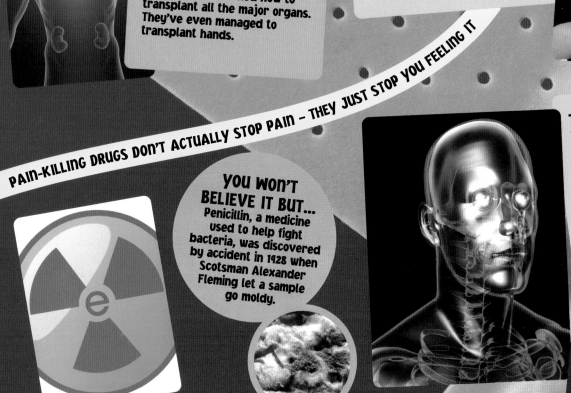

THAT'S HANDY
X-rays were discovered by a German called Wilhelm Roentgen in 1895. During an experiment, he noticed that a beam he was working with made a fluorescent screen glow, even with something in front of it. He went on to take x-ray photos of his wife's hand and the insides of metal objects.

CURIE CURES
Marie Curie worked with her husband, Pierre, investigating the effects of radioactivity during the late 1800s and early 1900s. Her work in using radiation to treat tumors still forms the basis of modern cancer treatments. She was also one of the first women to make her mark on the world of medicine.

LACK OF VITAMINS
You've probably heard of pirates calling each other 'scurvy dogs'. Scurvy was actually a common disease among sailors, caused by a lack of vitamin C during long sea voyages in the 1800s. People with scurvy would become tired and weak, and their gums would swell up and bleed.

A FEVER IS PART OF YOUR BODY'S DEFENSES. GERMS DON'T LIKE HOT TEMPERATURES

HOW DO YOU CURE A COLD?
You don't. Despite being one of the most common diseases, there is no cure. The cold is a virus which causes coughing and blocks up your nose. While some medicines ease these symptoms, the best thing to do is wait for your body's natural defenses to beat it.

YOU WON'T BELIEVE IT BUT...
The Incas carried out successful brain surgery over 1,000 years ago, using basic tools – and this was before anesthetic was developed.

THANKS BE TO HORACE

We should be thankful to American dentist Horace Wells, who is now regarded as one of the fathers of modern anesthetics. Before the development of anesthetic in the 1840s, surgeons started operations on the basis that their patients would pass out from the sheer pain.

GNARLY GNASHERS

Going to the dentist can be scary, but just be thankful you didn't have to go in years gone by. Rotten teeth were often pulled out with no pain relief, and replaced with false ones made from ivory, bone or the teeth of young calves.

WHAT ARE TONSILS?

We've all heard of them, but do you know what tonsils do? They're at the back of your throat, and look like two smallish lumps. Their job is to block bacteria from entering through the mouth. If infected, they can swell up. When that happens, the tonsils have to come out.

PIN CUSHION?

Acupuncture is a Chinese medical tradition which treats illnesses by inserting very thin needles into 'acupuncture points' on the body. A point on your thumb, for example, could help to heal a sore knee. Some martial artists use these points to win fights because they can be very painful.

TOUGH BREAK

If you break a bone, a doctor will use a cast or a splint to keep it straight. This doesn't heal it. Your body starts producing new bone cells almost immediately at the point where the break is. As long as the two ends are kept straight, the bone fixes itself.

THE MAGIC CURE

In the 1830s, ketchup was sold as a medicine called Dr Miles Compound Extract of Tomato. It was reputed to cure almost anything, from baldness to liver disease. This was pretty good going, considering that just fifty years earlier the tomato was generally thought to be poisonous.

YOU WON'T BELIEVE IT BUT...

In 2001, an American doctor shocked the medical world by performing the world's first head transplant on a monkey.

THE BRAIN IS NOT PAIN SENSITIVE, SO YOU COULD POKE A FINGER IN YOUR BRAIN AND NOT FEEL IT

WHY DOES ICE MELT?
Heat (or thermal) energy is related to an object's temperature. One reason we absorb chemical energy from food is so our bodies can turn it into heat, and if you hold an ice cube in your hand, it melts because it is taking that thermal energy from you.

AMERICA CONSUMES ALMOST A QUARTER OF THE WORLD'S ENERGY

YOU WON'T BELIEVE IT BUT...
The oil we rely on for our energy and power was formed from the rotting bodies of fish and plants millions of years ago, even before the dinosaurs were around.

WHAT MAKES A MONKEY SWING?
Known as kinetic energy, this is the energy that builds up in a moving object. If you put a monkey on a swing and gave it a push, you'd transfer energy from your muscles into the monkey's motion energy.

DON'T GO CHANGING
During the transfer of heat energy, objects can change their form. You've got examples of this all around you – steam, water and ice. The molecules in steam are very hot and move around, making it a gas. But ice has molecules that barely move at all, making it solid.

FUTILE ATTRACTION
Magnetism is associated with the motion of electric charges. One end of a magnet is called a north pole and the other end a south pole. The force between the different poles attracts, whereas the force between like poles repels. That's why magnets sometimes stick to each other, and sometimes jump apart.

CHOCOLATE FUEL
Chemical energy is what holds the atoms in a molecule together. When a molecule is broken down, this energy is released and transferred into another form. So when you eat a chocolate bar, your body breaks it down and absorbs the energy inside.

80 PERCENT OF CARS IN BRAZIL RUN ON ETHANOL – A FUEL MADE FROM CORN

YOU WON'T BELIEVE IT BUT...
Benjamin Franklin, one of America's founding fathers, first harnessed electricity in the 1750s. He used a kite with a metal key attached to 'catch' a bolt of lightning.

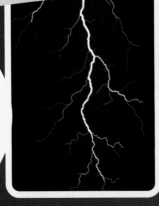

THE FULL FORCE
Energy is the force that makes everything happen, and it is present in every single atom in the entire universe. It's in your shoes, your chair and your food. Even this book is full of energy. Without it, nothing would ever move or grow.

BUBBLE TROUBLE
All energy transfer happens at a molecular level. When you boil a kettle, the thermal energy from the kettle heats up the water molecules, making them move about more rapidly. This is why boiling water bubbles and sloshes about all by itself.

MAKE IT ZAPPY
Electrical energy can move from one object to another. Try rubbing a balloon against your hair. See how it stands on end? Static electricity has moved from the balloon to you. Then rub the balloon on your sweater and place it on a wall. It will stick because the electricity has moved from you to the balloon.

YOU WON'T BELIEVE IT BUT...
On average, we use around five percent of the energy we get from our food. The rest is wasted as heat energy from our sweating bodies.

WE USE 80 MILLION BARRELS OF OIL EVERY DAY TO POWER CARS, HEATING, LIGHTS AND INDUSTRY

YOU WON'T BELIEVE IT BUT...
Some farmers collect the methane gas produced by animal dung as a natural fuel to power their homes and farms.

DIETING FOR SCIENCE
Energy in food is measured in calories – those things that people avoid when dieting. Calories are simply the amount of energy contained within the molecules of an object, such as a peanut. We extract them by digesting the peanut, but the same calories would be released if you set it on fire.

IN MOTION
Kinetic energy is the energy of motion. For every action there is an opposite and equal reaction. It is like stepping off a skateboard – you go forward and it will roll backwards.

SINCE 2002, HOMES IN ICELAND HAVE USED HEAT ENERGY FROM DEEP UNDERGROUND AS A NATURAL ALTERNATIVE TO ELECTRICITY

WANT TO SWAP?
The amount of energy in the universe can never increase or decrease, it can only change form. Kinetic, heat, and electrical are all forms of energy. Right now, your body is busy using several of these different energies just by reading this book.

POWER INTO LIGHT
Power is how we describe the speed at which energy is changed from one form to another. For example, a 100-watt light bulb can convert 100 watts of electrical energy into heat energy every second. This heats up the filament inside the bulb, which creates the light.

In 1982, LUCY BARMBY OF CALIFORNIA PATENTED A DIET MASK, WHICH FEATURED A GRILLE THAT STOPS THE WEARER FROM EATING

A GRAVE MISTAKE

In 1868, Franz Vester of New Jersey patented a mechanism to prevent people being buried alive. A string ran from the inside of the coffin, through the soil, and up to a bell on the grave. In the event that the inhabitant had been buried alive, they could ring the bell.

YOU WON'T BELIEVE IT BUT...

The first electrical tattooing machine was invented in 1891 by New Yorker Samuel O'Reilly.

SMELLS SO GOOD

Nobody knows the name of the person who invented the world's first underarm deodorant, but we know that they trademarked their cream in Philadelphia in the USA in 1888, and sold it under the brand name 'Mum'.

VICTORIA CALLING

Next time you turn on the radio you should thank Gugliemo Marconi, who invented the world's first wireless telegraph system in 1896. One of the first people to test his wireless telegraph system was Queen Victoria, who used it to call the Prince of Wales on his yacht.

A MATCH MADE IN... ENGLAND?

In 1827, an English chemist called John Walker found that a stick coated in chemicals could be set on fire if struck on a rough surface. Called 'congreves' these were extremely flammable, and when Swedish inventor Gustaf Erik Pasch created 'safety matches' in 1844, he gave them the name which they are known by to this day.

In 1994 EDWARD DOUGHNEY OF THE UK PATENTED A TINY RUBBER LADDER TO HELP SPIDERS OUT OF BATHS

THE BEAR NECESSITIES

In 1902, US President Teddy Roosevelt hit the headlines for refusing to shoot a bear cub while hunting. So Morris Michtom, a New York toymaker, made a stuffed one as a joke. He asked Roosevelt if he could name it after him, and the teddy bear was born.

YOU WON'T BELIEVE IT BUT...

The first mechanical lawn mower was patented in 1830 by an Englishman, Edwin Beard Budding.

NEAT AND TIDY
Before Johan Vaaler, people had to hold papers together with waxed ribbons or sharp pins. In 1899, Vaaler came up with the idea of bending a piece of wire in such a way that it could grip both sides of a sheaf of paper. We know it as the paperclip.

LET'S STICK TOGETHER
The world-famous LEGO bricks were invented in Denmark in 1949 by Ole Kirk Christiansen. Originally called Automatic Binding Bricks, they were renamed in 1954 using the name of Christiansen's toy company. The word LEGO is made up of the Danish words 'LEg GOdt', which mean 'play well'.

IN 1998, A NAPPY WAS PATENTED FOR PET BIRDS THAT ARE ALLOWED TO FLY FREELY ROUND THE HOUSE

DONE WITH THE DISHES
Josephine Cochrane invented the dishwasher in 1886. Cochrane was a wealthy lady from Shelbyville, Illinois, USA, who loved to throw dinner parties, using her best china. However, she found that her servants kept chipping the china while doing the washing up, so she did it herself. Because Cochrane hated the task so much, she invented the dishwasher in her garden shed to do it for her.

TRUTH OR DARE?
John Larson invented the lie-detector back in the 1920s. Also known as a polygraph, lie detectors work by recording changes in things like heart rate and perspiration. Many psychologists now say they are inaccurate, and some courts refuse to admit lie detector results as evidence.

YOU WON'T BELIEVE IT BUT...
John Pemberton invented Coca-Cola in 1885, but his business associate Frank Mason Robertson thought of the name. He came up with Coca-Cola because the original recipe contained Coca plant leaves and Kola nuts, but thought it looked and sounded better if Kola was spelt with a 'C'.

HOLLYWOOD ACTRESS HEDY LAMARR (1914-2000) INVENTED A TORPEDO GUIDANCE SYSTEM WITH HER FRIEND GEORGE ANTHEIL

CHOOSE YOUR CHEWS
While trying to turn the sap of the Mexican sapodilla tree into rubber for boots or tires, Thomas Adams began chewing on a spare piece of the gummy material. He found it didn't taste all that bad, and in 1869, he became the owner of the world's first chewing gum factory.

SAY CHEESE
On a summer's day in 1827, Joseph Niépce made history by becoming the first person to take a photograph. The image was captured on material that hardened in light and was permanent. It was no good for taking quick snaps though – the exposure time was over eight hours.

YOU WON'T BELIEVE IT BUT...
The sandwich is named after the Earl of Sandwich (1718-1792) who was fond of eating slices of beef between pieces of toast.

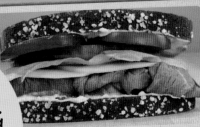

LOTS OF LEMURS
Lemurs only live on the African island of Madagascar. There are many types – the smallest is the pygmy mouse lemur, which only weighs 1oz/30g – less than a small candy bar.

KOKO, A GORILLA IN CALIFORNIA, KNOWS 1,000 WORDS IN SIGN LANGUAGE TAUGHT BY HER TRAINER

SWINGING KING
Orangutan King Louie calls himself the 'king of the swingers' in the film *The Jungle Book*. But in reality it's the gibbon that's the master. Using just its arms, it can swing on branches through the forest at speeds of up to 35mph/56kph, covering up to 50ft/15m with each swing.

YOU WON'T BELIEVE IT BUT...
The biggest primate ever was the prehistoric gigantopithecus. It lived from five million until 100,000 years ago and was 10ft/3m tall.

MONKEYS IN SPACE
It seems incredible and cruel to us today, but we put monkeys into space before humans. Many of them died, either of suffocation or shock. The first monkeys to return safely from space were Miss Baker, a squirrel monkey, and Able, a rhesus monkey, who were on the same rocket in 1959.

YOU WON'T BELIEVE IT BUT...
Male proboscis monkeys have the longest noses of all primates – the noses flop around on the monkeys' faces.

THE PYGMY MARMOSET IS THE SMALLEST MONKEY IN THE WORLD

YOU BIG BABOONS
While they lived in large numbers throughout Africa, baboons were very special animals to some of our ancestors. In Egypt, before the time of the pharaohs, people believed baboons were dead humans. They even worshipped a baboon god called Babi, which may be where they got their name.

HUMAN DNA IS 98 PERCENT IDENTICAL TO CHIMPANZEE DNA

AN INTERESTING TAIL
There are over 264 species of monkey, split into two distinct groups. Old World come from Africa and Asia, while New World live in South America. Many New World monkeys have a distinctive tail that they can use to grip things, almost like another hand – it's called a 'prehensile tail'.

THE ARM SPAN OF AN ORANGUTAN CAN MEASURE UP TO 7FT/2M

MALE MANDRILLS
Mandrills are large monkeys that are native to Africa. They are colorful creatures as not only do the males have an orange-yellow beard and flashes of blue and red on their dog-like snouts, but their bottoms are bright blue as well. The bluer the bottom, the more grown-up the mandrill.

YOU WON'T BELIEVE IT BUT...
With the exception of marmosets, which don't have thumbnails, all primates have fingernails just like us.

RIGHT AT HOME
'Man of the jungle' is what the name orangutan means in the language of Sumatra, the jungle-covered Asian island this ape calls home. The orangutan spends most of its life up trees and even sleeps above ground in a huge nest.

FINGER FOOD
A primate called the Aye-Aye has a very long middle finger, which it uses to scoop insect larvae from inside trees. First, it taps the bark of a tree and listens for insect larvae inside; then it makes a hole using its teeth and, finally, it fishes around for food.

YOU WON'T BELIEVE IT BUT...
There were up to two million chimpanzees in Africa just 100 years ago. But, because humans have cut down their forest homes, there are now no more than 150,000.

SIGN OF INTELLIGENCE
While movies such as *King Kong* portray gorillas as angry, violent monsters, they are actually gentle giants. They're highly intelligent, too – some have even been taught to communicate with humans and each other through sign language.

MEAT-EATERS
Tarsiers are the most carnivorous (meat-eating) of all primates; in fact, they are the only primates who never eat plants. Their diet consists entirely of other living creatures. They mostly eat insects but they have also been known to eat birds, snakes, bats and scorpions.

WHAT IS A DESERT?

Deserts don't have to be hot – many are actually extremely cold because there are no plants to hold heat to the ground – but they are all places in which very little rain or snow falls. Scientists agree that a desert is a place in which less than 10in/250mm of rain falls in a year. One-third of the Earth's land surface is desert.

HOME FROM HOME FOR SOME

It's tough for any creature to live for a day in desert, never mind a lifetime, but many species make it their home. Kangaroo rats in Death Valley save moisture by not panting or sweating like other animals, and the Mojave squirrel makes it through the dry season by hibernating for months.

THE SAHARA MIGHT BE HOT BUT IT'S HOME TO AROUND 1,200 SPECIES OF PLANT

DEATH VALLEY DANGER

In the US, the green of Death Valley is the lowest point below sea level in North America at -282ft/-86m, which is also one of the hottest and driest places on Earth, according to NOAA. The heat and the lack of moisture in the air have combined to make the normal environment unsuitable for normal life, making it one of the hottest places on Earth.

SANDSTORMY WEATHER

Sandstorms can create winds that blow at up to 75mph/120kph. These whip the sand up into a huge cloud. The storms can last for hours and, as well as getting sand into people's lungs – which leads to breathing problems – can result in people getting lost. And watch out for sand avalanches.

YOU WON'T BELIEVE IT BUT...

Picked up by the wind, sand from the Sahara has been found throughout Europe, as far north as the United Kingdom.

YOU WON'T BELIEVE IT BUT...

More people are killed in Death Valley every year in car accidents than from the heat, because the roads are narrow, twisting and gravel-sided.

WALKABOUT...

... is when a male Australian aborigine – aged just 13 – goes alone into the desert to prove he is a man. Using the techniques of his ancestors – such as knowing where to dig for water and how to find the soft parts of desert plants – the boy is expected to survive for six months. Although rare, this practice still occurs today.

EACH YEAR WE LOSE SIX MILLION HECTARES – 12 MILLION SOCCER PITCHES – BECAUSE OF GROWING DESERT

BIGGEST, HOTTEST

The biggest hot desert, the Sahara, covers an area of North Africa that's almost as big as the United States. Scientists believe it's been a desert for five million years. It can get as hot as 136°F/58°C during the daytime and as cold as 22°F/-6°C at night.

LOCUST LIFE

Incredibly, some animals thrive in the desert heat. The locust, not the most cuddly of creatures, benefits from bright light and heat too. A swarm in 1889 was estimated to cover an area the same size as the Grand Canyon.

THE GREAT DESERT
The name 'sahara' comes from Arabic, and means, appropriately, 'great desert'. The people who live there – the Tuareg – are very proud of the region.

WHAT'S THE DRIEST DESERT?
The Atacama desert of Chile in South America. It's 100 times drier than California's Death Valley and it once went almost 40 years without rain.

YOU WON'T BELIEVE IT BUT...
Sometimes sand dunes are as high as 1,000ft/300m – the size of a really big hill.

FOUR PERCENT OF HUMANS LIVE IN DESERT REGIONS

DOWN UNDER
44 percent of the land in Australia is officially desert. This is known collectively as the Outback, which covers 10 individual deserts.
This also accounts for Australia's relatively small human population. It is almost as big as the USA but home to just 20 million people. New York City has more than eight million people.

YOU WON'T BELIEVE IT BUT...
When in the desert, each person requires two gallons/7.5 liters of drinking water every day to stop dehydration of the body.

IS A DESERT ALWAYS DEADLY?
No. The Kalahari, which can be found in southern Africa, is home to other, more 'traditional' animals such as leopards, cheetahs and antelope. Several game reserves exist to protect the wildlife there, not from the heat, but from their true foe – hunters.

ONLY ABOUT ONE-QUARTER OF THE WORLD'S DESERTS ARE MADE OF SAND

DESERT LIVING
People have lived in the desert for thousands of years. In 500 BCE, one civilization, the Garamantes, even built towns in the desert. For water, they dug shafts into the mountains to access trapped water reserves.

WHAT A MOVER

Mercury is the closest planet to the Sun and is a lot like our own Moon. It is covered in craters and has no atmosphere. The planet moves quickly across the sky - it only takes 88 Earth days (each with 24 hours) to orbit the Sun, compared to our 365.

NO PRESENTS

If you lived on Pluto, it would be a long wait for your birthday. One Plutonian year equals 248 Earth years - so Pluto takes approximately 2.5 Earth centuries to orbit the Sun once. A single Pluto day is 153 hours long.

YOU WON'T BELIEVE IT BUT...

With a pair of good binoculars, you'll be able to see Saturn's rings yourself.

VENUS AND EARTH ARE THE TWO CLOSEST PLANETS. THEY ARE 'ONLY' 25 MILLION MI/43 MILLION KM APART

VOLCANIC VENUS

Venus is called the morning star because it's the brightest object in the sky, after the Moon. Unlike the Moon, it's a planet - the second closest to the Sun. It's similar to Earth in many ways - size, gravity and mineral composition. But it's covered in volcanoes.

MOUNTAINS OF MARS

Mars is the fourth planet from the Sun, and the one we know most about. It's also known as the Red Planet and is a world of mountains, valleys and volcanoes, just like Earth. But its atmosphere is so poisonous that it has been unable to sustain life of any sort.

JUPITER HAS 63 MOONS THAT WE KNOW ABOUT - THERE MAY BE MORE

YOU WON'T BELIEVE IT BUT...

Space probes have shown that Titan has lakes near its north pole - the only lakes found anywhere except Earth.

WHAT'S AN ASTEROID?

Asteroids are rocks in space that float in orbit around the Sun. They can be the size of a pebble or almost as big as planet Earth (130,000mi/210,000km across). Nearly all asteroids are found in the 'asteroid belt' between Mars and Jupiter. There are hundreds of thousands of them.

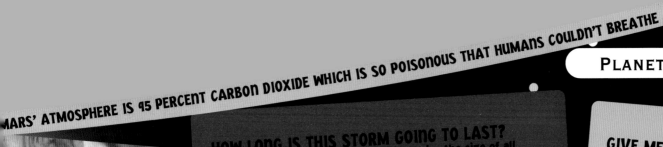

HOW LONG IS THIS STORM GOING TO LAST?
Jupiter is so huge that it's more than twice the size of all the planets and moons combined. It's known as a 'gas giant' because it is mostly hydrogen gas. Its famous 'red spot' is a storm that has been raging for at least 300 years.

GIVE ME A RING
Saturn is a gas giant like Jupiter, although it is much smaller. Even so, it is still 95 times bigger than the Earth. It is best known for its 'rings' – these are actually small rocks and lumps of ice that have been captured by the planet's gravity.

SATURN'S MOONS
As well as the chunks of rock and ice in its rings, Saturn has 56 known moons but most of them are very small – 30 are less than 6mi/10km across while 13 are more than 60mi/100km in diameter.

YOU WON'T BELIEVE IT BUT...
Mars is red because it's covered in iron oxide – better known as rust.

FEELING BLUE?
The eighth planet in the Solar System is another gas giant, Neptune. Like Saturn, Neptune has rings, but they're very faint. It's 17 times bigger than Earth, and its atmosphere includes the 'blue gas' methane which in turn makes the whole planet look blue.

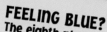

IS IT A MOON, OR A PLANET?
Saturn's main moon, Titan, is about 50 percent bigger than our own, which means that it is bigger than Mercury. It is also the only moon in the Solar System to have its own atmosphere.

GEE, PLUTO
In 2006, scientists at the International Astronomical Union changed their definition of a planet. On the basis of its small size, it was decided Pluto is a 'dwarf planet' which means it no longer lines up with Saturn, Mars and the others.

YOU WON'T BELIEVE IT BUT...
Uranus is the only planet to have been discovered using a telescope – others were spotted with the human eye.

PLANET SPOTTING
In ancient times, our ancestors knew about Mercury, Venus, Mars, Jupiter and Saturn. Once strong telescopes were invented, astronomers started to discover more, including Uranus, just beyond Saturn, which was spotted by Sir William Herschel in March 1781.

THE AVERAGE PERSON'S SKIN WEIGHS TWICE AS MUCH AS THEIR BRAIN

YOU WON'T BELIEVE IT BUT...
When you breathe deeply after exercise, you're making sure you're taking in extra oxygen to replace what you've used.

WALKIE TALKIE
At around nine months, a baby will learn to crawl and, after a year or so, will probably be able to walk. By age two, babies can talk, run, open doors and kick a ball and by five, will be able to read, write and even dance.

WHY DO EARS GROW BIGGER?
Although most of your body stops growing by your late teens, your ears grow throughout your life. As skin gets less elastic and faces take on a fuller shape, it is claimed that gravity works on earlobes so they hang down more.

LITTLE BIG HEAD
When you are born, your head is about a quarter of the length of your body. But by the time you're an adult, it's only about an eighth of your body-length. No, your head hasn't shrunk – your limbs have just grown a lot longer.

REACHING YOUR PEAK
After adolescence, your body harnesses the growth you have experienced during your early and teenage years. Regular exercise, relaxation, sleep and healthy diets and lifestyle all help maintain strength, and combat the effects of wear and tear of everyday living on your body and its organs.

IT'S ESTIMATED THAT MOST DUST PARTICLES IN A ROOM ARE MADE UP OF DEAD

YOU WON'T BELIEVE IT BUT...
Without any water, you'd only survive for a few days – you lose it in sweat and urine.

WHY DO TEENS GET ZITS?
During puberty, teenagers experience hormone surges which may be a bit of a shock to the system and can result in such skin outbreaks as spots. These surges can be profound and confusing for both boys and girls, though they usually subside after the age of 18.

WEAR AND TEAR
Eventually, internal wear and tear take its toll on our bodies. It is estimated that every second, around 50 million cells die in each human body, and between 500,000 and 1 million skin cells die every day and are replaced, even though we have billions of cells overall. However, muscle and nerve cells never die.

FINGERNAILS GROW FOUR TIMES AS FAST AS TOENAILS

HELLO, CAN YOU HEAR ME?
Older people tend to hear and see less well than younger people. This is because the ears lose some sensitivity, especially to high-pitched sounds, while the eyes lose some of their flexibility.

TO LONG LIFE
Average life expectancy is much longer these days than in the past. This is because of improved health care, diet, medicines, hygiene, living conditions and resistance to disease. In the year 1850, people routinely died by 40. Now the average is closer to 80.

HEY, WHAT'S THAT?
A baby can see, hear and has certain reflexes. For example, it can grasp at something put in its hand, and move its head if touched. By six months, it can sit up if helped, and will inquisitively turn its head around, fascinated by things.

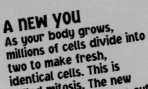

A NEW YOU
As your body grows, millions of cells divide into two to make fresh, identical cells. This is called mitosis. The new cells replace old worn out ones. So the 'you' of a few years ago has been completely updated and renovated since then.

YOU WON'T BELIEVE IT BUT...
Fingerprints have a function – they provide traction for the fingers to grasp things.

CHINA ACCOUNTS FOR NEARLY A QUARTER OF THE WORLD'S SIX BILLION POPULATION

YOU WON'T BELIEVE IT BUT...
Sleep is essential for healthy growth, but your nerve cells never sleep because they are needed even when you are resting.

COCK-A-DOODLE-WHAT?
The substance in your joints that makes them springy and helps protect the bones is called 'a long sugar molecule' with the name Glucosamine. It's exactly the same as the substance which makes the stuff inside your eyeball gooey. Both of them can be replaced by an extract from the comb of a rooster.

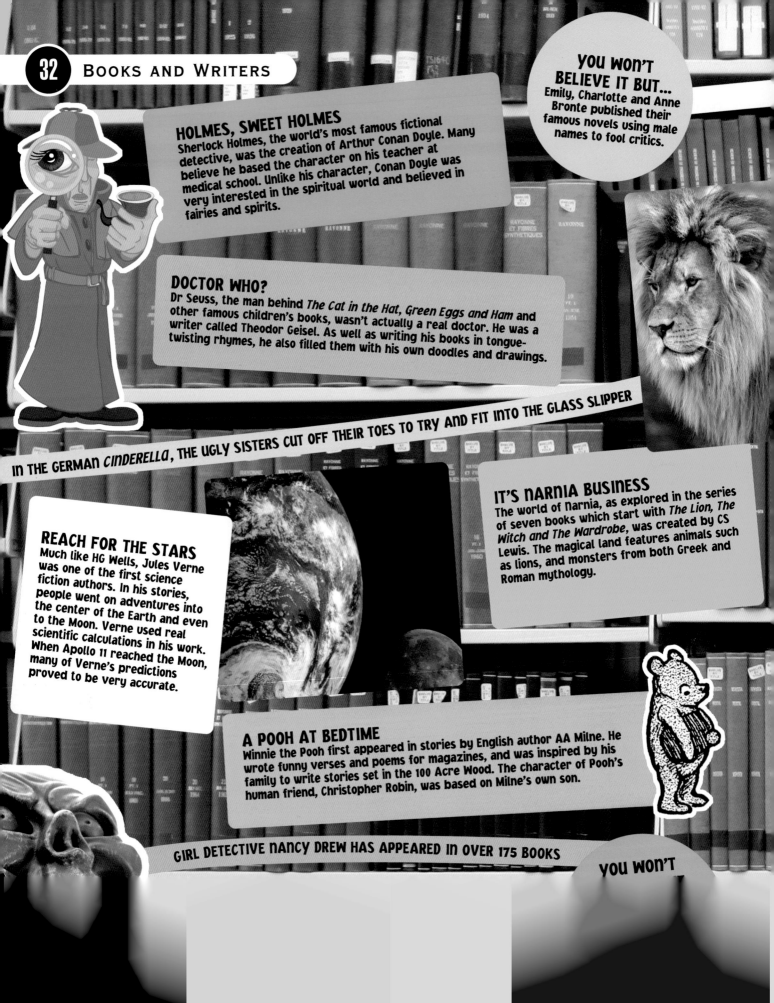

HOLMES, SWEET HOLMES
Sherlock Holmes, the world's most famous fictional detective, was the creation of Arthur Conan Doyle. Many believe he based the character on his teacher at medical school. Unlike his character, Conan Doyle was very interested in the spiritual world and believed in fairies and spirits.

YOU WON'T BELIEVE IT BUT...
Emily, Charlotte and Anne Bronte published their famous novels using male names to fool critics.

DOCTOR WHO?
Dr Seuss, the man behind *The Cat in the Hat*, *Green Eggs and Ham* and other famous children's books, wasn't actually a real doctor. He was a writer called Theodor Geisel. As well as writing his books in tongue-twisting rhymes, he also filled them with his own doodles and drawings.

IN THE GERMAN *CINDERELLA*, THE UGLY SISTERS CUT OFF THEIR TOES TO TRY AND FIT INTO THE GLASS SLIPPER

IT'S NARNIA BUSINESS
The world of Narnia, as explored in the series of seven books which start with *The Lion, The Witch and The Wardrobe*, was created by CS Lewis. The magical land features animals such as lions, and monsters from both Greek and Roman mythology.

REACH FOR THE STARS
Much like HG Wells, Jules Verne was one of the first science fiction authors. In his stories, people went on adventures into the center of the Earth and even to the Moon. Verne used real scientific calculations in his work. When Apollo 11 reached the Moon, many of Verne's predictions proved to be very accurate.

A POOH AT BEDTIME
Winnie the Pooh first appeared in stories by English author AA Milne. He wrote funny verses and poems for magazines, and was inspired by his family to write stories set in the 100 Acre Wood. The character of Pooh's human friend, Christopher Robin, was based on Milne's own son.

GIRL DETECTIVE NANCY DREW HAS APPEARED IN OVER 175 BOOKS

YOU WON'T

YOU WON'T BELIEVE IT BUT...
The Bible is the best-selling book ever. It is estimated that six billion copies have been sold and it has been translated into 2,000 languages.

LOVE AND MARRIAGE
Jane Austen was one of the first female authors to achieve widespread success and acclaim. Her novels, such as *Pride and Prejudice* and *Sense and Sensibility*, were often about young women. Austen used her books to poke fun at the manners of her time.

ELEPHANTS & TURTLES
Discworld is a flat world, balanced on the backs of four elephants, who are balanced on the back of a giant turtle. It's the setting for many books by Terry Pratchett, one of Britain's most popular authors. Discworld was originally created to make fun of other fantasy novels, but has since become a huge success.

ROCK AND ROALD
Roald Dahl was the British author responsible for *Charlie and the Chocolate Factory*, *James and the Giant Peach* and other stories. He began writing as a child, in a secret diary that he hid at the top of a tree in a tin box. He would sit up in the tree and write all day.

An ANCIENT STORY
A Japanese noble woman called Murasaki Shikibu is believed to have written the world's first novel in 1007. *The Tale of Genji* tells the story of a prince searching for love and wisdom. The English translation is more than 1,000 pages.

RUSSIAN TO THE END
War and Peace is regarded as one of the greatest books ever written, and is also one of the longest. It was written by Leo Tolstoy, and tells the stories of many characters living in Russia in the 19th century. The story is such an epic that the book is 560,000 words long.

WITH 1.5 MILLION WORDS, *REMEMBRANCE OF THINGS PAST* BY MARCEL PROUST, IS THE WORLD'S LONGEST NOVEL

YOU WON'T BELIEVE IT BUT...
James Bond author Ian Fleming wrote the children's story, *Chitty Chitty Bang Bang*, about a magical flying car.

FAST SCRIBBLER
Britain's Dame Barbara Cartland wrote more than 723 novels during her long life. This averages out as a novel every two weeks – an incredibly short space of time in which to write a book. No other author has ever written as many novels.

you won't BELIEVE IT BUT...
Bats make up around 20 percent of the world's mammal species.

BRILLIANT BATS
Bats are incredible. They are the only mammals (warm-blooded creatures who feed milk to their young) which can fly, but also the only ones to use echo-location – bouncing their high-pitched squeaks off objects so they can navigate at night and find prey. There are nearly 1,000 species of bat.

UNUSUALLY FOR MAMMALS, FEMALE HARES ARE BIGGER THAN MALES

YOU GO COLUGO
The Colugo is the correct name for a gliding mammal that lives in the forests and jungles of Southeast Asia. It is usually referred to as a 'flying lemur' but this is misleading as it can't fly, and it is not a lemur.

THE BOUNCING MOUSE
The smallest rodent is the pygmy jerboa that lives in the deserts of Africa and Asia. A bizarre-looking creature, it's like a cross between a mouse and a kangaroo. Although it can look quite long because of its tufted tail, its body is tiny – the smallest ever was only 2in/5cm.

OH, RATS!
Rats are medium-sized rodents that are born survivors. Highly intelligent, they live off our trash – you're never far away from one in a city. There are 56 rat species, among the most common of which is the brown rat. Though rats can carry disease, if properly looked after they make excellent pets.

THERE ARE 289 DIFFERENT SPECIES OF SHREW

BUNNY BREEDERS
Rabbits are common, both as pets and in the wild where they live in burrows and breed quickly. It only takes a litter of baby rabbits on average 31 days to grow inside the mother before birth, compared to nine months in humans.

you won't BELIEVE IT BUT...
Despite their front teeth, rabbits and hares aren't rodents – their family of animals is called 'leporidae'.

ARE YOU NUTS?
Some squirrels are so nuts they think they can fly. They can't, but they can glide. When they jump from the tops of trees, flaps of skin extending between their front and back legs catch the wind. Once airborne, using their tails, they can steer very accurately.

DINOSAUR FOR DINNER

There are over 2,000 species of rodent – that's 42 percent of all the mammal species. Their success is down to their front teeth – great for gnawing – and the fact they're not fussy about their food. They've been around for a long time – the earliest rodent fossils date back up to 56 million years ago.

MAGIC FINGERS

The common raccoon of America has incredibly sensitive paws. When it is fishing for prey in streams it feels around for fish, crabs and other tasty morsels – as though it can 'see' with its fingers. However, if the fish are not biting it will happily raid a dustbin for scraps.

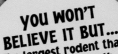

YOU WON'T BELIEVE IT BUT...

The largest rodent that ever lived in North America was the giant beaver. It was 8ft/2.5m long and died out 10,000 years ago.

THE STAR-NOSED MOLE HAS 22 TENTACLES ON ITS NOSE

YOU WON'T BELIEVE IT BUT...

Capybaras hide under water from their predators. They are excellent swimmers, and can sleep with their noses just above the surface.

CAN YOU HARE ME?

Hares are closely related to rabbits – both sharing the same fantastic floppy ears. Hares are much larger and are faster runners, and they don't live in underground warrens. Instead, they live in nests above ground. They also have a powerful kick that rabbits could only dream of.

ALARMED PORCUPINES WILL RAISE THEIR SPINES AND RUN BACKWARDS AT ATTACKERS

WATER PIG

The capybara, also known as the 'water pig', is the world's largest rodent. It lives in and around rivers in South America and parts of Florida. Though it looks a lot like a guinea pig, it is far bigger – adults weigh over 100lbs/45kg, the same as an 11-year-old boy.

SAFETY IN NUMBERS

Meerkats are a sociable type of mongoose from South Africa. Although they spend a lot of time digging and searching for food, there are always up to 30 members of the group on lookout duty. They stand on their back legs, eyes peeled for predators such as eagles.

TOTAL CONTROL
Computers today control most electronic devices – the traffic signals on the street, the bank machine that gives you money, even the engines of new cars. Computers are everywhere, and can handle almost any task.

CUSTOM COMPUTERS
Many PC owners like to personalize their computer with desktop pictures, but others go even further – and customize the shape of the PC itself. Dedicated computer geeks have managed to fit working PC components inside a gingerbread house and even a toilet.

USE YOUR NOODLE
You can buy all sorts of weird computer gadgets, thanks to small sockets called USB ports that let computers 'talk' to lots of different electronic devices. So your PC could run a fan, vacuum cleaner, seat warmer, or lava lamp. In Japan, you can even buy a computer-powered noodle strainer.

CHATTERBOTS
One way to test artificial intelligence was created by computer scientist Alan Turing. He suggested interrogating a human being and compter using nothing but textual messages. If the interrogator couldn't figure out who was the computer and who was the human, then the computer could be classed as 'intelligent'.

YOU WON'T BELIEVE IT BUT...
Thanks to a computer chip implanted in the brain, a man in the US who is paralyzed can 'think' his television on and off.

IS THERE ANYBODY OUT THERE?
Did you know your computer could help to discover alien life? *SETI@Home* is the world's largest computer project, tapping into the unused processing time of over three million ordinary home PCs to process the vast amounts of data needed to identify intelligent signals from the stars.

YOU WON'T BELIEVE IT BUT...
A computer managed to win Time magazine's 'Man of the Year' for 1982 – a great victory for machines?

HAS THE COMBINED POWER OF A 1.5MI/2.4KM-HIGH PILE OF LAPTOPS

BIG BYTES

Computers measure information in bytes. If you type one letter in a word processor, it takes one byte of computer memory to store. A kilobyte is 1,024 bytes, while a megabyte is 1,048,576 bytes. The first computers could only store a few kilobytes of data; now they store thousands of times that amount. An average PC now has a memory of around 500 megabytes.

THE ANTIKYTHERA MECHANISM IS AN ANCIENT GREEK CALCULATING DEVICE OVER 2,000 YEARS OLD

YOU WON'T BELIEVE IT BUT...
The computer that guided the first astronauts to the Moon had less computing power than a GameBoy.

WARNING
There are thousands of computer viruses, but most are easily blocked. One of the worst was MyDoom, released in 2004. It spread incredibly quickly using email and in just a few days it made millions of copies around the world. It is estimated that a new virus is discovered every 18 seconds. They can cause vast amounts of damage such as deleting files on your computer or changing data.

ARE COMPUTERS SMARTER THAN US?
Computers can only do what we tell them to do, but several computers have been created to try and beat world champions at chess. The first to succeed was *Deep Blue*, which defeated Gary Kasparov. So computers can be smarter than us... but only if we make them.

CAN COMPUTERS READ?
Computers don't have eyes but can 'look' at things using a scanner. There is even software that can teach your computer to recognize the way we write. If you had this, your computer could 'read' your handwriting.

Carton Size

WHAT A BRAINBOX
You already own the greatest computer in the world, and it's free. It's in your head. As advanced as computers are, the human brain has loads more processing power – plus it can imagine. So while a PC might be fast, remember who's in charge.

YOU WON'T BELIEVE IT BUT...
IBM boss Thomas Watson thought that the world would only ever want five computers – that was in 1943.

A BOUNCING BABY... COMPUTER?
The first modern computer was nicknamed Baby. It was invented in Manchester in 1948 by Tom Kilburn, and filled an entire room. Despite its size, Baby could only store 1,024 bits (128 bytes) of information. That's not even enough to remember all the letters on this page.

Help

URL: http://www.internet.com

THERE ARE NOW MORE THAN 100 MILLION WEBSITES ON THE INTERNET

YELLOW NEWSPAPERS
Why do old newspapers turn yellow? It's because of a substance called lignin, which reacts to light and air, gradually changing the color of the paper. Newsprint is in such high demand that it has to be cheap to produce – and paper containing more lignin is cheaper than other types of paper.

MANY FAMOUS NOVELISTS, SUCH AS CHARLES DICKENS, STARTED OUT IN NEWSPAPERS

FIRST EDITION
Julius Caesar first introduced a type of newspaper in ancient Rome. He wanted to keep the public up to date on the Roman Empire, and would display large boards around the city filled with political news, criminal trials and public executions.

YOU WON'T BELIEVE IT BUT...
The biggest single issue of a newspaper weighed 12lbs/5.4kg – more than a six-month-old child.

SAVING TREES
It takes 500,000 trees to produce each week's Sunday newspapers in the US. If just a single run of the Sunday *New York Times* were entirely recycled then 75,000 trees could be saved. If all newspapers were recycled then 250,000 trees per year would survive.

THE WORLD'S LONGEST RUNNING COMIC STRIP, *THE KATZENJAMMER KIDS*, DATES FROM 1897 IN THE US

YOU WON'T BELIEVE IT BUT...
About 52 million newspapers are produced every day in America – enough to cover the Moon in a year. That's still less than the number produced in China, the world's biggest market at 48 million.

A MONSTROUS READ
The world's biggest newspaper is the *Yomiuri Shimbun*, and is published in Japan. Its staff and reporters are treated like celebrities. A staggering 14 million copies are sold every day. If you stacked them on top of each other, one day's worth would stretch 40mi/64km into the sky.

YOU WON'T BELIEVE IT BUT...
Most newspapers are recycled and end up as part of another newspaper.

BUZZ OFF
Everyone knows that paparazzi are photographers who follow celebrities, but the term was first used in a 1960 film called *La Dolce Vita*. A news photographer in the film was called Paparazzo, and the name stuck. It was originally an Italian slang word meaning mosquito, or annoying insect.

THE WORLD'S OLDEST EXISTING NEWSPAPER HAS BEEN PUBLISHED IN SWEDEN FOR OVER 400 YEARS

ANYONE GOT A CLUE?
Roger Squires is the world's most prolific crossword compiler. In May 2007, he published his 66,666th crossword – which meant that he had created an astonishing two million clues since the 1960s. The 75-year-old also holds the record for the longest word ever used in a crossword – a 58-letter Welsh town.

BREAKING NEWS
The first American newspaper to have more than one page was called *Publick Occurrences; both Foreign and Domestick*. It was published in Boston for the first and last time in 1690. Its publishers were keen to publish monthly, but the authorities disapproved and closed it down for not being licensed.

HOT OFF THE PRESS
The first printed newspaper ever published was in 1605. Johann Carolus' *Relation* was distributed to the residents of Strasbourg (which was then in Germany, and now in France).

PRIZE WRITERS
Joseph Pulitzer was a newspaper publisher in the 19th century who created a prize to encourage better journalism. The Pulitzer Prize is now like the Oscars of the newspaper industry. The newspaper with the most prizes is the *New York Times*, having won over 90 times.

YOU WON'T BELIEVE IT BUT...
In 2001, Indian Pooran Chandra Pande had a record-breaking one hundred and eighteen of his letters published in a single newspaper.

A GRAVE THEORY
Gravity is the universal law by which all objects are attracted to each other – the larger the object, the greater the pull. Gravity pulled together the atoms that make up our planet, it keeps the Moon orbiting the Earth, and it makes your pencil fall to the ground.

HOW DO ROLLER COASTERS WORK?
Ever wondered why you feel weightless on theme park rides? It's because of Newton's third law (see opposite page). As the ride plummets down, your bottom isn't pressing down on the seat with your full weight. As a result, you feel lighter than you actually are.

YOU WON'T BELIEVE IT BUT...
The Earth's atmosphere is around 56mi/90km high. Falling from this height, it would take a grown adult up to half an hour to hit the ground.

WASHED OUT
Next time your sandcastle gets washed away by the sea, blame the Moon. It's the Moon's gravity that pulls the Earth's oceans, making the tide go in and out. Some sea creatures can sense this pull, and use it to figure out when to sleep.

FALLING FAST
According to a popular story, the 16th century scientist Galileo discovered that all falling objects accelerate at the same speed. Before this, it was believed heavier objects fell faster. Galileo made his discovery by climbing up the Leaning Tower of Pisa and throwing things from the top.

THE WEIGHT OF THE EARTH IS APPROXIMATELY 6,000,000,000,000,000,000,000,000KG

IN A SPIN
In science fiction films, ever wondered why space stations are always shaped like rings? It's because a circular space station can create its own gravity, if it spins fast enough. However, even a space station one mile wide would have to spin around once every minute to stop astronauts floating.

THE MOON HAS ABOUT ONE SIXTH OF THE EARTH'S GRAVITY. THIS IS WHY ASTRONAUTS LOOK SO BOUNCY AS THEY WALK

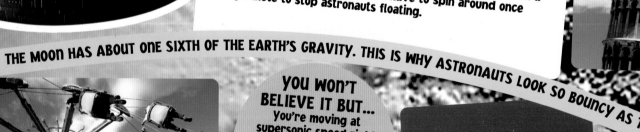

YOU WON'T BELIEVE IT BUT...
You're moving at supersonic speed right now. That's because the Earth revolves at 1,000mph/1,600kph while orbiting the Sun at over 67,000mph/ 108,000kph.

SPEWING FOR SCIENCE
To train astronauts in zero gravity, NASA built a special plane that became known as the Vomit Comet. Flying in it felt so weird passengers were often sick. When it was retired in 2004, NASA claimed to have mopped up over 285gal/ 1,000l of puke.

HEAD-SPINNING SCIENCE
If you've ever ridden a merry-go-round you'll have experienced something called centrifugal force. It's the force that occurs on a spinning object that pushes things away from the center of the spin. Try putting some dried peas on a turntable and see what happens when it speeds up.

A REAL WISE GUY
Sir Isaac Newton, born in England in 1643, is regarded by many as the most important figure in modern science. His theories about gravity helped establish the three rules that define all motion in the universe (see below) – and it all started because he saw an apple fall from a tree.

HOW FAST CAN YOU GO?
The land speed record challenges engineers to create vehicles that can cover one kilometer in the fastest possible time. In 1848, the record was 39mph/63kph, slower than today's cars. By 1997, the fastest speed had rocketed up to an amazing 760mph/1,223kph.

YOU MOVE MORE SLOWLY UNDERWATER BECAUSE THE LIQUID'S MOLECULES CREATE MORE RESISTANCE THAN THOSE IN THE AIR

NEWTON'S FIRST LAW
An object won't move unless it is affected by another force. For instance, a ball won't suddenly roll away on its own unless someone kicks it. When objects do move without someone actually pushing them, it's because they're affected by gravity or some similar physical force.

NEWTON'S SECOND LAW
The acceleration of a moving object is determined by the force applied to it, and is in the same direction. In other words, the harder you push a toy car, the faster it will move, and it will always roll in the direction you pushed it.

YOU WON'T BELIEVE IT BUT...
Greek mathematician Archimedes first identified the properties of gravity and motion, over 2,000 years ago.

YOU WON'T BELIEVE IT BUT...
To blast off into space, you'll need to be moving at 6.9mps/11.2kps to escape the Earth's gravity.

THE 16TH CENTURY SCIENTIST GALILEO WAS HELD UNDER HOUSE ARREST FOR DISCOVERING THAT THE EARTH ORBITED THE SUN, NOT THE OTHER WAY AROUND

NEWTON'S THIRD LAW
Every action has an equal and opposite reaction. When you sit on a chair, your bottom pushes down on the chair, but the chair also pushes you back with a force equal to your weight. If it didn't, you'd squash it flat.

THERE ARE 33 LETTERS IN THE RUSSIAN ALPHABET: 21 CONSONANTS, 10 VOWELS, AND TWO PRONUNCIATION SIGNS.

TIGER TIGER
Most of the world's wild tigers live in Asia. They are the largest cats on Earth and they used to be quite common, but the spread of human cities and hunting has cut their numbers in the wild to less than 7,000. They are fearsome predators, but no match for humans.

IT'S RAINING, IT'S POURING...
Monsoons, where rain pours down continually, are common in Asia. The Indian monsoon season arrives between June and September and most of the country's rain falls in this short time. In one storm in 2005 almost 3ft/1m of rain fell in just one day.

YOU WON'T BELIEVE IT BUT...
Thimphu in Bhutan is the only capital city without traffic lights – most of the 50,000 residents don't like them.

ANY SPARE ROOM?
Shanghai, in China, is the world's most populated city, with over 20 million people squeezed into its many buildings and streets. Asia is also home to the world's second biggest city, with Mumbai in India groaning at the seams with more than about 18 million inhabitants – that's 30 times the population of Washington D.C.

WATCH YOUR FEET
The Asian elephant weighs the same as a forklift truck. However, it is still considered small by elephant standards. It has the longest tail of any land mammal though – excluding the tuft of hair on the end, the tail can be 5ft/1.5m.

YOU WON'T BELIEVE IT BUT...
Indonesia is made up of around 18,000 islands – so it is a challenge to visit different parts of the country.

INDIA INVENTED THE NUMBER SYSTEM OVER 1,700 YEARS AGO

WHERE DID IT GO?
Can you lose a city? Surprisingly, yes, because the city of Angkor in Cambodia was considered lost for several hundred years before a French botanist rediscovered it in 1858. However, legend suggests that the Cambodian king found the city whilst hunting elephants.

POPULAR WHEELS
Japan's Toyota Corolla has been the most popular car in its home country for 36 of the last 40 years. It's also the best-selling car worldwide; since the first one was made in 1966, over 32 million have been sold.

A KATANA IS A TRADITIONAL JAPANESE SWORD

GO EAST
Japan is one of the world's most technologically advanced nations. The characters that make the word Japan literally mean 'sun origin', which is why it is called the Land of the Rising Sun. It is actually made up of over 6,000 separate islands – and a lot of bridges.

ALL ABOARD
For one of the world's longest train journeys, hop on the Trans-Siberian train. It travels from Europe all across Asia, and the tracks are longer than the Great Wall of China. The railway is so long, some journeys last over a week.

DO YOU SEA?
The South China Sea covers an area of 1.4 million sq mi/ 3.6 million sq km, and is the biggest sea in the world. It's also the busiest, with over half of the world's trading ships traveling across it carrying cargo such as coal and iron ore, as well as oil in massive supertankers.

SILK IS A VALUABLE CLOTH, AND CHINA PRODUCES OVER HALF OF THE WORLD'S SUPPLY

WHAT A CROWD
Asia is the world's largest continent, and the most populated region on Earth. Aside from China and Russia, it's got India too. Other big nations are Japan, Thailand, and Indonesia. In all, over 44 countries make up Asia, and it is home to more than half the people in the world.

NEW YEAR CELEBRATIONS...
The Chinese New Year usually takes place sometime in late January or early February.

ROOM FOR ONE MORE?
The smallest Asian region is Macau, a tiny country that belongs to China. At only 11 sq mi/28 sq km in size, its half a million inhabitants are packed in pretty tightly. In fact, its Asia's most densely populated region with over 6,450 people per sq mi/18,000 people per sq km.

THE ASIAN CONNECTION
Most of the world's major religions began in what we now call Asia. Buddhism comes from China, while Hinduism started in India. Islam was founded in Arabia in the seventh century. Even Christianity and Judaism have their roots in Israel, on the western edge of Asia.

BLAZING TENNIS BALLS

Ace tennis players can hit a ball faster than the top speed of an average family car. American Andy Roddick holds the record for the fastest serve – a smashing 153mph/246kph recorded in the 2004 Davis Cup. In 2006, Dutch player Brenda Schultz-McCarthy clocked 130mph/209kph qualifying for the Cincinnati tournament – the fastest serve by a woman.

THE GREATEST?

The boxer Muhammad Ali has been called the greatest athlete of the 20th century. He was famous for his nimble movements and rhyming phrases. He took part in 61 fights, and won 56 of them. Ali could punch so hard that he knocked out 37 of his opponents.

WHAT'S THE OLDEST SPORT?

Wrestling is one of the oldest sports in the world, with ancient versions in China, India and Egypt taking place up to 4,000 years ago. However, almost every nation records some form of wrestling taking place during its history.

YOU WON'T BELIEVE IT BUT...

Extreme ironing is a 'sport' in which participants iron clothes in extreme locations – including on mountain tops and underwater.

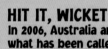

HIT IT, WICKET

In 2006, Australia and South Africa played what has been called the greatest one-day cricket match of all time. Australia set a new world record by scoring a whopping 434 runs, a score that seemed impossible to beat. Amazingly, South Africa managed to score 438 runs – with only one ball left before the end of the match.

THE NOT-OLYMPICS

The World Games is an event that takes place every four years. It is made up of sports that have not been allowed into the Olympic Games. The sports range from well-known pastimes such as karate and waterskiing to some very strange events like rock 'n' roll dancing, lifesaving and korfball.

IN THE SOUTH-EAST ASIAN SPORT KABADDI (LIKE TAG) PLAYERS CAN ONLY ATTACK FOR THE LENGTH OF ONE BREATH

YOU WON'T BELIEVE IT BUT...

Before he played for Manchester United, the 11-year-old David Beckham was their mascot.

BET ON BECKHAM

David Beckham is one of the most popular soccer players in the world. He signed for Manchester United in 1991, and went on to be the captain of England's national team. But he was a star on the pitch long before then. By the age of eight, he'd scored 100 goals for his local team.

YOU WON'T BELIEVE IT BUT...
Soviet gymnast Larissa Latynina won 18 Olympic medals during the 1950s–1960s – the most in any one sport.

CRUNCH TIME
Rugby is a very physical game that was invented at Rugby School in England. Concussion and other head injuries are common, as are broken bones and sprained ankles.

IS IT A MAN?
William Perry was an American football player in the 1980s. He weighed as much as five of your friends, and was so big that people called him 'the Fridge'. He used his giant size to stop other players getting past him. He was so famous he released his own rap records, and even had his own GI Joe action figure.

THE AVERAGE PROFESSIONAL SOCCER PLAYER CAN KICK THE BALL AT OVER 70MPH/112KPH

BASKET FANTASTIC
Given America's passion for the sport, you might expect that most basketball records would be held by American players, but Swedish player Mel Wermelin pulled off a slam-dunking miracle in 1974. In a regional tournament, his team won by 272 points to nothing. Aged just 13, Wermelin had scored every single point.

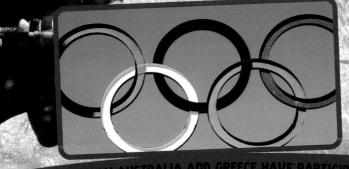

SINCE 1896, ONLY AUSTRALIA AND GREECE HAVE PARTICIPATED IN EVERY MODERN OLYMPIC GAMES

WHOLE LARA TALENT
Brian Lara is a cricket player from the West Indies. He broke a lot of world records and led his national team in many international cricket tournaments. He is most famous for his high-scoring batting. In 1994, in a three-day match, he scored more than 500 runs without being bowled out.

YOU WON'T BELIEVE IT BUT...
The modern game of American football has its roots in English rugby, although rugby players do not wear padded kit.

SKY-HIGH SLAM-DUNKS
Michael Jordan is often called the greatest basketball player of all time. He used to play for the Chicago Bulls. He was so good that he scored more than 10 points in 866 games in a row. He was especially famous for his slam-dunks and could jump so high that his nickname was 'Air Jordan'.

WHEN WERE THE MIDDLE AGES?
The Middle Ages officially began in 476 CE, when the Roman Empire fell in Western Europe. Elsewhere in the world, however, the Roman Empire continued to exist for nearly another thousand years. The empire's final end in 1453 CE marks the end of the Middle Ages.

YOU WON'T BELIEVE IT BUT...
In medieval Europe, people stretched hours depending on the time of the year. For example, in summer (as the sun goes down later), the length of an 'hour' increased to about 150 minutes.

BATTLE OF EYE-STINGS
No sooner had the English King Harold defeated the Vikings than the Norman noble William the Conqueror invaded and beat him at the Battle of Hastings in 1066. Legend has it, Harold was struck in the eye with an arrow. The defeat saw Britain fall under Norman rule.

A CUNNING EMPEROR
The Eastern Roman Empire was also called the Byzantine Empire. One Byzantine emperor, Leo VI, went out in disguise without his identity papers to test the city's police. He was arrested, and promptly rewarded the police for doing their job so well.

SHRIEK THAT TUNE
The shawm was a musical instrument, which made a penetrating and shrieking sound, and was used by military bands marching into war. A member of the woodwind family, it has evolved into the far more pleasant-sounding oboe that musicians use today.

SIGN, OR ELSE
King John took over from his brother Richard the Lionheart but he was a terrible ruler. In 1215, English barons forced John to sign the Magna Carta, ensuring people's liberties under common law and making the King subject to the law of the land.

IN THE MIDDLE AGES, IT WAS COMMONLY BELIEVED THAT DISEASES WERE CAUSED BY BAD SMELLS

BLACK DEATH STRIKES
During the 14th century, a horrible disease called the Black Death spread across Europe. Those unlucky enough to catch it suffered swollen glands, blackened skin and death within days. The Black Death is thought to have killed around 25 million people and wasn't fully wiped out in England until the Great Fire of London in 1666.

YOU WON'T BELIEVE IT BUT...
The increasing popularity of underwear in the later Middle Ages meant there were more rags available for turning into parchment for books. This made books cheaper to produce, and helped popularize reading.

LET IT OUT
Doctors thought that having 'too much blood' caused many diseases. In order to 'cure' their patients, they would carry out bloodletting – the removal of what they considered to be excess blood. They would do this by attaching leeches to the patient's body to suck the blood out of them.

A KNIGHT'S TALE

Knights often boiled their armor to make it tougher. The armor, made from leather, was placed in a large pot and boiled in a mixture of beeswax. This process resulted in the leather taking on a consistency similar to wood, protecting the wearer against bludgeoning.

OXFORD UNIVERSITY FORBADE STUDENTS FROM BRINGING BOWS AND ARROWS TO LECTURES

YOU WON'T BELIEVE IT BUT...

It was quite common for animals to be tried for injuring humans. The French parliament once executed a cow.

YOU WON'T BELIEVE IT BUT...

Legend has it that Lady Godiva rode naked on a horse through the UK city of Coventry to save its people from having to pay taxes.

COOKING UP TROUBLE

Most people in the Middle Ages lived in wooden houses with empty holes for windows. Because people cooked their food on an open fire, they had to be careful when making dinner – a gust of wind through the window could send sparks inside and burn the house down.

BELIEVE IT OR NOT

If you think your bedroom is messy, try living like they did in the Middle Ages. Rubbish was thrown everywhere, dead animals littered the streets and people would throw toilet waste onto the street too. Food was contaminated and often rotten, and urine was used for washing clothes.

SAFETY FIRST

From about 1300 CE, knights wore armor made from solid metal plates. This offered good protection, but was very heavy. The average suit of armor could weigh at least 40lbs/18kg, the weight of a typical bodybuilder's dumbbell.

AN ARROW ESCAPE

The weapon of choice for armies was the longbow. A longbow could fire an arrow 750ft/228m – over twice the length of a soccer field. An arrow from a longbow could shoot through a wooden door 3in/7.5cm thick.

MEDIEVAL LORDS OFTEN HELD THEIR GREAT FEASTS IN THE MORNING, NOT IN THE EVENING

YOU WON'T BELIEVE IT BUT...
People believe that dogs can only see in different shades of gray but they can actually see violet, indigo, blue, yellow and red.

YOU WON'T BELIEVE IT BUT...
Ultraviolet, just beyond the visible spectrum, is the wavelength in sunlight that can tan or burn our skin.

SOUND WAVES TRAVEL AT 1,088FT PER SECOND – A JUMBO JET CAN COVER 762.6FT PER SECOND

OVER THE RAINBOW
Ever wondered why you only see rainbows when the sun shines on a rainy day? It's because when the light shines through the moist air it is broken down into the seven colors of the spectrum, which then appear as a ring in the sky.

SPECTRUM OF LIGHT
Light moves in waves, and different waves have different lengths. To our eyes, these different wavelengths show up as different colors. All these colors together are called the spectrum. We can only see colors in the middle of it. At either end are infrared or ultra-violet light, which we cannot see as their wavelengths are too low or too high for our eyes to pick up.

WHY IS THE SKY BLUE?
The color of the sky is influenced by the light from the Sun and what happens when it hits molecules in our atmosphere. Sunlight is made up of many different colors but the molecules scatter more blue light from the Sun towards our eyes than other colors.

WHAT IS SOUND?
Just like light, sound is simply a form of energy moving in a wave. Sound travels by vibration, and these change depending on what the sound is traveling through. Next time you have a bath, put your ears below the water and knock on the tub. It sounds completely different.

CAN YOU UNDERSTAND ME?
When you speak, your vocal cords vibrate and make the sounds. Your mouth and tongue then form these sounds into the words you want to say.

WHY ARE EARS SO SQUIGGLY?
It's not just to make us look funny. Our ears are there to direct sounds towards the eardrum, and the weird looking folds and ridges make this happen. Your eardrum vibrates when the sound waves reach it, and your brain translates so you can understand what you heard.

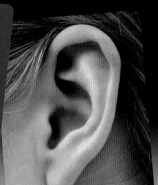

YOU WON'T BELIEVE IT BUT...
If a person is color blind, it means they have a genetic defect in their eye so that they see certain colors differently to people without the condition, or they may not be able to distinguish certain colors.

BREAKING THE BARRIER
While it's impossible for us to travel faster than light, we can travel faster than sound – somewhere around 760mph/1,223kph. Jet planes often break this sound barrier. When they do, the sound of the jet can only explode behind it. This is called a sonic boom.

WHAT IS LIGHT?
Light is made up of tiny particles called photons, moving in waves. The more photons in the wave, the brighter it is. When you twist a dimmer switch you're changing the amount of photons in the bulb. The light isn't getting brighter, there's just more of it.

THE BLUE WHALE'S CALL IS ALMOST AS LOUD AS A FIREWORK

SEE-THROUGH SOUND
We can use sound waves to look inside people. Ultrasound waves are very high frequency, so we can't hear them. They can pass through the human body, and hospitals use special ultrasound machines to read the echoes that bounce off the things inside.

170dB/C 4
Persist Off
2D Opt:HSCT
Fr Rate:Surv

–5

–10

PROFILE

YOU WON'T BELIEVE IT BUT...
Outer space is silent. With no air to vibrate, sound waves cannot travel, so even rockets go very quiet.

MIRRORS WORK IN THE SAME WAY AS ECHOES – BUT THEY BOUNCE LIGHT WAVES BACK AT YOU

ECHO, ECHO, ECHO
When sound waves hit a solid object, some of the waves travel through it, but some bounce back. Stand in front of a solid wall and shout something at it. You should hear your sound waves bounce back, but you probably already know it as your echo.

NOW THAT'S FAST
Light travels at a staggering 299,792,458mps/482,455,453kps. Even at this speed, the sheer distance between objects in space means light takes a long time to get to us. The light from the Sun is seven minutes old when you see it, and the light from distant stars can be thousands of years old.

LIGHT IS WHITE
The seven colors of the visible spectrum are red, orange, yellow, green, blue, indigo and violet. Normally we can't see them because when they're all mixed together they appear as white.

UNDERWATER ERUPTIONS
The ocean floor is full of cracks where underwater volcanoes spew out magma from the Earth. The minerals within this lava also add to the oceans' salt content. Around 75 percent of all magma eruptions happen underwater.

FLOAT ON
Located between Israel, Jordan and the West Bank, the Dead Sea was once part of an ancient sea that was cut off and then shrank, with the remaining water getting saltier all the time. It is famous for being so salty you can float in it without moving.

YOU WON'T BELIEVE IT BUT...
As well as containing salt, scientists estimate that our oceans contain 20 million tons of gold in small, non-extractable concentrations.

AN AGE IN AQUARIUS
Aquarius is the world's only underwater research laboratory. It's 4mi/5.6km off the coast of Florida and 65ft/20m under the sea. Scientists spend long periods inside the laboratory, with the longest mission lasting 14 days.

BLUE PLANET
You don't have to travel very far in space before Earth becomes one color – the blue of its global ocean. Water makes up 71 percent of the planet's surface. Of this, only three percent is fresh water that we can use.

THE OCEANS COVER AN AREA OF AROUND 224 MILLION SQ MI/361 MILLION SQ KM

YOU WON'T BELIEVE IT BUT...
The highest tides are found in Canada's Bay of Fundy – the difference between tides is more than a three-storey building due to the unique shape of the bay.

MIND THAT ICEBERG
Iceberg Alley is an area of the North Atlantic where icebergs break off from Greenland's glaciers and enter the ocean. They often float into shipping lanes and can be extremely dangerous.

THE LOST CONTINENT
In the 18th century, Captain Samuel Wallis was sent by the British Navy to find a continent that all learned men believed lay somewhere in the Pacific Ocean. They were wrong: the Pacific is largely empty. But the trip wasn't wasted as Wallis came across the island of Tahiti.

THE PACIFIC OCEAN'S NAME COMES FROM THE LATIN 'MARE PACIFICUM', WHICH MEANS 'PEACEFUL SEA'

WHY IS SEAWATER SALTY?

The oceans are salty because of the rain. Rain is made slightly acidic by carbon dioxide in the air. This acidity dissolves the minerals, mainly salt, in rocks, which are washed into the rivers and then into the sea. And that's why it's salty.

FREAKY FISH

Most fish and sea plants live fairly near the surface of the ocean in the Euphotic zone (down to 1,600ft/500m), but the bizarre angler fish lives in the pitch black depths at 3,000ft/900m. It has a small light dangling on a stalk from its head to attract prey.

FLAT AS A PANCAKE

At the deepest point in the ocean, the pressure created by the water is massive – more than 11,318 tons per square meter. This is equivalent to one person attempting to hold up 50 jumbo jet passenger planes.

SWALLOWING AMERICA

The Pacific Ocean is not only the largest in the world, but also the deepest as well. It is more than 30 times the size of the continental US and its deepest point, the Marinas trench, could swallow almost 24 Empire State Buildings, one on top of the other.

YOU WON'T BELIEVE IT BUT...

Giant waves called tsunami, created by earthquakes, can travel as fast as a jet airplane through the Pacific Ocean.

DISAPPEARING OCEANS

More than 10 oceans have disappeared forever because of continental drift. The Bridge River Ocean, between America and the Pacific islands, was a notable casualty and closed forever around 115 million years ago. Another victim, the Tethys Ocean – that spanned from Europe to Asia – used to split an enormous supercontinent called Panagea in two.

YOU WON'T BELIEVE IT BUT...

The area of the Pacific Ocean is greater than all the land masses of the Earth combined.

CELEBRATING SEA GODS

Since ancient times, the sea has inspired awe and legend. Many cultures worshipped gods: the Greeks worshipped Poseidon, who later became the Romans' Neptune. Seafaring warriors, the Vikings, had several sea gods. Chief of them was Ægir, who caused storms, calmed seas, and brewed beer.

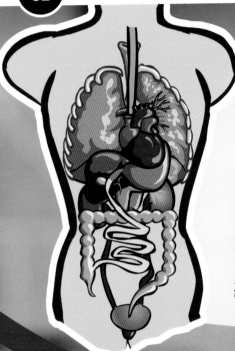

YOU WON'T BELIEVE IT BUT...
Eating an average meal, you swallow up to 300 times. Or at least you should.

WHAT'S THE SMALL INTESTINE?
The small intestine hangs in folds and is full of wrinkles. Food stays here for up to six hours and it's where most of it is absorbed by your body. If you were to lay the small intestine out flat, it would be about 22ft/6.7m long – it is called 'small' though, because it is only about 1in/3cm wide.

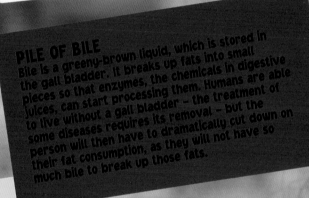

KEEP THEM CLEAN
Your teeth contain nerves and blood vessels in an inner soft pulp. They are covered with enamel, the body's hardest substance.

THE LIVER PERFORMS AROUND 500 FUNCTIONS

DOWN THE HATCH
As food passes through you, it is broken down into tiny pieces by the process of digestion and dissolved in your blood. The digestive tract, or alimentary canal, is a tube that actually runs all the way from your mouth to the hole in your backside (the anus). In an average lifetime, this tract will process the weight of five large trucks.

PILE OF BILE
Bile is a greeny-brown liquid, which is stored in the gall bladder. It breaks up fats into small pieces so that enzymes, the chemicals in digestive juices, can start processing them. Humans are able to live without a gall bladder – the treatment of some diseases requires its removal – but the person will then have to dramatically cut down on their fat consumption, as they will not have so much bile to break up those fats.

YOUR TONGUE CAN ONLY TASTE SWEET, SOUR, SALTY AND BITTER

TOUGH TUBE
The 1ft/0.3m tube that goes from our mouth to our stomach is called the esophagus. You can still swallow if you are upside down, because of the strong muscles in the esophagus. This isn't recommended.

WHAT'S IN POO?
Feces are what's left after your body's absorbed everything that is useful to it. It includes waste pigments, water, dead cells and bacteria, and is excreted via the rectum through the anus.

WHY ARE MY TEETH DIFFERENT SHAPES?
Teeth are different because they all have different jobs. There are four types: incisors, for cutting; canines, for tearing; premolars, for crushing; and the big flat molars at the back for grinding.

BELLY UP
Gastric juices in your stomach carry on breaking up food. The stomach lining has little folds called rugae, which go flat as your stomach fills up. Food remains in your stomach for up to four hours. The adult stomach can hold 0.4gal/1.5l of material.

YOU WON'T BELIEVE IT BUT...
Even thinking about food makes you salivate – your body is getting ready to digest what you eat.

YOU WON'T BELIEVE IT BUT...
Each meal, along with your food, you swallow about one pint/500ml of air – which makes you burp.

ROLE OF SALIVA
In your mouth, food mixes with saliva, which helps it slip down easily. Spittle also starts to break down your food, and helps to keep your mouth and teeth clean. You make one to three pints a day.

HUNGER ALARM
Your stomach growls when you're hungry because your brain tells it to – the stomach is trying to digest something but there is nothing in it to eat. The vibrations in your empty stomach are what you hear as growling.

WHAT A WASTE
Your large intestine has a tiny tube coming off it called an appendix, which doesn't actually do anything. It may have been useful to our ancestors, but for us it can be a pain – quite literally – because it may get infected and need to be removed. Wisdom teeth don't do anything helpful, either.

YOU WON'T BELIEVE IT BUT...
Your stomach makes about 0.53gal/2l of hydrochloric acid a day, which would seriously burn your skin if it touched the outside of your body.

YOUR COLON CONTAINS ABOUT 400 DIFFERENT KINDS OF BACTERIA

WHEN DO MY TEETH CHANGE?
Your first set of teeth appear at around six months old. These are baby teeth, and there are 20 of them. Between age six and 12 these are replaced by permanent teeth, of which there are normally 32.

THE AVERAGE HUMAN PRODUCES UP TO 10,000 GALLONS OF SALIVA IN A LIFETIME

MARTIN LUTHER KING JR

This African-American campaigner was the leader of the civil rights movement and is famous for fighting for equal rights among races. He was awarded the Nobel Peace Prize for his efforts, but was assassinated in 1968.

GANDHI

Mahatma Gandhi became famous because of his belief in non-violence as a way to protest. The Indian spiritual leader urged people not to resort to violence to get what they want. He helped India gain independence in 1948, as well as inspiring millions of people around the world to fight peacefully for their freedom.

YOU WON'T BELIEVE IT BUT...

Stranded by a flight cancellation, Richard Branson decided to charter a jet liner – and Virgin Atlantic Airways was born.

SIR WINSTON CHURCHILL

British Prime Minister from 1940, Winston Churchill is a key figure in history because of his role in World War Two, inspiring the Allied Forces to go on to victory. He was known for his 'never surrender' attitude and his rousing speeches.

EXPLOSIVE STUFF

Swiss chemist, industrialist and inventor Alfred Nobel is best known for founding the Nobel Prize awards, which recognize excellence in a number of different fields. But he certainly wasn't solely concerned with peaceful achievements. He spent most of his life studying and manufacturing explosives and was the inventor of dynamite.

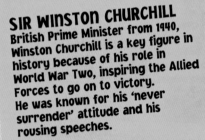

YOU WON'T BELIEVE IT BUT...

William Shakespeare is the world's most famous playwright, but we still don't know his exact birthday – the date, April 23rd, 1564 is actually a guess.

MAHATMA GANDHI WOVE HIS OWN CLOTHES ON A CHARKA, A TRADITIONAL INDIAN SPINNING WHEEL

ALL RIGHT?

Together, The Wright Brothers, Orville and Wilbur, built the world's first successful fixed-wing aircraft. However, they only flew together once, in 1910 at Huffman Prairie, Ohio, because they wanted to make sure that if one of them crashed and was killed, the other would be able to continue their work.

LEONARDO DA VINCI

Perhaps best known for his paintings (such as the *Mona Lisa*), Italian Leonardo da Vinci (1452-1519) was also an inventor, sculptor, scientist, mathematician, architect and writer.

GENGHIS KHAN

In 1206, warrior Genghis Khan founded the Mongol Empire, one of the biggest empires ever assembled. He united Mongolia and got the people on his side but not by being nice – he was one of the most feared rulers of all time.

GEORGE WASHINGTON

In 1789, George Washington was declared the first President of the United States. He'd become a much respected figure; during the War of Independence, the future of the nation rested on his soldiers. As Commander-in-Chief of the Army , he was instrumental in defeating the British.

A MEAL MACHINE

Henry Ford may be most famous for making the first mass-produced car – the Model T Ford – but he also liked to experiment with unusual materials. He was fascinated by what you could make from soybeans and in 1941 made a car body entirely out of plastic derived from them.

PLATO

Plato was one of the most important figures in Ancient Greece. Born around 428 BCE, Plato may have coined the term 'philosophy', which means love of knowledge.

RL BENZ INVENTED THE AUTOMOBILE, BUT HIS WIFE BERTHA MARKETED IT. IN 1888, SHE DROVE 50 MILES TO SHOW THE WORLD THAT THE VEHICLE WAS RELIABLE

ALEXANDER THE GREAT

Student of the famous Greek scholar Aristotle, Alexander the Great (356-323 BCE) well deserved his title, having conquered vast swathes of land, including Persia, Egypt, Greece and northern India. He was ruthless but had such respect for other cultures, he let his conquered subjects keep their traditions. He founded 70 cities, a number of them called Alexandria.

YOU WON'T BELIEVE IT BUT...

By the age of 17, Bill Gates had sold his first computer program – to his old high school.

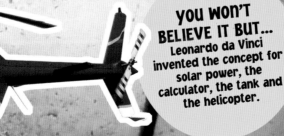

YOU WON'T BELIEVE IT BUT...

Leonardo da Vinci invented the concept for solar power, the calculator, the tank and the helicopter.

YOU WON'T BELIEVE IT BUT...
According to one story, Thomas Edison may have invented the word 'hello', in 1877, as the preferred way of answering the telephone.

IT'S FOR YOU
The telephone was invented by a Scot called Alexander Graham Bell. He was fascinated by the idea of transmitting speech down wires. In 1876, Bell made the world's first phone call when he said to his assistant: "Mr Watson – come here – I want to see you."

YOU WON'T BELIEVE IT BUT...
Before phones and email, messages had to be carried by a messenger on horseback and could take weeks, or even months, to arrive.

AROUND THE WORLD, OVER A BILLION PEOPLE ARE NOW BELIEVED TO HAVE ACCESS TO THE INTERNET

FESTIVE CHEER
On December 3rd, 1992 Richard Jarvis of Vodaphone received an excellent Christmas present – the first commercial text message ever sent. It read (predictably) 'Merry Christmas' and was sent by Neil Papworth of Sema Group using his computer. Jarvis received it on his Orbitel 901 handset.

1 new message

LOGGING ON
The internet was invented by the US military in 1969. They spent years researching ways to allow computers to talk directly with each other using telephone lines. The early internet looked nothing like the one we use today. There were no web pages, just scientists writing to each other.

FAST AND FURIOUS
A recent study estimated that a colossal 171 billion emails are sent every day, which works out at about 2 million per second. However, they are not all sent by individuals with something to say, because between 70 and 72 percent were calculated to be spam or viruses.

SEEKING SOFTWARE
An Israeli software company created the first instant messaging program to be aimed at the general public. They launched ICQ – a shortened version of I-Seek-You – in 1996 and sold out two years later for the princely sum of $407/£203 million. Helping people communicate is big business.

CAN YOU CRACK THE CODE?
People use codes to keep secret information safe. Letters can be turned into numbers, or whole words can be replaced with code. One of the most famous codes is Morse Code, which uses dots and dashes instead of letters.

SINGTONES ARE RINGTONES THAT USE YOUR VOICE, BUT ALTER IT TO MAKE YOU A BETTER SINGER

HEY! OVER HERE!

Before telephones, people used different ways of communicating messages over long distances. Early humans banged drums. Sailors used flags to pass information from ship to ship. Trained pigeons have also been used to carry messages.

GOING MOBILE

The world's first commercial mobile phone went on sale in 1984. The Motorola DynaTAC 8000X weighed seven times more than modern mobile phones. If you wanted one, it cost $8,000/£4,000 for the privilege. That's about 20 times the cost of phones today.

COMPUTER PROGRAMMER RAY TOMLINSON SENT THE FIRST EMAIL – TO HIMSELF – IN 1971

CONNECTING YOU NOW

The early telephone networks were controlled by enormous switchboards. Each line came into a socket and lines were connected by the operator plugging in a short cord between two sockets. As phones became more popular, automatic switchboards were introduced, allowing people to call each other directly.

YOU WON'T BELIEVE IT BUT...

Alexander Graham Bell also invented the photophone, which transmitted speech through sunlight. It actually worked, but not on cloudy days.

BLAZING THUMBS

The blazing thumbs of 13-year-old Morgan Pozgar have earned her the title of first-ever American Texting Champion. To win the title and cash prize she texted at the speed of light – or to be precise, with a message speed of 42 seconds for a 151-character phrase.

CAN I LEAVE A MESSAGE?

As telephones became widespread, people began missing phone calls. Willy Müller was the first to suggest a solution. He created an automatic answering machine in 1935. Unfortunately, his machine was 3ft/90cm tall.

IN 2006 THERE WERE AROUND 1.1 BILLION PEOPLE USING EMAIL

YOU WON'T BELIEVE IT BUT...

Early telephone operators were able to hear every conversation they connected.

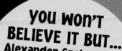

ROCK ON TV
Rock band Queen were unable to appear live on UK chart show *Top of the Pops* to perform their hit single *Bohemian Rhapsody* in 1975. So they spent a few hours putting together a short film that could be played instead. In just one afternoon, they'd invented the modern pop video.

HOT ROD
The biggest ever concert crowd didn't turn up to see Madonna, or U2, or any of today's biggest stars. The record was set on New Year's Eve in 1994, when Scottish rocker Rod Stewart threw a free concert on a beach in Brazil. An amazing 3.5 million people attended.

WHERE'S THE KING?
Elvis Presley, the American singer known as the 'King of Rock and Roll', died of a heart attack in 1977 at the age of 42, but many fans believe he's still alive. There is even an official Elvis Sightings Society that asks people to write in if they think they see him walking around.

YOU WON'T BELIEVE IT BUT...
The world's biggest selling music single of all time is *Candle in the Wind*, Elton John's tribute to the Princess of Wales. It sold over 37 million copies.

AN ALBUM MUST SELL 500,000 COPIES TO BECOME A GOLD DISC IN THE US

RAP INVENTED
Rap music was created in New York in the 1970s by combining elements of soul, funk and reggae. The first rap song to reach the charts was *Rapper's Delight* by the Sugarhill Gang.

YOU WON'T BELIEVE IT BUT...
Three hit songs have had titles consisting of just one letter or number – 7, U and X.

THE FIRST BOY BAND?
When The Beatles became famous in the 1960s, they attracted crowds of screaming girls wherever they went. Many people have called them the world's first boy band. The Beatles' hit song *Yesterday*, is the most recorded song in history with over 3,000 versions recorded by other artists.

U2 HAVE MORE GRAMMY AND BRIT AWARDS THAN ANY OTHER POP GROUP

MONEY WELL SPENT
In the 1960s, the Motown record label was known as Hitsville USA. It specialized in R&B and soul. The label, which was eventually worth millions, was set up by a young music fan called Berry Gordy with just a few hundred dollars. Between 1961 and 1971, Motown released 110 top ten hits in America alone.

ROCK LOUDER
Many rock bands have tried to claim the title of being the world's loudest rockers. The three main contenders are The Who, Metallica and Manowar. Scientific tests at their concerts have recorded sound levels of around 130 decibels – that's like standing next to a jet fighter taking off.

A MONSTER HIT
Michael Jackson first became famous when he was just 11 years old, singing with his brothers as the Jackson 5. He went on to release *Thriller*, which is still the best-selling album of all time. During the record-breaking 14-minute video for the title song, Michael spectacularly transformed into a werewolf.

IN 2006, THERE WERE OVER 500 MILLION LEGAL MUSIC DOWNLOADS IN AMERICA ALONE

BACK TO THE FUTURE
Michael and Janet Jackson's music video *Scream*, was the most expensive ever made, costing more than $7/£3.5 million. Its futuristic setting required pricey special effects – like a computer-generated spaceship.

MOUSE MATES
They may be three of the biggest names in pop, but Justin Timberlake, Britney Spears and Christina Aguilera all knew each other before they became celebrities – and it's all thanks to Mickey Mouse. They all worked together as singers on the *New Mickey Mouse Club* TV show in the early 1990s.

IN 1992, 'I WILL ALWAYS LOVE YOU' MADE WHITNEY HOUSTON THE FIRST WOMAN TO CONCURRENTLY TOP THE UK, US AND AUSTRALIAN SINGLES CHARTS

THE SONGBIRD
Mariah Carey's vocal range spans five octaves, and she is the only female artist to have 17 number one songs on the US Billboard Hot 100 chart. In 2001 Mariah signed a recording deal with Virgin for a staggering $80/£40 million.

YOU WON'T BELIEVE IT BUT...
Jimmy Osmond was just nine years old when his 1972 hit, *Long Haired Lover From Liverpool*, reached the top of the UK charts.

YOU WON'T BELIEVE IT BUT...
The first song to be converted into an mp3 was *Tom's Diner* by Suzanne Vega.

FASTEST SELLING MP3
The iPod is the fastest selling mp3 player in history. 100 million iPods of all varieties were sold between November 2001 and April 2007. In that time, more than 10 different variations on the iPod have been launched, including a limited edition range featuring the engraved signature of Madonna.

GREECE HAS MORE THAN 3,000 ISLANDS – BUT ONLY 140 ARE INHABITED

FORGET CHEERING
For thousands of years, Greeks traditionally accompanied their local bands by enthusiastically throwing their plates on the ground and smashing them.

READY, STEADY, GO
The Greeks loved sports and held a huge athletic competition every four years in the city of Olympia. This eventually became known as the Olympic Games.
Competitors took part in running, boxing, chariot racing and more to win the coveted laurel wreath – all in the nude.

VOTE FOR ME
In 508 BCE, the capital city of Athens became home to the first democracy – a system that lets the people decide on their government. However, women, slaves, foreigners and men under 18 were excluded from the system.

PLAY TIME
Greeks invented the modern play and performed their shows in open-air theaters. They were either tragedies or comedies and actors wore bright masks, so those at the back could follow the action. Some theaters held up to 20,000 people.

GREEKS BEARING GIFTS
Ancient Greeks built what is considered by many to be the foundation of Western civilization and formed many ideas and beliefs that we still live by today. The Romans thought so too, and adopted many of their ideas.

YOU WON'T BELIEVE IT BUT...
Because production of 'Feta' cheese goes back 6,000 years, it has been officially recognized as a uniquely Greek product and only Greece can use the name.

HUNDREDS AND THOUSANDS
300 warriors from the Greek state of Sparta fought tens of thousands of invading Persians in the battle of Thermopylae. The Spartans held off the Persians for three days, but were eventually defeated by Emperor Xerxes' huge army.

EUREKA
Greece was home to some of history's greatest inventors. Archimedes made many scientific and mathematical discoveries and he invented many new weapons and contraptions. Legend has it that he set up mirrors and turned the reflection of the sun on approaching Roman ships setting them on fire. Archimedes also came up with the mathematical ratio Pi.

TALK TO ME
Oracles were women the Greeks believed could speak to the gods. The Oracles went into a kind of dream and spoke in a very strange language, which the priests then translated for the audience.

THE PARTHENON WAS A TEMPLE COMPLETED IN 432 BCE AND ITS REMAINS STILL STAND TODAY

HIT OR MYTH?
According to Greek mythology, there were a dozen gods, called the Twelve Olympians. The Greeks thought Zeus and the other gods such as Poseidon and Apollo lived on Mount Olympus in northern Greece, using the mountains themselves as thrones.

YOU WON'T BELIEVE IT BUT...
The ancient Greeks invented the first 'proper' hat 2,500 years ago. Called a 'Petasos', it had a wide brim and was worn for traveling, to shield the wearer from the weather.

YOU WON'T BELIEVE IT BUT...
Once the Romans took over, the Olympics stopped for 1,500 years, until they were revived in 1896.

FIGHTING PHALANX
Greeks were fine soldiers and often had to defend their land from invading armies. One winning tactic was called a phalanx. Hundreds of men would pack closely together behind overlapping shields and then stick out their long spears and move forward together in formation.

NIKE WAS THE GODDESS OF VICTORY AND WATCHED OVER THE OLYMPIC CONTESTS

DOCTOR, DOCTOR...
Hippocrates was a legendary Ancient Greek doctor. If you were sick, he would take a sample of your urine and test it – by tasting it! Despite his odd treatments, medics today still swear by his oath to do no harm.

TROY STORY
A famous Greek legend is the Siege of Troy. Paris, a prince, eloped to Troy with the Spartan king's wife Helen, causing 10 years of fighting. The war was won when Greek warriors hid inside a giant wooden horse that they gave the Trojans as a present. They jumped out at night and opened the city gates, letting the rest of the Greek troops in.

PLASTIC NOT FANTASTIC
Modern society has come to rely on plastic for a great number of things, such as bottles and bags. However, plastic is made from oil and there are concerns that such items use up valuable oil resources.

CAN IT
Tons of new aluminum is produced every year, creating great clouds of greenhouse gases and pollution in the process. A lot of this is used for canned goods. If we do buy a can, it's important we recycle it.

GARBAGE MEANS GROCERIES
In Philadelphia, an electronic chip has been embedded into recycling trash cans. When full, the cans are weighed by the garbage truck to see how much has been recycled. Recycle enough and you earn Recycle Bank Dollars which can be spent on groceries, clothes and more. The system works too – the pilot scheme using 2,500 residents saw the recycling figure jump from six to 90 percent.

A LOAD OF RUBBISH
An average European home produces 1,177lbs/534kg of household rubbish every year, and an average of 22 percent is recycled, although this varies from country to country; one of the most impressive recyclers is Belgium, which recycles 53 percent of its household waste.

EVERY PERSON IN THE UK THROWS OUT THEIR OWN BODYWEIGHT IN RUBBISH EVERY SEVEN WEEKS

PANDA FOOD FLOORING
An eco-friendly alternative to using rainforest hardwoods is bamboo, the favorite food of pandas. It can be used for many things including flooring, but doesn't require the whole plant to be killed. You just cut the tops off and it grows back.

YOU WON'T BELIEVE IT BUT...
There are companies 'recycling' old computers by distributing them to developing nations. Computer Aid International has shipped over 90,000 used PCs to more than 100 countries.

80 PERCENT OF AN AVERAGE CAR CAN BE RECYCLED

LIGHT FANTASTIC
Energy-saving light-bulbs might cost more money than regular ones, but they last far longer – 15,000 hours as opposed to an old-fashioned bulb's 1,000 hours. More importantly, they use less electricity, which means less pollution.

YOU WON'T BELIEVE IT BUT...
Recycled paper makes 73 percent less air pollution than paper coming direct from trees.

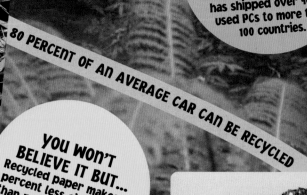

APE APOCALYPSE
The activities of humans are threatening thousands of animal species with extinction. One group that is threatened is the great apes, such as gorillas, chimps and orangutans. Some experts predict that there might be none left by 2030.

YOU WON'T BELIEVE IT BUT...
Recycling just one aluminum tin saves enough energy to power a TV for three hours.

NO MATTER HOW MANY TIMES GLASS IS RECYCLED, IT NEVER BECOMES LESS CLEAR

SAVE THE ANIMALS
Man has caused the extinction of at least 500 species of animal, most of them this century, and this alarming trend looks set to continue. At least one species dies out every year, about 5,000 are classified as endangered, and many more probably become extinct without anyone realizing.

DON'T WASTE WOOD
Just because wood is natural, it doesn't mean we can be careless about how we use it. Trees take years to grow, and harvesting new wood uses more fuel than recycling old wood.

IS FLYING BAD FOR THE ENVIRONMENT?
It is, and environmental campaigners are concerned that pollution caused by air travel will continue to grow. In Europe, aircraft pollution nearly doubled between 1990 and 2006 – and it's still increasing.

FLUSHED WITH SUCCESS
Water is becoming scarcer in many Western countries and the process of making it drinkable costs precious energy. One simple way of saving water is to put a house-brick in the cistern of your toilet. This causes the water level to rise so you use less when you flush.

YOU WON'T BELIEVE IT BUT...
On average, 16 percent of the price of a product goes to pay for the packaging, most of which just goes in the bin.

DEFORESTATION
Rainforests are the oldest living ecosystems on Earth and are home to more than half of the planet's plant and animal species, despite covering only six percent of the world's surface. That percentage is falling because people wanting to clear the forests – to sell the lumber and farm the land – are cutting down about 2,000 trees per minute.

PLASTIC TAKES AROUND 500 YEARS TO DECOMPOSE

GONE FISHING

Humans have always liked eating fish. Hooks made from animal bone have been found, showing that our Stone Age ancestors were fishing hundreds of thousands of years ago.

BONY BODY

Coral reefs look like they're made of stone but are actually a sort of skeleton worn on the outside by creatures called corals. As the creatures reproduce, more coral is produced, which forms a reef. In turn, this becomes home to thousands of sea creatures.

SWORD OF THE SEA

The Swordfish gets its name from the huge spike on the end of its nose. It uses this to kill fish for food and to defend itself against sharks.

POACHED PUPFISH

One of the rarest fish is the Devil's Hole Pupfish. It only lives in a small natural pond in Death Valley, one of the hottest places on Earth. The water is the same temperature as your bathwater. Only about 80 of these fish are known to still exist.

AT ONLY 0.3IN/0.8CM LONG, THE PHILIPPINE GOBY IS THE SMALLEST FISH

IN MISSOURI IT IS ILLEGAL TO FISH FOR CATFISH BY HAND

YOU WON'T BELIEVE IT BUT...

Corals are part of the family of animals called 'cnidarians', which also includes jellyfish and sea anemones.

YOU WON'T BELIEVE IT BUT...

There are at least 24,600 known species of fish.

FOOD FOR THOUGHT

Fish aren't just tasty to eat, they're also incredibly good for you. They're packed full of vitamins and minerals and many experts now say we should eat fish at least twice a week.

THE SALMON'S STRUGGLE
Pacific salmon are born in fresh water, but spend most of their lives in the ocean. They end their lives by swimming hundreds of miles back upriver against the current to the place where they were born, where they fertilize eggs and then die.

you won't BELIEVE IT BUT...
40 percent of all fish species live in fresh water, yet less than three percent of the Earth's water is fresh water.

HORNED DEVIL
The biggest of the Rays, the Manta Ray, is also called the 'Devil Ray' because it has two small horns on either side of its head. It measures up to 23ft/7m across and weighs in at 6,613lbs/3,000kg - the same weight as a female Asian elephant.

THE SHARK IS THE ONLY FISH THAT CAN BLINK WITH BOTH EYES

WHAT KIND OF FISH IS THAT?
When a Coelacanth was caught off the coast of South Africa in 1938, scientists were amazed – they thought it had been extinct for 65 million years! This has caused some people to wonder if any other prehistoric beasts are swimming around down there.

FISH HAVE BEEN AROUND FOR 500 MILLION YEARS

LIGHT SNACK
The bizarre Anglerfish lives deep in the ocean, at about 3,000ft/900m. Because there is no light down there, it has a dangling 'lure' that glows in the dark. This is used to attract other fish that it then eats.

you won't BELIEVE IT BUT...
The glow of the Anglerfish's 'lure' is caused by millions of bacteria that live on it.

RIDE A SEAHORSE
Seahorses are strange fish. Not only do they look like horses but it is the male seahorse that carries the young, not the female. Once the eggs are fertilized, it's the male who keeps them in a special pouch until they hatch.

SWEET DREAMS
Fish are just as keen on napping as humans, but it's always hard to work out when they are asleep because they have no eyelids. However, a species of parrotfish found on the Great Barrier Reef sleeps so soundly that the fish can be picked up and handled by divers without stirring.

A FISHY STORY
The Climbing Perch (or Gourami) can 'walk' short distances on land by using its gills as supports and pushing itself along with fins and tail. It doesn't walk for fun though – only out of necessity when its water source dries up and it needs to find another one.

HOORAY FOR BOLLYWOOD

Put Bombay and Hollywood together, and you get Bollywood – the nickname given to India's incredibly busy film industry. It turns out almost 1,000 movies every year, many more than the big Hollywood studios.

TITANIC TAKINGS

Kate Winslet and Leonardo Di Caprio's doomed love affair in the movie *Titanic* left audiences weeping, but movie bosses smiling. That's because the film, written and directed by James Cameron, is the most successful movie of all time, having earned almost $2/£1 billion worldwide.

YOU WON'T BELIEVE IT BUT...

The most common line in movies is "Let's get outta here!" A study found that, at one point, it was spoken in four out of five American films.

THANKS TO HARRY POTTER, DANIEL RADCLIFFE WAS A MILLIONAIRE BEFORE HIS 15TH BIRTHDAY

ARNOLD SCHWARZENEGGER MADE $30/£15 MILLION FOR THE THIRD *TERMINATOR* MOVIE.

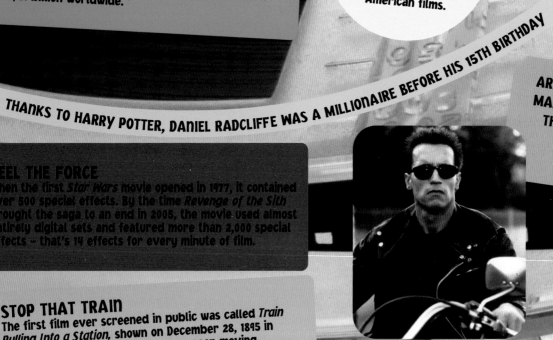

FEEL THE FORCE

When the first *Star Wars* movie opened in 1977, it contained over 500 special effects. By the time *Revenge of the Sith* brought the saga to an end in 2005, the movie used almost entirely digital sets and featured more than 2,000 special effects – that's 14 effects for every minute of film.

STOP THAT TRAIN

The first film ever screened in public was called *Train Pulling Into a Station,* shown on December 28, 1895 in Paris. The audience, who had never seen moving pictures before, fled in terror, fearing the train would come out of the screen and run them over.

THE BIGGEST MOVIES EVER?

It took Peter Jackson over eight years to bring the epic story of *The Lord of the Rings* to the big screen, but spare a thought for the people behind the scenes. They had to make 48,000 pieces of armor, 10,000 arrows, and 1,800 rubber Hobbit feet.

ELEMENTARY, DEAR DRACULA

Bloodsucking menace Dracula may be one of our most famous and feared film characters but he comes second in terms of movie appearances to Sherlock Holmes. Holmes is Hollywood's favorite character, making 200 movie appearances. Dracula made around 160 appearances.

HOW MUCH?
Back in 1991, the world gasped when *Terminator 2* became the first movie to cost more than $100/£50 million to produce. In 2007, movies like *Spider-Man 3* and *Pirates of the Caribbean* cost nearly three times that amount.

THE WORLD'S LONGEST MOVIE RUNS FOR 87 HOURS AND IS CALLED *THE CURE FOR INSOMNIA*.

IF YOU UNWOUND THE FILM FOR A 90-MINUTE MOVIE, IT WOULD BE OVER 7,800FT/2,400M LONG.

EYE-BOGGLING
The Sylvia Park cinema in New Zealand is the home of the largest traditional cinema screen in the world, measuring an amazing 43ft/13m high and 98ft/30m across. That's as tall as a house, and as long as a blue whale.

ROAR POWER
Casino Royale marked James Bond's 21st official movie outing, but even 007 needs to try harder to catch the king of the sequels. Japanese movie monster Godzilla first appeared in 1954 and, by the time the studio officially retired him 50 years later, he'd starred in an amazing 28 movies.

HOW DO MOVIES WORK?
When you watch a moving film, what you're actually seeing are incredibly fast sequences of still images, each slightly different to the last. When projected at 24 images per second, your brain fills in the gaps and is tricked into thinking the pictures are moving.

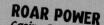

PATIENCE IS A VIRTUE
Animated films take much longer to produce than normal movies. Disney's *Snow White and the Seven Dwarves*, the first feature-length cartoon, was drawn by hand and took three years to complete. If Pixar's *Cars* (2006) was made using just one computer, it would have taken over 2,000 years to finish.

PIONEERING PROJECTIONISTS
Auguste and Louis Lumiere are hailed as the true pioneers of modern cinema. In the late 19th century, they invented a new method of projecting film and entertained the public with short movies.

YOU WON'T BELIEVE IT BUT...
Many people think that the *Wizard of Oz*, made in 1939, was the first color film. In fact, filmmakers were experimenting with color from the 1840s.

YOU WON'T BELIEVE IT BUT...
Legend has it that the golden statue presented at the Academy Awards got its Oscar nickname because it reminded one of the Academy staff of her Uncle Oscar.

PRESSING AHEAD
It was not until Johannes Gutenberg was involved in the building of the first printing press and the invention of movable type in the 1440s and 1450s that books could be printed in large numbers. Before that, it was a long, slow process as letters were carefully placed using wooden or metal blocks, and each sheet of paper was then pressed on top.

YOU WON'T BELIEVE IT BUT...
Chindogu, meaning 'weird tools' is the Japanese term for bizarre and outrageous inventions.

YOU WON'T BELIEVE IT BUT...
Some historians believe that, in the 1200s, Ghengis Khan invented the burger by keeping patties of meat under his saddle.

IN 1981, A PATENT WAS ISSUED FOR A TRUMPET THAT DOUBLED AS A FLAMETHROWER

A RIVETING INVENTION
Nevada-based tailor Jacob Davis invented the riveted jean in 1871 when a customer asked him to make a pair of trousers for her husband who often burst out of his pants at the seams. Davis added rivets to these trousers so they'd last longer, and his invention soon caught on with cowboys who wanted hard-wearing clothes.

TIME TO JET
The first airplane to fly under jet power was a German Heinkel HE-178 in 1939 and the first passenger jet was the de Havilland Comet, which started flying in 1949. The basic concept of a turbine engine was first patented in England in 1791 by a British engineer called John Barber.

YOU WON'T BELIEVE IT BUT...
During World War One, Minnesota-based mechanic Charles Strite was so fed up with burnt toast that he invented a machine which would toast bread and then stop automatically when it was done. His invention, the pop-up toaster, was patented in 1919.

THE BIG PONG
Many centuries before guns even existed, Chinese chemists were experimenting with gunpowder to create fireworks and explosions. The job was dangerous, and very smelly. To get one of the key ingredients – potassium nitrate – the poor scientists had to work with piles of animal dung.

A PATENT IS AN EXCLUSIVE RIGHT GRANTED TO SOMEONE TO USE OR SELL AN INVENTION

DRIVEN TO DISTRACTION
The first wireless remote-controlled toy cars were produced and sold by an English company called Mardave Racing in the 1960s. The company is still going today.

BIKINI BOMB
In 1946, engineer Louis Reard and fashion designer Jacques Heim introduced the bikini at a Parisian fashion show. It was named after Bikini Atoll, a small outcrop in the Marshall Islands where, a few days previously, nuclear weapons tests had been carried out – the men thought their invention was so daring that the reaction it provoked would be similar to the impact of a nuclear bomb.

A CUT ABOVE THE REST

If Earle Dickson's wife had been more careful, the sticking plaster might never have been invented. She was so accident-prone that Dickson began preparing bandages in advance by sticking pieces of gauze on a roll of tape. By 1921, his idea was on sale around the world.

IN AMERICA ALONE, THERE ARE ALREADY MORE THAN SEVEN MILLION PATENTS

YOU WON'T BELIEVE IT BUT...
The art of making music by scratching records was invented by a Brookyln DJ called Grand Wizzard Theodore in 1975.

CLICK-CLACK-FIZZZZZZ!
Years ago, if you wanted to open a canned drink, you had to punch two holes in the top. Ermal Fraze invented a tear-off strip in the early 1960s, but it was only when Omar Brown and Don Peters added a ring to it in 1965 that the modern can was born.

TIME TO PLAY?
Next time you start up your games console, you're taking part in a pastime that's been around for over 50 years. Written way back in 1952, by Alexander Douglas, the OXO computer game was tic-tac-toe played on a tiny black and white screen.

US PRESIDENT THOMAS JEFFERSON INVENTED A COAT HANGER, A FOLDAWAY BED AND A CALENDAR CLOCK

THE WRITE STUFF
The disposable ballpoint pen was patented in 1888 by John J Loud but, unfortunately, it leaked. Years later Laszlo Biro, a journalist from Hungary, created one using thicker ink. He took his idea to the British government, and the Royal Air Force used the first Biro pens in 1944.

MILITARY MICROWAVE
Did you know the microwave started life as a military radar? Its cooking properties were discovered when Percy LeBaron Spencer left a bar of chocolate next to a radar device, and saw it melted. He tried popcorn next and, as well as having a tasty snack, he revolutionized cooking forever.

YOU WON'T BELIEVE IT BUT...
Before Mary Anderson invented the windshield wiper in 1903, drivers had to lean out of their car and use their hands.

BATTERIES WEREN'T INCLUDED
The electrical battery was created over 200 years ago when an Italian physicist called Alessandro Volta lowered sheets of copper and zinc into salt water, creating an electrical current. After he died the volt, a unit of electrical power, was named in his honor.

YOU WON'T BELIEVE IT BUT...
Time-traveling adventurer *Doctor Who* is the world's longest-running science fiction TV series, having debuted in 1963, three years before *Star Trek*.

WOO-HOO
The Simpsons is the longest-running sitcom in US TV history, and also the longest running animated series. Homer and family first appeared in short cartoon sketches on *The Tracey Ullman Show* way back in 1987. Creator Matt Groening named the characters after his own family.

LOOK, I'M ON TV
In October 1925, William Edward Taynton, a 20-year-old office boy, was asked to sit in front of a camera by Scottish inventor John Logie Baird. He didn't know it at the time, but he had just become the first person ever to appear on television.

EVERYBODY'S WATCHING
The most successful pre-recorded show came when almost 106 million American viewers tuned in for the final episode of popular sitcom *M*a*s*H* in 1983.

BILLION FOR BAYWATCH
The most watched TV show in the world is *Baywatch*, the saga of Californian lifeguards that launched the career of Pamela Anderson. Running from 1989 to 2001, it has been broadcast in over 100 countries and has attracted over a billion viewers.

WORTH THE WAIT?
In 1999, the Dragon King of the tiny Buddhist country of Bhutan, located high in the Himalayan mountains, lifted a national ban on television, making it officially the last nation on Earth to receive regular TV broadcasts.

THE WORD 'TELEVISION' WAS FIRST OFFICIALLY USED AT THE 1900 EXPOSITION UNIVERSELLE IN PARIS

CAN YOU SEE?
Today, television screens keep getting bigger and bigger, but spare a thought for people who bought the very first television sets. Housed in a large wooden cabinet, the flickering black and white screen was no bigger than a playing card.

BUT DID HE WATCH THEM ALL?
The famous TV producer Aaron Spelling holds the world record for most hours of television produced. During his career, he created over 200 shows – including *Charlie's Angels*, *Starsky & Hutch* and *Dynasty* – adding up to 3,842 hours of primetime viewing.

IN THE US, IN 1952, MR POTATO HEAD BECAME THE FIRST TOY TO BE ADVERTISED ON TV

TV TOO
The first TV cartoon was *Crusader Rabbit*. The superhero bunny appeared on US television in 1949 and ran for 195 episodes until 1951. Before *Crusader Rabbit*, cartoons were only shown in cinemas before the film started.

YOU WON'T BELIEVE IT BUT...
The longest-serving actor in a TV series is William Roache in UK soap opera *Coronation Street*. He has been playing the part of Ken Barlow for over 45 years.

PRICEY PERFUME
Chanel perfume spent around $36 million/£18 million to produce a TV ad starring the actress Nicole Kidman, making it the most expensive ever produced at the time. The famous perfume doesn't appear anywhere in the advert.

SOAP OPERAS ARE SO CALLED BECAUSE THEY WERE ORIGINALLY SPONSORED BY SOAP COMPANIES

YOU WON'T BELIEVE IT BUT...
The first ever TV ad was broadcast in 1941 in the United States for the Bulova Watch Company. It paid just $9/£4.50 for the privilege.

YOU WON'T BELIEVE IT BUT...
The world's longest running television show is *Meet the Press*, an American news show that started in 1947.

COSTALOTTASAURUS
One of the most expensive TV documentaries ever made was the BBC's *Walking with Dinosaurs*. The award-winning computer graphics which brought the prehistoric beasts to life cost $9.9/£5 million for six episodes. That's $61,111/£32,000 for every minute.

THE AVERAGE VIEWER IN THE US WILL SPEND OVER 68 DAYS PER YEAR WATCHING TV

SHE EARNS HOW MUCH?
TV's highest paid star is Oprah Winfrey, who earns an estimated $225/£112.5 million every year from her television productions. Her chat show, which has been running since 1986, is the most successful show of its kind in television history and has won over 40 Emmy Awards over the course of its run.

SOMETHING FISHY
If SpongeBob SquarePants and his under-sea friends in Bikini Bottom seem to have a ring of truth about them, it's probably because creator Stephen Hillenburg is a qualified marine biologist and an expert on underwater life. He demonstrated the show to TV producers using a real aquarium.

DEEP DOWN
The deepest cave is the Voronya cave in Georgia, in the former Soviet Union. In 2005, a team of 60 people spent many days climbing down into its depths. When they could go no further, they were an astonishing 7,000ft/2,140m below the Earth's surface.

YOU WON'T BELIEVE IT BUT...
In folklore, caves were the best place to find dragons – but such myths may simply have been born out of locals mistaking large lizards for something more fearsome.

IS ANYBODY THERE?
The Movile cave in Romania contains an eco-system that exists without sunlight. 47 unique species of animal, from the tiniest microbe to a blind spider, live in the cave. It was cut off from the outside world five million years ago, leaving the animals to adapt to their surroundings.

NEVADA DESERT HAS AN ELEPHANT-SHAPED ROCK 'CARVED' BY EROSION

FAIRY CHIMNEYS
Cappadocia in Turkey has a remarkable landscape. As a result of millions of years of volcanic activity, the region is covered in volcanic rock. Because this is soft, it has been weathered away by the wind and rain, creating weird shapes that are known as fairy chimneys.

FEELING BOULDER
A boulder is generally accepted to be a rock that is so large that one person alone could not move it. However, the official definition of a boulder is of a rock that has a diameter of more than 10in/25.6cm, so they are not necessarily huge.

WORLD'S BIGGEST ROCK
The largest rock in the world can be found in the Australian outback and is called Mount Augustus (also known by its Aboriginal name, Burringurrah). The rock is 2,352ft/717m high, about 5mi/8km long and estimated to be about 1,000 million years old.

TAKE THE TUBE
Some caves are the result of lava tubes that were forced up by volcanoes. Kazumura cave in Hawaii is both the longest, at 214,845ft/65,500m, and deepest, at 3,612ft/1,101m, lava tube in the world.

WHAT A FIND
In 1940, four teenagers stumbled on one of the most remarkable archeological finds while they were playing in caves in southwestern France. The Lascaux caves contain the best-preserved examples of Stone Age art, depicting bulls, antelopes, horses and many other animals. They were painted around 17,000 years ago.

YOU WON'T BELIEVE IT BUT...
Moon rock is thought to be worth about four times as much as diamond – a raisin-sized piece of moon rock was valued at $5 million/ £2.5 million.

YOU WON'T BELIEVE IT BUT...
Kentucky, USA, boasts the longest known cave system in the world – the Mammoth Caves cover 365 explored miles and are about 10 million years old.

NATURE'S PAINTBRUSH
In Hayden, Western Australia, there is a gigantic 46ft/14m high and over 350ft/107m long 'wave'. This dramatic 500 million-year-old structure looks like an enormous surfer's wave, and is the result of water and wind erosion.

ROCKS ARE CATEGORIZED ACCORDING TO THEIR DIAMETER OR PARTICLE SIZE

FEELING HARD?
Some rocks are hard, while others are so soft we can easily scratch them away. In 1812, mineralogist Friedrich Mohs developed a scale of hardness. The human fingernail has a hardness score of 2.2, a copper penny about 3.2 and a knife blade 5.1.

AMAZING CAVE FOSSILS
Paleontologists often find the fossils of ancient animals that died trapped in caves. One of the best examples is in Nullarbor Plain in Australia. It contained hundreds of fossilized skeletons, some of huge beasts that lived 400,000 years ago. Scientists think the animals fell in through holes in the ground.

STONEHENGE IN THE UK WAS ERECTED OVER 4,100 YEARS AGO

CAVE CONDO
Although we tend to think of Stone Age man living in caves, they are also proving popular with modern day dwellers. Caves are being refurbished and sold as homes in countries such as Spain. These cave homes come fully equipped, are environmentally friendly, and are low maintenance.

WORK OR PLAY?
Many people enjoy going into caves and exploring them, even if the caves are difficult or dangerous to navigate. Exploring caves for fun in this way is called potholing or caving. However, when scientists go into caves to carry out research, it is called speleology.

DANCE TRANCE
To celebrate their religious beliefs, the Aztecs thumped large temple drums that could be heard for miles around. Participants danced themselves into a trance while worshipping their gods, including Xochipilli, the god of music and dance.

YOU WON'T BELIEVE IT BUT...
It's estimated that up to half of the Aztec population may have been wiped out by smallpox in 1520 and 1531.

AZTECS USED COCOA BEANS AND COTTON CLOTH AS CURRENCY

YOU WON'T BELIEVE IT BUT...
The Aztecs believed that warriors killed in battle spent four years in paradise, then returned to earth as a hummingbird or butterfly. This is because hummingbirds and butterflies fly and drink nectar from flowers, which the Aztecs considered to be the ultimate life of luxury.

GODS' GREAT PYRAMID
In the center of the capital city of Tenoch was a huge temple that towered 100ft/30m above the people below. At the peak of the Great Pyramid were two shrines: one for Huitzilpochtli, the god of war and sun, and one for Tlaloc, the god of rain and fertility.

IT IS ESTIMATED THAT 20,000 PEOPLE WERE RITUALLY SACRIFICED EVERY YEAR

EAGLE EYED
In 1325, migrating Aztecs saw a beautiful eagle sitting on a prickly pear, with a snake in its claws and its wings outstretched against the sun. They had been told in a vision to seek this and built the capital city of Tenochtitlan on that very spot.

CALENDAR CONFUSION?
The Aztecs had two calendars. They had a 365-day year, split into 18 months of 20 days, with five extra days at the end that were considered unlucky. The Aztecs also followed a 260-day ritual that featured numbers and symbols depicting the gods, which told them what to do.

AZTECS' END
In 1521, it took 75 days of fighting for the Spanish military to conquer the Aztec captial city, Tenochtitlan, and bring an end to the age of the Aztecs. The Spaniards built Mexico City in Tenochtitlan's place.

YOU WON'T BELIEVE IT BUT...
Aztecs drank an alcoholic drink made from plants called Pulque, but it was illegal to get drunk before the age of 70.

THE AZTEC POPULATION WAS OVER 19 MILLION

LET'S PLAY BALL
The Aztecs loved playing a ball game called Ulama. Many players would join together in specially built courts to hit a rubber ball with their hips. It is still played in some areas of Mexico and is one of the oldest sports in the world.

NOW YOU'RE TALKING
Early Aztecs did not communicate by writing, but did speak a language called Nahuatl, which is still spoken in some forms today. They also used hieroglyphs and pictures on beautifully painted paper, made from the pounded bark of fig trees.

SCHOOL'S OUT
Aztecs thought education was extremely important. They were one of the first civilizations to make going to school compulsory for every boy and girl. Boys learned practical skills like fishing, while girls learned crafts and housekeeping.

ALL HAIL BIRD-SNAKE
Aztecs worshipped many gods, but perhaps the most well known is Quetzalcoatl. He was a feathered serpent who was a god of wind, creativity and fertility. Some people still believe he lives in caves in deepest, darkest Mexico.

THE AVERAGE LIFE EXPECTANCY OF AN AZTEC MAN WAS 37 YEARS

GORY END FOR PRISONERS
The Aztecs took prisoners of war to the top of the Great Pyramid, cut out their hearts, cut off their heads and threw the bodies down the steps to cannibals below.

WHAT'S FOR DINNER?
The Aztec people had a very varied diet. A typical meal would consist of maize and beans with tomato or chillies, but Aztecs also ate fish and insects. High-ranking Aztecs were also known to dine on human flesh.

AHOY THERE...

The Pirates of Penzance is one of the world's most famous and enduring musicals – it was first performed in 1880 and remains popular to this day. It was written by Gilbert and Sullivan, who were famous for creating operas that were full of jokes and funny songs.

THE WORD 'THEATER' COMES FROM THE GREEK WORD 'THEATRON', MEANING 'PLACE OF SEEING'

WHERE IS BROADWAY?

Broadway is the name given to New York's theater district, where some of the world's most successful and famous shows are staged. Shows can run for many years – *The Phantom of the Opera* has been running at Broadway's Majestic Theater since 1988.

BETTER BRING A PILLOW

The world's longest play is *The Warp*, by Neil Oram, and it runs for an exhausting 22 hours. It was performed in London in 1979, is made up of 10 shorter plays, and tells the story of an ancient English mystic and his journey through life. The world's shortest play is *Breath*, by Samuel Beckett, which has no actors, and lasts just 35 seconds.

JACKIE CHAN: OPERA STAR?

When you think of opera, you probably think of large men, singing loudly. However, Chinese opera is full of acrobatics and kung fu displays, and that's why martial arts megastar Jackie Chan learned his amazing skills from the Peking Opera School.

YOU WON'T BELIEVE IT BUT...

In Japanese Kabuki theater, the actors use elaborate make-up to look like animals and monsters.

SAY WHAT?

The phrase 'break a leg' comes from the early days of the stage, when actors believed that wishing someone good luck would tempt fate and make their performance worse. They wish for something bad to happen, like a broken leg, in the hope that the opposite will happen and the performance will go well.

YOU WON'T BELIEVE IT BUT...

Cirque du Soleil's 'KÁ' is reputedly the most expensive stage production ever. It is performed at the MGM Grand Hotel in Las Vegas and cost $165 million/£80 million to set-up.

YOU WON'T BELIEVE IT BUT...

When a stage is described as being 'in the round', it means that the audience sits in a circle surrounding the actors.

IT'S BEHIND YOU
Want to see a play where you can yell at the actors? Then you should go to a pantomime, the traditional form of festive British shows where well-known fairy tales such as *Aladdin* are brought to life, with the audience expected to join in by shouting and singing along.

THE PLAYS OF WILLIAM SHAKESPEARE CONTAIN AN AMAZING 884,647 WORDS

THE CURSED PLAY
It is rumored that William Shakespeare included real magic spells in his play *Macbeth*, and many actors still refuse to mention it by name, preferring to call it 'the Scottish play'. The superstition says that the name of the play angers the witches, and they'll curse the actors if it is spoken aloud.

THE GREATEST WRITER EVER?
William Shakespeare, born in England in the 16th century, is often considered to be the greatest writer in the history of literature. His work has been translated and performed in many of the world's languages. Some people don't believe he wrote all of the plays that bear his name.

TO BE OR NOT TO BE?
The most famous, and most quoted, play in the English language is Shakespeare's *Hamlet*. It tells the story of the Prince of Denmark, who must reclaim his throne after his evil uncle murders his father, the king.

DON'T SPOIL THE SURPRISE
Agatha Christie's murder mystery *The Mousetrap* is the world's longest running play, having been performed in London since November 1952. The cast changes every year, and the audience is asked to promise not to give away the ending to anyone who hasn't seen it.

THE SCARIEST STORIES EVER?
The Grand Guignol was a venue in Paris that opened in 1847. It specialized in performing gruesome horror stories, and the actors used meat and blood from the local butcher's shop to create the gory special effects that made it famous.

TWINKLE TOES
The world's greatest ballet dancers are as fit as Olympic athletes and soccer players. They can dance and walk on their toes for extended periods, and are trained to appear as if they are floating and flying on stage.

YOU WON'T BELIEVE IT BUT...
Actors always refer to the stage from the audience's point of view, so when they 'exit stage right', they're actually going to the left.

RAIN PAIN
The most rain to fall in a 24-hour period was 73.62in/186.44cm in Reunion Island in the Indian Ocean on 15-16th March, 1952 – that's the same height as the average US male.

HURRICANE, TYPHOON OR CYCLONE?
The name given to a storm where the wind blows at over 74 mph/119 kph depends on where it occurs. In the North Atlantic Ocean, North Pacific Ocean and the South Pacific Ocean, they are hurricanes. Typhoons happen in the northwest Pacific and cyclones rage in the Indian Ocean.

YOU WON'T BELIEVE IT BUT...
The fastest recorded temperature rise took place on January 22, 1943 in Spearfish, South Dakota at 7.30am. In two minutes, the temperature rose by 80°F/27°C from -4°F/-20°C to 45°F/7°C.

IF ALL OF THE ICE IN ANTARCTICA MELTED, THE SEA WOULD RISE BY ABOUT 200FT/61M

HURRICANE EXPENSIVE
America's worst hurricane was Katrina in 2005. Because it hit highly populated areas, it was also the most expensive storm on record. It is estimated to have been responsible for $81/£40 billion in damage.

STRIKE-POD
In 2006, teenager Jason Bunch had a lucky escape as he listened to music on his iPod, while mowing the lawn outside his home in Denver, Colorado. When lightning struck, it passed through his headphones and blasted into his ears. He lost some hearing but only had to spend two nights in hospital.

THE SPEED OF SNOW
Falling snowflakes usually move at between 1-5mph/1.6-8kph. Raindrops are a little faster, but not by much – when no wind is present, they fall at between 7-18mph/11-29kph, depending on the size of the raindrop. Raindrops can't go faster than 18mph/29kph, though, because at any speed above that, they are broken up by friction with the air.

YOU WON'T BELIEVE IT BUT...
In the southern hemisphere, 99 percent of tornadoes spin clockwise – but in the northern hemisphere, 99 percent rotate counterclockwise.

THE MOST INTENSE HURRICANE ON RECORD IN THE ATLANTIC WAS WILMA IN OCTOBER 2005

SURPRISE STORM
The south of England was hit by its worst hurricane in over 200 years in 1987 when London was blasted by 93mph/151kmh winds. Repairs cost $2/£1 billion.

TWISTER
A tornado is a column of swirling air that sweeps across the land, sucking everything it comes across into its violent vortex. Around 800 tornadoes are reported in the US on average every year.

HOT AND COLD
The hottest recorded place on the planet is El Azizia in Libya. Its temperature peaked at 136°F/57.8°C on 13th September, 1922. Surprisingly, the coldest place on earth is technically a desert too. On the 21st July 1983, Vostock in Antarctica had a recorded temperature of -129°F/-89°C.

THE LONGEST RAINBOW LASTED FOR THREE HOURS ON 14 AUGUST, 1979, OVER WALES

STORMY WARNING
The future looks stormy. Climate scientists warn us that global warming may be making our weather more extreme, causing more hurricanes, tornadoes, floods and – in hot places – droughts than ever before.

FLASH OF NATURE
At sunset, you may be able to see the 'Green Flash.' A rare phenomenon, it occurs when the Sun sets below the horizon and, due to refraction of its rays on the water, a flash of green light may appear at the exact instant it sinks below the horizon. Be careful not to look directly at the Sun.

YOU WON'T BELIEVE IT BUT...
The largest snowflake ever found was nearly the size of a basketball. It was reported to have fallen in Bratsk, Siberia in 1971.

ENERGETIC WEATHER
The climate can provide amazing amounts of energy. A one-day hurricane releases an amount of energy equivalent to all the electricity used in America for approximately six months. Since man started using fossil fuels, they have produced an amount of energy equal to only 30 days of sunlight.

YOU HAVE A ONE-IN-THREE MILLION CHANCE OF BEING STRUCK BY LIGHTNING

STARRY, STARRY NIGHT
Astronomers can't agree on how many stars our galaxy contains, but it's at least 200 billion. It's called the Milky Way because the most distant stars look like a milky powder across the night sky.

MIND THAT HOLE
Black holes are what happens when massive stars collapse in on themselves. Their gravity becomes so strong that nothing can escape them – even light, hence the name black hole. If a spaceship went near one, it would be crushed to atoms.

NICE NEBULA
When stars explode, they give off a huge dust-cloud called a 'nebula'. These eventually form new stars, which is why not all stars are as old as the Universe. Our own Sun, for instance, is quite young – between 4.5 and 5 billion years old.

YOU WON'T BELIEVE IT BUT...
The Pistol Star is obscured by a dust-cloud so it isn't visible in our night sky. However, it is by far the brightest known star.

HOW BIG IS THE UNIVERSE?
We don't know. But it's so mind-bogglingly big that astronomers measure it in light years. The fastest thing in the Universe is light, which travels at 299,792,458 meters per second – that's 9,460,530,000,000km. A light year is simply how far light travels in a year.

YOU WON'T BELIEVE IT BUT...
Greek philosopher Democritus first suggested the Milky Way was made up of distant stars – in the third century BCE.

SEEKING OUT THE STARS
Thanks to ultra-powerful telescopes, scientists now know that there are planets orbiting stars other than our own Sun. Known as 'exoplanets' or 'extra-solar' planets, their number is growing all the time.

ASTRONOMERS THINK THAT HALF OF THE STARS IN THE UNIVERSE COME IN TWOS – KNOWN AS 'BINARY SYSTEMS'

OVER 100 TONS OF SPACE DUST LAND ON EARTH EVERY DAY

METEOR SHOWER
Bits of rock, metal and dust that burn up and glow brightly for a few seconds as they enter the Earth's atmosphere are called meteors. Meteors that do not completely burn up before hitting the Earth are called meteorites.

YOU WON'T BELIEVE IT BUT...
On 28th June 1911, over 40 stone-sized meteorites hit Nakhla, Egypt. The rocks, estimated to be approximately 1.3 billion years old, landed over a 2.5mi/4km area.

PISTOL PACKS HEAT
The Pistol Star is 25,000 light years away from us at the center of the Milky Way, and produces the same energy in six seconds as the Sun does in a year.

WHICH WAY IS THAT?
A galaxy is a collection of billions of stars. In turn, these galaxies – which can be of different shapes – are formed into clusters, all spinning through space. We live in a galaxy called the Milky Way.

ANDROMEDA, THE NEAREST GALAXY TO OUR GALAXY, IS ABOUT 2 MILLION LIGHT YEARS AWAY

MOST SCIENTISTS AGREE THAT THE UNIVERSE IS 14 BILLION YEARS OLD

DEATH OF A STAR
When a star has used up all its fuel, it explodes into a 'supernova' – thousands of times brighter than it was before. Scientists estimate that this happens about every 100 to 300 years in our galaxy.

RED STAR GAZING
Humans have been watching the skies from our earliest days, which is useful to our scientists. It appears that Chinese astronomers saw the star Betelgeuse as white 2,000 years ago, while the Greeks later saw it as red. From this we can work out when Betelgeuse turned into the red giant of today.

OUR NEAREST NEIGHBORS
The nearest stars to our own Sun are the three stars of Alpha Centauri. The closest, Proxima Centauri, is 4.22 light years away, while the others, Alpha Centauri A and B, are a little further off, about 4.35 light years. That's next door in space terms.

YOU WON'T BELIEVE IT BUT...
The speed of light means we can't see light from objects that are further away than the Universe is old. This means we can't even see how big the Universe is.

TAKE TO THE SKIES

In 1903, American brothers Orville and Wilbur Wright became the first people to pilot an aircraft. The plane, called the Flyer, was the brothers' own creation.

A TITANIC LOSS

The passenger ship Titanic was said to be unsinkable, but it hit an iceberg in the Atlantic Ocean on its maiden voyage in 1912 and sank. Just over 700 people survived, but around 1,500 passengers died, including Captain Edward John Smith, who went down with his ship.

VOTES FOR ALL

Before World War One, women in Britain could not vote in elections. Emmeline Pankhurst set up a movement called the Suffragettes to campaign for votes for women. In 1928, all women over 21 were finally granted the right to vote.

THE 1995 EARTHQUAKE IN KOBE, JAPAN, CAUSED DAMAGE WORTH 10 TRILLION YEN ($100/£50 BILLION)

APARTHEID ENDS

When the South African National Party came to power in 1948, they declared that whites would have more rights than other races. This apartheid (meaning 'apartness') was condemned around the world and was finally abolished in 1994, when black political prisoner Nelson Mandela was elected president of South Africa.

QUAKE DAMAGE

In 1906, the American city of San Francisco was struck by a massive earthquake. It only lasted for around one minute, but created a split in the ground 270mi/434km long. The quake also started a fire, which destroyed over 250,000 buildings.

SIRIMAVO BANDARANAIKE BECAME THE WORLD'S FIRST FEMALE PRIME MINISTER IN SRI LANKA IN 1960

YOU WON'T BELIEVE IT BUT...

In 1900, the world population was just 1.6 billion. One hundred years later, the number of people had rocketed to 5.9 billion.

BURGER BONANZA

The iconic McDonald's chain opened its first restaurant in 1955 in Des Plaines, Illinois, from where it expanded to operate over 20,000 restaurants in 100 countries across every one of the world's continents except Antarctica. Since its first day, McDonald's has sold over 100 billion hamburgers worldwide, and now makes almost seven million pounds of fries worldwide in an average day.

DEFEATED
When Nazi dictator Adolf Hitler invaded Poland in 1939, Britain, France, America, Russia and Japan joined the fight. Allied forces won and Hitler killed himself in 1945, just before Germany surrendered.

SCRIPT SLIP-UP
When he stepped onto the lunar surface, Neil Armstrong, the first man on the Moon, was supposed to say "That's one small step for a man, one giant leap for mankind." He accidentally left out the "a" and the phrase "one small step for man" is now world famous.

TRIVIAL TREASURE
The best selling board game, *Trivial Pursuit*, actually lost money when it was first released – it cost $75 to make each game but they were sold in shops for $15 to raise brand awareness.

YOU WON'T BELIEVE IT BUT...
Years after he died, scientists analyzed the brain of Albert Einstein, the greatest scientist of the 20th century, and discovered the section that determines mathematical skill was enlarged.

SIR EDMUND HILLARY AND TENZING NORGAY WERE THE FIRST MEN TO CONQUER MOUNT EVEREST, IN 1953

YOU WON'T BELIEVE IT BUT...
In 1928, Scottish scientist Sir Alexander Fleming nearly threw away some mouldy equipment but, when he examined the fungus more closely, he discovered penicillin, a vital medicine.

YOU WON'T BELIEVE IT BUT...
In China's first nationwide census of 2000, the population was recorded at just under 1.3 billion.

BERLIN WALL FALLS
In November 1989, the wall separating West and East Berlin was torn down and Germany, which had been split into two countries after World War Two, was once again unified.

CUP CRIME
In 1966, the trophy of the soccer World Cup was stolen from a museum in England. It was found a week later under a hedge in South Norwood, London by a dog called Pickles. Pickles became a national hero, starred in a film, and even had his own agent.

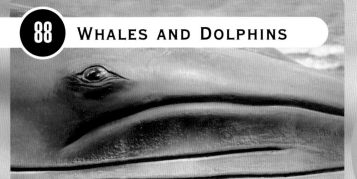

BIG BLUE
The biggest animal in the world is the Blue whale. A baleen whale, it eats small shrimps and fish. It really is humungous – weighing in at 180 tons and measuring up to 100ft/33m in length – as long as a passenger jet.

YOU WON'T BELIEVE IT BUT...
The pilot whale gets its name from when fishermen used to follow it to locate shoals of herring in the ocean.

DOLPHINS SOMETIMES SAVE HUMANS FROM SHARK ATTACKS

THE SEA'S UNICORN
The male narwhal is one of the most striking-looking whales because it has a tusk sticking out from the middle of its forehead. This tusk is actually a tooth, which can grow up to 10ft/3m. It is thought that the whale uses it to fight other male narwhal competitors. The narwhal's tusk can grow up to 10ft/3m long, which is even longer than an African elephant's tusk.

BIRTH DANGER
Baby whales must breathe as soon as they leave their mother's womb or they risk drowning. As soon as the baby is born, the mother and other friendly whales will whisk it to the surface so it can take its first breath.

SENSE OF PORPOISE
The six types of porpoise are closely related to dolphins. They are generally smaller and can be recognized by their rounded heads, compared to dolphins' large, melon-shaped bump. They aren't as playful or as clever as dolphins and don't react well to living in captivity.

ANCIENT WHALES
Experts believe that the bowhead whale may be the longest-living mammal in the world – they have been known to live for 211 years. People have been able to roughly figure out their ages because 19th century harpoon heads have been found lodged in some of them.

DOLPHINS CAN JUMP AS HIGH AS 16FT/5M OUT OF WATER

THE LONGEST JOURNEY
The grey whale's migration is believed to the longest undertaken by any mammal. Their yearly round-trip is estimated to be a staggering 12,500mi/20,1167km. They start on the North American Pacific Coast and migrate down to Baja California, Mexico.

YOU WON'T BELIEVE IT BUT...
In 1820, a sperm whale attacked and sank a whaling ship, inspiring writer Herman Melville's classic novel *Moby Dick* about a white sperm whale.

BIG BRAIN
The sperm whale has the biggest brain of any animal alive in the world today. Its brain weighs more than 20lbs/9kg – which is about four times heavier than a human brain. Of course, size isn't everything when it comes to judging intelligence.

YOU WON'T BELIEVE IT BUT...
Sperm whales can go deeper than any other mammal, diving to an incredible 7,200ft/2,200m beneath the waves.

BIG HEAD
The sperm whale is an odd-looking animal – its huge, square-shaped head makes up about a third of its total length, which can be as much as 60ft/18m – almost as long as a tennis court. They are the biggest-toothed animals in the world.

NAME THAT TUNE
Whale song is the name given to the haunting sound whales make. Sound carries better underwater and whales have very good hearing – meaning they can communicate over vast distances. Scientists don't know much about whale song, but some believe it is a far more complex language than any used by other animals.

WHALES HAVE GREASY TEARS TO PROTECT THEIR EYES FROM SALT WATER

DASTARDLY DOLPHINS
Don't be fooled by the smile of a dolphin. Recent studies show that dolphins are often very violent, and not just when hunting. They fight one another and weaker species, such as porpoises, and often kill for no reason. They cause massive internal injuries by ramming with their hard noses.

IT'S SHOWTIME
Fun-loving dolphins are among the most intelligent animals, at least the equal of the cleverest dogs. They can be trained to do complex tricks. There are 37 species of dolphin, ranging in size from Maui's dolphin up to the massive orca.

TOM THE TRAITOR
Old Tom was the name of a killer whale in charge of a pod (group) of killer whales that often helped whalers off the coast of Australia in the 1920s. He and his pod would herd whales into one spot for the whalers so they could be caught.

MAD MAZE-MUNCHER
The chomping maze-muncher known as Pac-Man was one of the first true video game characters, first appearing in arcades in 1974. His original name was pakku-man, taken from 'paku paku', a Japanese phrase for an eating motion. His distinctive design started out as the Japanese symbol for mouth.

POPULAR HERO
Mario, Nintendo's cheerful plumber mascot, is one of the most popular videogame characters of all time. He started life as the hero of the game *Donkey Kong*, and has appeared in over 100 others since. In his first outing he didn't have a name – he was just called Jumpman.

THE VIDEO-GAMING BUSINESS IS THOUGHT TO BE WORTH $30/£15 BILLION

YOU WON'T BELIEVE IT BUT...
It is rumored that Lara Croft was originally going to be a man, until her designer thought it would be better to have a strong, confident female character.

ANOTHER WORLD
Many gamers spend hours playing massive multiplayer online role-playing games, or MMORPGs. One of the most popular has over eight million registered players.

VOICE OF THE STARS
Voiceover work for videogames is attracting big names these days – major A-list Hollywood stars who have lent their voices and digitalized their faces for video games include Pierce Brosnan, Willem Dafoe, Dame Judi Dench and Samuel L Jackson.

CAN GAMES BE GOOD FOR YOU?
Researchers have claimed that videogames can help develop important skills. People who play a lot of videogames have been found to be more alert, more aware of what is going on around them and quicker to react.

YOU WON'T BELIEVE IT BUT...
When the classic arcade game *Space Invaders* was launched in Japan in 1978, the government had to quadruple the amount of yen coins produced to cope with the demand to 'feed' the machines.

THERE HAVE BEEN OVER 50 VIDEOGAMES BASED ON THE *STAR WARS* MOVIES

MARIO FLOP
The first-ever movie based on a videogame was the 1993 $45/£22 million production *Super Mario Bros* based on the famous Nintendo game. However, the film only made $20/£10 million at the box office and no sequel was made.

PLAYING FOR KEEPS
Some players become so good at their favorite games that they're able to become professional 'cyber athletes', and take part in organized tournaments. American Jonathan Wendel, five-times World Champion, plays under the nickname FATALITY and has earned over $500,000/£250,000 from playing games since he started in 1999.

IT'S A BLOCKBUSTER
When the Xbox shoot-em-up *Halo 2* went on sale in 2004, it sold nearly 2.5 million copies in America alone in its first 24 hours. It brought in $125/£63 million, making more money in one day than movies like *Harry Potter* or *The Matrix*.

BUILD UP YOUR MENTAL MUSCLES
Tetris is one of the world's most popular videogames, having appeared on virtually every console since it was created in 1985. It's much more than a simple puzzle – mathematicians have shown that a long game of *Tetris* is one of the most complex tasks your brain can tackle.

MUSIC FROM *FINAL FANTASY* HAS BEEN TURNED INTO A FULL CLASSICAL MUSIC CONCERT

YOU WON'T BELIEVE IT BUT...
In 1980, a 12-year-old boy called Eric Furrer played *Space Invaders* for almost 40 hours, taking only seven 15-minute breaks. He scored over a million points.

TOP SELLER
Launched in 1994, Sony's PlayStation became the best-selling videogame console in history, sales reaching over 100 million worldwide in 2005.

NINTENDO HAS BEEN AROUND FOR OVER 100 YEARS, AND ORIGINALLY MANUFACTURED PLAYING CARDS

IT'S AMAZING
The first home videogame console was released in America in 1972. The Magnavox Odyssey came with 12 simple sports and maze games on plastic cartridges. Because it couldn't draw background graphics, each game came with a plastic sheet that you had to stick on the TV screen.

YOU WON'T BELIEVE IT BUT...
It can take a decade to produce a single videogame, but on average it takes between one and three years, and the development process can cost tens of millions of dollars. The most expensive game ever made was *Shenmue* and it is claimed that it cost $70/£35 million.

WHAT ARE GERMS?
Bacteria and viruses are the main germs that invade the body to make you unwell. Bacteria are microscopic and found everywhere. Viruses are strands of DNA that invade cells in the body to live.

FALSE TEETH
Archeologists have discovered false teeth, dating back to the first century CE, with gold wire used to hold the false teeth together.

YOUR LINES OF DEFENSE
Your body tries to keep germs out. But if they do get in, there are serious lines of defense in place – from the hairs and mucus in your nose, to the wax in your ear and hydrochloric acid in your stomach.

THE LIVER IS THE ONLY ORGAN YOU CAN TRANSPLANT JUST PART OF, AND BOTH THE DONOR'S AND RECIPIENT'S PARTS WILL GROW BACK TO FULL SIZE

YOU WON'T BELIEVE IT BUT...
The brain sends out electrical signals up to 37 hours after death.

HOW GERMS ARE SPREAD
When a fly feeds on dung or decomposing matter, germs can stick to its body and spread to food that the fly descends on. This is just one way that germs can be spread. They can be passed from one thing to another by air, touch, animals, or even water.

HOW BADDIES ATTACK
As Britney once sang, 'toxic' is not good for you. Harmful bacteria make chemicals called toxins, which cause disease, such as throat infections, typhoid, and cholera. Viruses make colds, flu, and other diseases by killing cells in your body.

SEVERE BURNS VICTIMS CAN BE TREATED WITH 'LIVING SKIN' GROWN FROM CELLS

TO THE RESCUE
Perhaps the best germ-fighting partnership in your body is your white blood cells and your lymphatic system. The latter is a network of organs and tubes containing lymph. This network recycle white blood cells so they can keep on battling infection.

YOU WON'T BELIEVE IT BUT...
It is claimed that the body part most commonly bitten by insects is the foot.

SNEEZE MARATHON
Briton Donna Griffiths had a sneezing fit that lasted 978 days. She began sneezing on January 13, 1981 and finished on September 16, 1983. It is estimated that she sneezed about one million times in the first 365 days.

YOU WON'T BELIEVE IT BUT...
It is claimed that, if you take a heart out of a human body, it will still beat for a while, even if it's cut into pieces.

WORMING THROUGH HISTORY
A tapeworm can grow to 50ft/15m long and live 20 years. They have been with us for about 2.5 million years.

IN THE AVERAGE LIFETIME, THE HEART BEATS AROUND THIRTY BILLION TIMES

BLOOD BANK
We have about 10–12pt/5–7l of blood being pumped round our bodies at any one time. To do this, the heart has to beat over 365 million times per year.

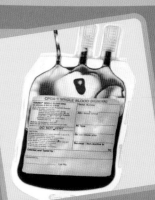

LIVE, STERILE MAGGOTS CAN BE USED BY DOCTORS TO HELP CLEAN DIRTY WOUNDS – THEY EAT THE DIRT AND DEAD TISSUE AND THE CLEAN WOUND CAN THEN HEAL

FLU FIGHTERS
There is a vaccine that can help prevent us from catching the flu but, as the bug is always changing, a different vaccine has to be made each year.

YOU WON'T BELIEVE IT BUT...
Most adult heartbeats are between 60 and 100 beats a minute, whereas a baby's is about 130 beats a minute.

BONE NUMBERS
Babies are born with about 300 bones in their body but, by the time they become adults, they will only have about 208 because some of our bones grow together as we get older.

WATER WORRY
Some people are allergic to water. This condition is known as 'aquagenic urticaria' or 'water urticaria'. Sufferers develop a blotchy rash when they come into direct contact with water, and can be affected by bath water, fresh water, sea water and even their own sweat.

YOU WON'T BELIEVE IT BUT...
Because tulips now grow everywhere, nobody knows exactly where they first came from.

TULIP MANIA
Many of today's common varieties of flowers were once rare. The tulip only became well known in Europe when it was introduced in the 16th century. Soon after the continent was gripped by 'tulip mania' – suddenly everybody was growing them.

SPREADING POLLEN
Flowers need to spread their pollen. One way this is done is by insects. To attract insects, many flowers produce sweet-tasting nectar. Bees, in particular, love this and, when they get back to their hives, they turn it into honey.

ROSE RECORD
The world's largest rose bush – now a tree – covers 8000 sq ft/2,438 sq m, is over 9ft/2.7m high and flowers every April displaying over a million white blossoms. It was planted in 1855 and can be seen at the Rose Tree Inn museum, Tombstone, Arizona.

YOU WON'T BELIEVE IT BUT...
$10,000/£5,000 was spent on one bouquet in New York, USA on August 27, 2004. It had 101,791 multi-colored roses and was 103ft/31m long – as long as a netball court.

THE HYDRANGEA ORIGINATES FROM JAPAN. ITS NAME MEANS 'WATER BARREL'.

THE STINKING CORPSE FLOWER IS ONLY FOUND IN SUMATRA

THE CORPSE FLOWER
It might be one of the biggest flowers in the world, but the Titan Arum isn't the most attractive. Its huge, purple flowers give off the stink of rotting flesh – which is where it gets its nasty name. It smells like this to attract insects.

A SUNNY DISPOSITION
As well as being beautiful, the sunflower is also a very useful plant – a single flower can produce up to 2,000 seeds and the stems can be used to fill life jackets.

TALL AND SPIKY
The tallest cactus in the world is the Pachycereus pringlei. It grows in Mexico and California and the biggest one recorded was 63ft/19.2m high. Its close relative, the Saguaro, lives in the same deserts and is almost as tall.

LONG LIFE, QUICK END
The rare South American Puya Raimondii plant grows to about 8ft/2.4m wide and can reach over 30ft/9m in height. Once the plant is about 150 years old, it will produce thousands of creamy-white flowers – after which, the plant dies.

IT IS ESTIMATED THAT, IN THE US, $2/£1 BILLION A YEAR IS MADE SELLING FLOWERS

IS IT A BEE?
No, it's a Bee Orchid. This flower has cleverly disguised itself as a female bee to attract male bees. It's a good way for the flower to trick the insect into spreading its pollen.

YOU WON'T BELIEVE IT BUT...
The hummingbird's main source of food is nectar from flowers.

FLOWERING GODDESS
The Aztec civilization in Mexico had a goddess of flowers called Xochiquetzal, who was always depicted surrounded by birds and butterflies, just like real flowers. As in Western culture, flowers were also linked with romance, and so Xochiquetzal was also the goddess of dancing and love.

PRICKLY PEAR PLEASE
If you're dying of thirst in the deserts of Mexico or the West and southwestern US, find yourself a prickly pear. This cactus is 90 percent water. It is also edible and can be put into stews.

YOU WON'T BELIEVE IT BUT...
The prickly pear has been found to have medicinal properties and can be used to treat diabetes.

FLOWER DEFENSE
Schipol Airport in Amsterdam uses flowers to protect its planes from bird strikes. It was discovered that the mice and other small mammals that the birds eat don't like the scent of daffodils or tulips. The surrounding fields have been planted with these flowers to move the animals away, and therefore, subsequently, the birds.

BLOWING YOUR TOP
In 1980, Mount St Helens, a volcano in the US state of Washington, erupted. The explosion blew the top off the mountain and caused the biggest landslide in recorded history. Traveling at over 70mph/112kph, rocks from the mountain slid over 20mi/32km.

THE WATERS OF LOUISIANA ARE HOME TO OVER 90 PERCENT OF THE WORLD'S CRAYFISH

FINDERS KEEPERS
Columbus may be credited with its discovery, but America was named after another European explorer, Amerigo Vespucci, who arrived there a few years later. Unlike Columbus, who thought he'd reached Asia, Amerigo realized he'd discovered a new continent. The new country was named America in his honor.

YOU WON'T BELIEVE IT BUT...
The first person ever to ride over Niagara Falls in a barrel and survive was Annie Edson Taylor, in 1901. A teacher, she was 63 years old.

A RIGHT STATE
The US is made up of 50 states. Over 200 years ago, there were 13 separate colonies ruled by the British, but after the American Revolution they joined together as the United States, governed from Washington DC. Unfortunately, it did not stop the states fighting each other in a civil war.

THAT'S A LOT OF PEOPLE
With over 300 million residents, the United States of America is one of the world's most populated countries. Only China and India are home to more people. The US population is rising, with a new American baby born every seven seconds.

ARKANSAS IS HOME TO THE ONLY ACTIVE DIAMOND MINE IN THE US

TAKE A BITE OF THE BIG APPLE
The largest and most famous city in America is New York City. Made up of five boroughs - the Bronx, Queens, Manhattan, Brooklyn and Staten Island - it is home to eight million residents, 468 subway stations, 1,200 schools, and 37,000 police officers.

YOU WON'T BELIEVE IT BUT...
More than 355 million pints/168 million liters of water go over the side of the Niagara Falls every minute.

MAKING A SPLASH
At 3,948ft/1,203m across, Niagara Falls is the one of the world's largest waterfalls. In 1948, the raging falls slowed to a trickle. The weather was so cold that the river above it had frozen.

YOU WON'T BELIEVE IT BUT...
The Empire State Building, in New York, is one of America's most famous buildings. It has 86 floors and, if you climbed the stairs to the top, you'd have gone up 1,860 steps.

COLOSSUS
The US covers a massive 3.7 million sq mi/9.5 million sq km, making it more than twice the size of the entire European Union. Canada, America's neighbor to the north, is even bigger. That covers 3.8 million square mi/9.8 million square km.

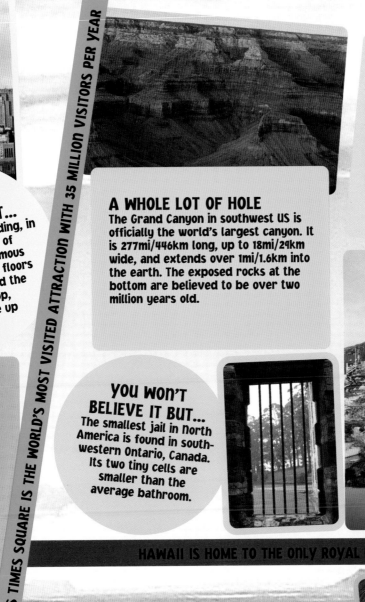

A WHOLE LOT OF HOLE
The Grand Canyon in southwest US is officially the world's largest canyon. It is 277mi/446km long, up to 18mi/29km wide, and extends over 1mi/1.6km into the earth. The exposed rocks at the bottom are believed to be over two million years old.

YOU WON'T BELIEVE IT BUT...
The smallest jail in North America is found in south-western Ontario, Canada. Its two tiny cells are smaller than the average bathroom.

A SHORE THING
The five Great Lakes are among the largest freshwater lakes on the planet. They are Lake Erie, Lake Huron, Lake Michigan, Lake Ontario and Lake Superior, the biggest and deepest of them all. If you straightened out their shorelines they would stretch halfway around the world.

NEW YORK'S TIMES SQUARE IS THE WORLD'S MOST VISITED ATTRACTION WITH 35 MILLION VISITORS PER YEAR

HAWAII IS HOME TO THE ONLY ROYAL PALACE IN THE US, AT LOLANI

SHORT AND SWEET
George Washington gave the shortest inauguration speech made by a president – a mere 133 words on March 4, 1793. The longest was made by William Henry Harrison on March 4, 1841 – an epic 8,443 words.

George Washington

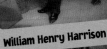
William Henry Harrison

ROAD RUNNER
Canada is the second-largest country in the world after Russia and it boasts the Trans Canada Highway, the world's longest national road at over 5,000mi/8,000km in length.

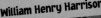

THE LONGEST WALL
Although some sections have collapsed, the Great Wall of China still stretches over 4,000mi/6,400km. That's longer than the width of the United States of America from New York to San Francisco. However, the Great Wall is not visible from space.

YOU WON'T BELIEVE IT BUT...
Buckingham Palace, the official home of Queen Elizabeth II, contains an astonishing 775 rooms.

MIGHTY MALL
West Edmonton Mall is the largest shopping mall in North America. It contains over 800 shops, and has its own hotel, swimming pool and roller coaster. Even this mega mall looks tiny compared to some in China, where there can be over 1,000 stores to choose from.

OPERATIC ARCHITECTURE
Opened in 1973, the Sydney Opera House, with its sweeping roof design, is one of Australia's best-known landmarks.

YOU WON'T BELIEVE IT BUT...
The first President to live in the White House was John Adams in 1800, shortly before it was completed. Construction began in 1792.

THE AVERAGE BRICK HOUSE IS MADE UP OF APPROXIMATELY 17,000 BRICKS

THE WORLD'S WEIRDEST BUILDING?
The Dancing House in Prague, built between 1992 and 1996, is one of the world's strangest-looking buildings. The front of the building is curved and twisted to look like two people dancing. It was originally called the Astaire and Rogers Building, after Fred Astaire and Ginger Rogers, two movie stars famous for their dancing.

SUPER-SIZED SPEEDWAY
If you get a seat at the back of the Indianapolis Speedway, USA, you'd better bring a telescope. The largest sporting venue in history, and home to the famous Indy 500 car race, it can comfortably seat over a quarter of a million people.

THE 111FT/34M MIRROR IN THE GREAT CANARY TELESCOPE IN THE CANARY ISLANDS IS BIGGER THAN A BLUE WHALE

TOWERING ACHIEVEMENT?
Until they were destroyed by terrorists, the twin towers of the World Trade Center were among the tallest skyscrapers in the world. The Freedom Tower that will replace them will be 1,776ft/541m tall, because 1776 was the year of the American Declaration of Independence.

THE RIVETING TOWER

The Eiffel Tower was named after its designer, Gustave Eiffel. Built for the 1889 Paris world exhibition, it was constructed to demonstrate that iron could be as strong as stone. It took two years for 132 workers to construct and contains 2,500,000 separate rivets.

CHILLING OUT

The Ice Hotel in Sweden, just 125mi/200km north of the Arctic Circle, is built from blocks of ice carved from the Torne River. Every spring the hotel closes – and melts. It is then rebuilt the next winter.

THE WORD ARCHITECT COMES FROM THE GREEK WORD 'ARKHITEKTON', MEANING A MASTER BUILDER

MONSTROUS MONUMENTS

The Yan Huang statues in China stand 347ft/106m tall and depict two of China's first emperors. However, they're small when compared to the Ushiku Amida Buddha near Tokyo. At 393ft/120m, it's taller than 20 giraffes and weighs more than 300 elephants.

SCOTLAND HAS ONE OF THE WORLD'S LARGEST TREE HOUSES, WHICH IS ALSO A RESTAURANT SEATING 120 PEOPLE

WHAT IS THE MYSTERY OF STONEHENGE?

Nobody is sure who arranged these prehistoric stones, or how they were able to move such enormous pieces of rock without modern machinery. Some people believe the site is an ancient calendar that uses the shadows of the sun.

HURRY UP!

The Cathedral of Saint John the Divine in New York is the world's largest cathedral – and it's probably going to get bigger. Construction on the cathedral began over 100 years ago and it is still not completed. Local people call it Saint John the Unfinished.

YOU WON'T BELIEVE IT BUT...

In 2005, a scale model was built of the Allianz-Arena football stadium using over one million LEGO bricks.

HOLIDAY FUN

The world's largest holiday resort is Disney World, Florida. Ever since it opened in 1971, it has been a popular holiday destination. It now features four separate theme parks, two water parks and, in 2004, had 40.7 million visitors.

YOU WON'T BELIEVE IT BUT...

Big Ben is not actually the name of London's famous clock tower. It's the name of the bell inside.

GENERAL GIANT
General Sherman was a general who became famous during the American Civil War. An army tank was named after him, and so is the world's largest living thing – a Giant Sequoia redwood tree in California. It is 275ft/84m tall – almost the size of the Statue of Liberty.

BIGGEST IN AUSTRALIA
A mountain ash, the Ada Tree, is the largest tree in Australia. It is very tall, standing 236ft/72m high, and very wide, with a circumference of 50ft/15m. Its root system spreads a vast distance underground. So it must be very hard to pull up.

WHO INVENTED THE CHRISTMAS TREE?
Legend has it that an English monk, Boniface, was spreading the gospel in Germany when he came across some pagans worshipping an oak tree. Boniface angrily cut it down and to everyone's amazement a fir tree sprang up in its place. The Germans, now Christians, started calling the fir 'Christ's tree'.

WHERE AM I? UNDER A TREE
The Bo Tree (also known as the Bodhi Tree) was a very old fig tree that grew outside a temple in India. It was under this tree that the Buddha sat meditating for 49 days until he 'arrived' at Bodhi or enlightenment – the name Buddhists give to the state where you understand your place in the universe.

HUMANS HAVE GROWN OLIVE TREES FOR 8,000 YEARS

YOU WON'T BELIEVE IT BUT...
The Talipot Palm tree lives for up to 60 years and produces a flowery spike 33ft/10m high – that's taller than a house.

YOU WON'T BELIEVE IT BUT...
The art of Bonsai – keeping trees deliberately small – was first developed in China over 1,000 years ago.

AIR FRESHENERS
Not only do trees provide oxygen for us to breathe but they protect us from the pollution we make. They absorb some of the poisons we put in the air, like car fumes, which means not so much goes into our bodies. They are natural air cleaners.

WHERE IS THE WORLD'S OLDEST TREE?
The location of the world's oldest tree is a secret – to protect it from vandalism. Named Methuselah, after a Biblical figure who lived for 969 years, it is somewhere in the White Mountains of California. It is over 4,700 years old.

YOU WON'T BELIEVE IT BUT...
The story of President George Washington chopping down the cherry tree as a child was never mentioned in his lifetime.

TREES LIVE LONGER THAN ANY OTHER ORGANISM ON EARTH

WHAT ARE MOON TREES?
The Apollo 14 mission in 1971 took hundreds of seeds into space to see if being planted in a weightless environment would make them grow differently back on Earth. Twenty years later, scientists were unable to see any difference between normal trees and 'moon trees'.

TRUCK HITS TRUNK
The Tree of Ténéré in the Sahara desert was famous for being the most isolated tree in the world. Its roots had to burrow 118ft/36m below the desert to find water. Despite its isolation it still came to a sticky end – a truck knocked it down in 1973.

OXYGEN MACHINES
Like all plants, trees 'breathe' in carbon dioxide and turn it into oxygen. The average tree produces 260lbs/118kg of oxygen a year – so two trees are enough to keep one person breathing for a full 12 months.

JUST ONE CANADIAN ASPEN TREE CAN BE CHOPPED UP TO MAKE ONE MILLION MATCHSTICKS

YOU WON'T BELIEVE IT BUT...
A mature oak tree can grow a quarter of a million leaves each year and produce up to 50,000 acorns.

WOOD YOU BELIEVE IT?
The Chapel Oak at Allouville-Bellefosse, France, is an ancient oak with an enormous 49ft/15m trunk. That's wider than two adult African elephants standing end to end. It's so large that two church chapels have been built inside the tree.

A KILLER CROP
The Strangler Fig tree, found in tropical climates such as Southeast Asia, wraps itself around another tree and steals its light, water and nutrients. Eventually, the host tree is squeezed to death and only the fig tree is left.

YOU WON'T BELIEVE IT BUT...
The composer JS Bach invented the note scale which all modern instruments use. For this reason, he is often called 'the father of modern music'.

BOY GENIUS
Many people call Wolfgang Amadeus Mozart a genius, and it's easy to see why. By the age of five he was not only playing the piano, but also composing his own short pieces of music. At eight he toured Europe, and by the age of 12 he had written two complete operas.

THE CONVENTION HALL ORGAN IN ATLANTIC CITY, NEW JERSEY, IS THE WORLD'S LOUDEST MUSICAL INSTRUMENT

VOLUME CONTROL
The full name of the piano is a pianoforte. The name is made up of two Italian words, with 'piano' meaning 'soft', and 'forte' meaning 'loud'. This is because a piano player can produce both quiet and loud music, depending on how the keys are struck.

FIGHT MUSIC
The Rite of Spring, a ballet by Russian composer Igor Stravinsky, used rhythms and ideas drawn from ancient folklore and was considered shocking compared to most music of the time. During the first performance on May 29, 1913, in Paris, fights broke out between people who hated it and those who loved it.

THE TUBA IS THE LARGEST – AND LOUDEST – BRASS INSTRUMENT

YOU WON'T BELIEVE IT BUT...
The saxophone was invented by a Belgian man called Adolph Sax around 1840. 'Phone' is the Greek word for 'sound', so a saxophone is literally 'the sound of Sax'.

SHUSH!
The composer John Cage is famous for a completely silent piece called 4' 3". The idea is to sit and listen to all the sounds around you for around four and a half minutes, making each performance different.

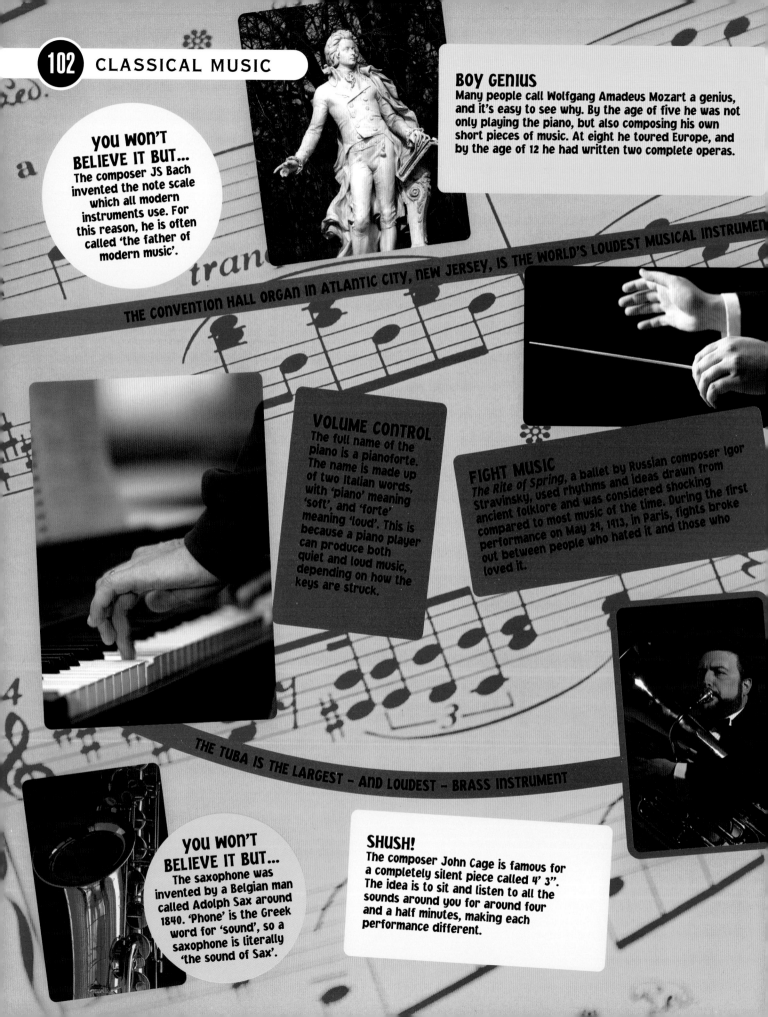

YOU WON'T BELIEVE IT BUT...

The world's largest piano was built in 1935. At over 11ft/3.3m in length it was longer than a car, and weighed about the same.

ORCHESTRA CONDUCTORS CAN EARN OVER $2/£1 MILLION A YEAR

ALL TOGETHER NOW

In total a large symphony orchestra can have more than 90 members all playing together. The most common instrument in any orchestra is the violin. It's common for around one third of a large orchestra, or around 30 musicians, to be made up of violinists.

MOODY BEETHOVEN

When Beethoven was composing, he would pay no attention to anything other than the music. No one was allowed to touch his manuscripts and to better feel the vibrations of the music, he worked sitting on the floor at a legless piano (of which he had several), often wearing only underwear. If anyone came to visit, he would ignore them, and he would pour ice-water over his head to keep himself awake.

YOU WON'T BELIEVE IT BUT...

In 1972, Beethoven's Ode To Joy, from his Ninth Symphony, was used during the launch of the European flag and, in 1985, it was adopted as the official anthem of the European Union.

AT 13 HOURS, VICTORY AT SEA HOLDS THE RECORD FOR BEING THE LONGEST SYMPHONY

YOU WON'T BELIEVE IT BUT...

Stradivarius violins are very rare. Only 650 of his instruments are believed to still exist. One sold at auction in 2005 for over $2/£1 million.

GET ON UP!

During performances of *The Messiah* by Handel, the audience always stands up for the Hallelujah chorus. This is said to be because, in the 18th century, King George II of England found the music so moving that he rose to his feet. According to British custom, the King's subjects had to stand as well, and the custom spread overseas.

A MUSICAL GIANT

The composer Rachmaninov was over 6.5ft/2m tall, and also had very big hands. He composed a lot of work for piano, and he was said to be able to reach across 13 keys of the piano with one hand. Because of this, it can be very difficult for piano players with normal hands to play his music.

HONK IF YOU LIKE MUSIC

The modern classical composer Steve Reich used to be a taxi driver in New York. Through his music, he attempts to recreate the experience of living in the city and often gets choirs to impersonate the sound of police car sirens with their voices.

YOU WON'T BELIEVE IT BUT...
The Incas of South America thought seabird droppings were so important that anybody caught killing seabirds was executed.

BIG BIRD
The African Ostrich is the biggest and tallest bird. It can't fly, but it can run at speeds of up to 45mph/72.5kph. Though they haven't caught on in many Western countries, they are farmed all over the world for their meat because it's very low in fat.

WHO ARE YOU CALLING COMMON?
The most common bird isn't the sparrow or seagull as you might expect, but an African species called the Red-Billed Quelea. It lives near the Sahara Desert and there are thought to be 1.5 billion of them.

THE LARGEST EGG IS LAID BY THE AFRICAN OSTRICH

CAN YOU HEAR HUMMING?
The smallest bird is the Bee Hummingbird. The tiny creature is native to South America and some Caribbean islands such as Cuba. It is only 2in/5cm long and it weighs just 0.06oz/1.8g. That's the same as a small coin.

DIVE, DIVE, DIVE
The Emperor Penguin is, as its name implies, the largest member of the penguin family. It can dive to depths of up to 1,853ft/565m, and it can hold its breath for an astonishing 22 minutes, all this in the freezing cold water of the Antarctic.

A SWIFT SLEEP
While most birds come home to a nest to sleep, the swift spends almost its entire life in the air. They catch and eat flying insects on the move, and when they need a rest they glide thousands of feet into the air to relax in warmer air currents.

BIRDS ARE WARM-BLOODED, LIKE MAMMALS

FASTEST OF THEM ALL
Peregrine Falcons aren't just the fastest of all birds – they are the fastest animals of all. They are found on every continent except Antarctica and, when swooping for prey, they can reach speeds of up to 200mph/320kph. That's almost as fast as Formula One racing cars.

LIKE A PLANE?
The wingspan of the Condor Vulture can be up to an impressive 10ft/3m - the height of a basketball net. This giant vulture lives high in the Andes Mountains of South America and in California.

YOU WON'T BELIEVE IT BUT...
An albatross's heart rate is the same when it's gliding with a good wind as when it's sitting still.

WHAT DID HE JUST SAY?
Some birds can mimic human speech, although they don't know the meaning of the words they're saying. The best of all is the budgerigar, a popular pet, which can learn almost 1,800 words.

YOU WON'T BELIEVE IT BUT...
There are at least 40 species of bird, including penguins and ostriches, which cannot fly even though they have wings.

ALBATROSS ADVENTURE
The widest wingspan belongs to the albatross, a sea bird. The creature hardly needs to flap its wings but can just glide on the wind. Scientists have recorded electronically-tagged birds traveling 2,600mi/4,184km in one trip. That's a long way to fly back.

THE DODO WAS RELATED TO THE PIGEON

DO YOU REMEMBER THE DODO?
The dodo's sad tale is a warning from history. A large, flightless bird native to the island of Mauritius in the Indian Ocean, it first became known to westerners in the 16th century. Within 200 years, they had all been killed for food. Hence, the phrase: 'dead as a dodo'.

CROP FERTILIZER
Guano, better known as seabird droppings, is one of the best natural fertilizers in the world. Traditionally collected from the coasts of South America and nearby islands – some of which are completely covered in poo – it's used on crops all over the world.

FLYING LIZARD
Fossils have been found of a lizard-like creature that had feathers – the oldest creature thought to be a bird. Called 'archaeopteryx', it had teeth in its beak and lived at the same time as the dinosaurs.

YOU WON'T BELIEVE IT BUT...
In just one second the Great spotted woodpecker can peck its beak more than 40 times!

THE BIGGEST BIRD EVER, THE 10FT/3M TALL ELEPHANT BIRD, BECAME EXTINCT IN THE LAST 1,000 YEARS

LIGHT SLEEPER
Some people can train themselves to survive with very little sleep. British yachtswoman Ellen MacArthur, who sailed around the world on her own in 2005, survived the trip on an average of 36 minutes' sleep at a time, totaling around five and a half hours a day.

HAIR POWER
A single human hair is less than half a millimeter wide. Despite being so thin, our hair is incredibly strong. The average human hair can support a weight of around 132lbs/60kg before snapping. That's equal to the weight of two healthy children.

IT IS COMMONLY BELIEVED THAT IT TAKES 17 MUSCLES TO MAKE YOU SMILE, 43 TO FROWN

YOU WON'T BELIEVE IT BUT...
When you are afraid, your ears secrete more ear wax (oil plus sweat). At the same time, your eyes widen and blood rushes to your muscles.

NERVOUS WRECKED
The brain is the nerve center of your body. Nerve impulses whiz to and from the brain at speeds as fast as a racing car. The fastest impulses recorded were traveling at 186mph/300kph.

THERE ARE TWO KINDS OF SLEEP
The first is REM (from which the pop group took their name), which stands for rapid eye movement, and is when intense dreaming occurs. During REM sleep your eyes move around and your brain is active. The second kind of sleep is non-REM, when your brain is much less active and any dreams are fleeting.

KEEPING A BALANCE
Your ears play an important part in your balance. The vestibular system (in your inner ear) sends your brain messages about whether your head is tilting forwards, backwards or sideways. The motion of being at sea can confuse your vestibular system – which is why some people suffer seasickness.

THERE ARE AROUND 550 HAIRS IN YOUR EYEBROW

BRAINY STUFF
When you are born, your brain weighs just under 1lb/0.5kg, about the same as a small baseball. An adult's brain weighs three times that and contains more than 10 billion nerve cells.

YOU WON'T BELIEVE IT BUT...
As a child, your sense of smell is at its best – you can detect up to 10,000 different smells.

DAYDREAM BELIEVERS
You can spend many hours a day daydreaming. Most of the time you don't notice you're doing it, like blinking. Positive daydreams can help you to work out what you want and aspire to. Nasty daydreams can be a good way of letting off steam.

SMELLING THE PAST
Your sense of smell is strongly linked to your memory, because the same part of the brain deals with smell, memory and feelings. So a whiff of newly cut grass can take you back instantly to a particular time.

YOU WON'T BELIEVE IT BUT...
Your eyes have 82-157 million light-sensitive cells in them – 75-150 million rods that see in black and white and seven million cones that see in color.

NIGHT VISION
While our eyes can see colors and detail better than most animals, our vision in darkness is worse than most of theirs. This must be why we invented the electric light.

HAIR FALLS OUT ALL THE TIME – THE AVERAGE HAIR LOSS PER DAY IS AROUND 100 STRANDS

CURLY OR STRAIGHT HAIR?
Your hair grows from follicles, little caves in your skin. The visible hairs – called shafts – are made of dead cells pushed up through the follicles. The shape of the follicle decides the shape of the hair. Cutting hair doesn't hurt, because it's dead.

YOU WON'T BELIEVE IT BUT...
Your tongue is covered with about 10,000 taste buds – these buds are sensitive to bitter, sour, salty and sweet tastes.

SHINE A LIGHT
Light rays enter your eyes through a hole called the pupil. They pass through the cornea (a clear layer) and a disk (the lens). These bend the rays to form an image on the back of the eye (the retina). The retina converts the images into nerve impulses, which the brain can understand.

WHY DO I GET HEADACHES?
Headaches are not actually pains in your brain, because the brain itself cannot feel anything. Swellings in the blood vessels and the muscles in your head and neck cause most headaches.

THE LARGEST AND DEEPEST OF THEM ALL

At its deepest point, the Pacific Ocean would cover Mount Everest with 1.2mi/2km to spare. It is the world's largest and deepest ocean, covering almost one-third of the Earth's surface. The North Pacific reaches up to the US while the South Pacific touches eastern Asia and Australia.

AUSTRALIA IS THE DRIEST INHABITED CONTINENT ON EARTH

ISLANDS IN THE SUN

Oceania is the name given to the islands of the Pacific Ocean, and includes the area known as Australasia. More than 10,000 islands are in Oceanic territory, including Australia, New Zealand and Papua New Guinea.

LAND HO!

No one is sure exactly how many islands there are in the Pacific Ocean. Experts believe there could be as many as 30,000 but, if you stuck them all together, they would still be smaller than the state of Alaska.

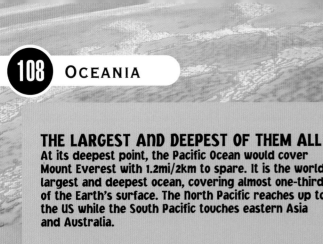

COLOSSAL CORAL

The Great Barrier Reef is made up of over 3,000 smaller coral reefs and stretches 1400mi/2,300km along the Australian coast.

YOU WON'T BELIEVE IT BUT... New Zealand became the first place to allow women to vote, in 1893.

ABOUT 20 PERCENT OF NEW ZEALAND'S RESIDENTS WERE BORN OVERSEAS

WHAT'S IN A NAME?

A New Zealand hill called Taumatawhakatangihangakoauauot-amateaturipukakapikimaungahoronukupokaiwhenuakitamatah u bears the longest place name in the world still in common use. It was named by a Maori chief in memory of his brother.

WHO ARE THE MYSTERIOUS MOAI?

Rapa Nui, also known as Easter Island, is a small triangular island with fewer than 4,000 inhabitants. It is most famous for the hundreds of giant stone figures, or moai, dotted around its coast. Some of the statues are over 1,000 years old and their purpose and origin remain a mystery.

YOU WON'T BELIEVE IT BUT...
Fijian rituals including the Meke dance depict the stories of the island's legends.

OUTBACK OUTLAW
Ned Kelly was one of Australia's most famous outlaws. He fought back against British colonial law in the 19th century, and was hunted down after he and his brothers shot and killed three policemen. The Kelly gang made their final stand in 1880, dressed in home-made suits of metal armor.

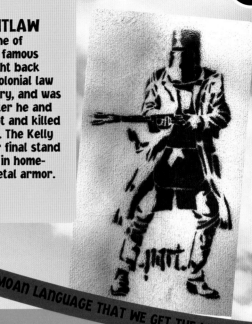

THE SAMOANS HAVE A TRADITION OF RITUAL MARKINGS, AND IT'S FROM THE SAMOAN LANGUAGE THAT WE GET THE WORD 'TATTOO'

GETTING MUSICAL
The didgeridoo is an Aboriginal wind instrument made from a hollow piece of timber – generally eucalyptus – that has been eaten out by termites working their way through the center of the branch or trunk. It can be difficult to master the didgeridoo, as it requires what is known as 'circular breathing' – the ability to breathe in through your nose and out through your mouth at the same time.

WILD DANCING
The Maoris are the original inhabitants of New Zealand, arriving from Polynesia over 1,000 years ago. Maoris would wear intricate patterns on their faces and bodies, and perform dances called 'haka'. These dances involve a lot of stamping and shouting. The New Zealand rugby team still uses them to scare its opponents.

PHOTOGRAPHER'S DELIGHT
Depending on the time of day and the atmospheric conditions, Ayers Rock in central Australia can dramatically change color, anything from blue to violet to glowing red. Many photographers set up for days and record its many changing colors.

YOU WON'T BELIEVE IT BUT...
Many animals such as the kangaroo, the koala bear and the duck-billed platypus are unique to this part of the world.

AUSTRALIA HAS MORE THAN 1,500 SPECIES OF SPIDER

KEEP ON RUNNING
The national bird of New Zealand is the kiwi, a flightless bird about the size of a domestic hen. Although they can't fly, they can outrun a human and use their sharp, four-toed feet to kick and slash enemies.

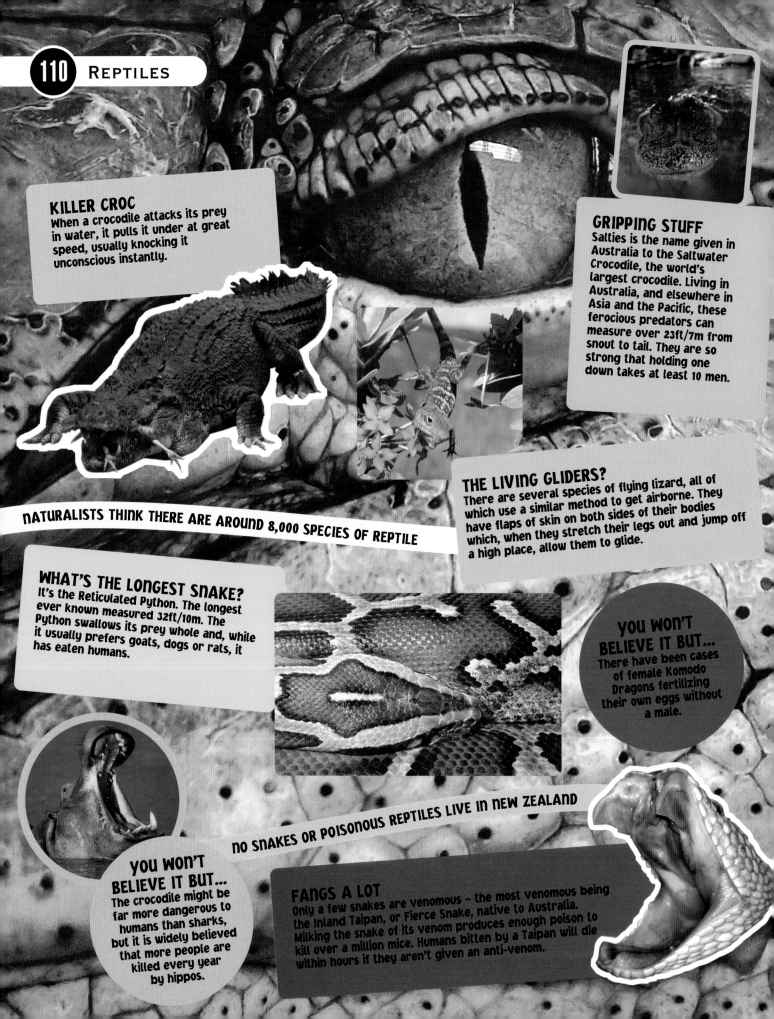

KILLER CROC
When a crocodile attacks its prey in water, it pulls it under at great speed, usually knocking it unconscious instantly.

GRIPPING STUFF
Salties is the name given in Australia to the Saltwater Crocodile, the world's largest crocodile. Living in Australia, and elsewhere in Asia and the Pacific, these ferocious predators can measure over 23ft/7m from snout to tail. They are so strong that holding one down takes at least 10 men.

NATURALISTS THINK THERE ARE AROUND 8,000 SPECIES OF REPTILE

THE LIVING GLIDERS?
There are several species of flying lizard, all of which use a similar method to get airborne. They have flaps of skin on both sides of their bodies which, when they stretch their legs out and jump off a high place, allow them to glide.

WHAT'S THE LONGEST SNAKE?
It's the Reticulated Python. The longest ever known measured 32ft/10m. The Python swallows its prey whole and, while it usually prefers goats, dogs or rats, it has eaten humans.

YOU WON'T BELIEVE IT BUT...
There have been cases of female Komodo Dragons fertilizing their own eggs without a male.

NO SNAKES OR POISONOUS REPTILES LIVE IN NEW ZEALAND

YOU WON'T BELIEVE IT BUT...
The crocodile might be far more dangerous to humans than sharks, but it is widely believed that more people are killed every year by hippos.

FANGS A LOT
Only a few snakes are venomous – the most venomous being the Inland Taipan, or Fierce Snake, native to Australia. Milking the snake of its venom produces enough poison to kill over a million mice. Humans bitten by a Taipan will die within hours if they aren't given an anti-venom.

IS THAT A FLYING SNAKE?

Some snakes appear to fly, although what they are actually doing is gliding. Incredibly, they flatten their bodies and throw themselves from the top of a tree and catch the wind. They are actually better at gliding than mammals like the Flying Squirrel.

YOU WON'T BELIEVE IT BUT...

Scientists thought there were only two poisonous lizards but have recently discovered that lizards like Iguanas and Monitor Lizards are mildly venomous.

BAD-TEMPERED TURTLES

A bite from a Snapping Turtle's beak, which it can deliver lightning quick, can easily snip off a finger. In case that wasn't enough, its tail is covered in sharp spikes, too.

SNAKES CANNOT HEAR SOUND – INSTEAD, THEY ARE SENSITIVE TO THE VIBRATIONS IN THE GROUND

TAKE IT EASY

Giant Tortoises aren't in a hurry. Not only are they huge reptiles – they can weigh up to 347lbs/180kg – they are also thought to live longer than any other animal, or humans, for that matter. It's amazing, but these giants can live for up to 175 years.

EGG-STREMELY DANGEROUS

The female Leatherback Turtle returns to the beach where she was born to lay her eggs. When they hatch, the baby turtles make a desperate drive for the sea, because predators like seagulls pick them off.

FEELING RUFF?

The Frilled Lizard, native to Australia and New Guinea, has an unusual ruff of skin around its neck. When it is scared, it opens its mouth and extends the ruff, making its body look far bigger to potential enemies.

HERE BE DRAGONS

The Komodo Dragon is the largest living lizard. Inhabiting the jungle regions of Indonesia, it can reach lengths of up to 10ft/3m and weigh as much as 300lbs/135kg.

PLAYING DEAD

The Grass Snake pretends to be dead by flipping on to its back when threatened. Its tongue flops out of its mouth and it releases a foul smell, tricking predators into thinking the snake has gone rotten.

IF A GECKO LOSES ITS TAIL, IT CAN GROW A NEW ONE

YOU WON'T BELIEVE IT BUT...

Leatherback Turtles can dive up to 3,609ft/1,100m – deeper even than the Sperm Whale.

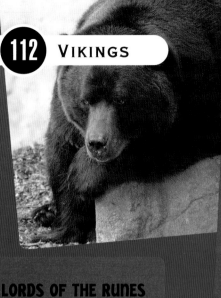

POLAR PETS
It was common for Vikings to keep bears as pets. Polar Bears were prized above all others, and considered noble gifts for Viking kings. Harold the Fairhaired was the first European king to keep captive polar bears in 880 CE.

YOU WON'T BELIEVE IT BUT...
It is thought Vikings enjoyed ice skating and used the carved leg bones of animals for blades.

VIKINGS AND QUEENS
Vikings were ruthless, but the men were put in their place by their wives. Women were highly respected and could divorce their husbands whenever they wanted. They learned how to use weapons in case of attack on their homes while the men were away.

LORDS OF THE RUNES
Vikings would write with ancient symbols known as runes, which they would carve into wood or stone. Runes were made up of straight lines because it was too hard to carve curves. They are still used as a secret mystic language today and even appeared in *The Lord of the Rings* books.

THE WORD 'VIKING' MEANS PIRATE OR RAIDER

FOOD FIT FOR VIKINGS
The Viking diet wasn't that different to ours. They would eat bread, fish, cheese, onions, cabbages, carrots and peas but they also enjoyed special Viking delicacies such as seagull meat.

FAST AND FURIOUS
Vikings were great sailors and built boats they called longships. They were very light and extremely fast, which helped the Vikings carry out their vicious raids. Each ship would carry 60 men and had an ugly figurehead at the front to scare their enemies.

YOU WON'T BELIEVE IT BUT...
Despite what you've seen in movies and on TV, Viking helmets did not have horns on them.

THE VIKINGS TRAVELED AS FAR AS RUSSIA, TURKEY AND EVEN NORTH AFRICA

VIKING SING-A-LONG

The Vikings loved a good party. They enjoyed singing and held lavish feasts where they would eat wild boar and deer. They drank beer from cattle horns, but because of their shape couldn't put them down and had to drink them in one go. This led to many a drunk Viking.

AN AVERAGE LONGSHIP WAS ALMOST AS LONG AS A MODERN-DAY TENNIS COURT

Valhalla

YOU WON'T BELIEVE IT BUT...
Some of our days of the week are named after Norse gods, for example, Thursday is 'Thor's day'.

VALHALLA THERE!
Before they became Christians, Vikings had their own religion, which is now known as Norse mythology. They thought that dying in battle would mean that they were carried off by beautiful warrior maidens called Valkyries to spend eternity with the gods in Valhalla.

NORSE NAMES
Names were very important to the Vikings – they gave names to everything from their ships to their swords. Vikings would also give each other wild nicknames such as Einar Belly-Shaker, Ulf the Unwashed, Harald Bluetooth, Ivar the Boneless and Sihtric the Squinty.

SHIRTS AND SKINS
Some Viking warriors were known as 'berserkers'. Some think these fearless fighters entered battle with no shirt or protective clothing, others think they wore clothing made from the skin of a bear. Either way, they were terrifying to their enemies and even their fellow Vikings, and were considered by many to have magical powers.

ASHES TO ASHES...
To honor their dead, Vikings held elaborate funerals. The corpse would be placed on a longship and set on fire, then pushed out into the ocean. It is said that if the color of the fire was the same as the sunset, the Viking had led a good life.

VIKINGS FOUNDED DUBLIN, THE CAPITAL OF THE REPUBLIC OF IRELAND, IN THE 9TH CENTURY

BRAVE NEW WORLDS
Vikings were fine explorers. They navigated using the sun, the stars and even fish and birds to seek out new land. Viking explorers even discovered Iceland and Greenland.

YOU WON'T BELIEVE IT BUT...
In Norse mythology, the great god Thor was the Lord of Thunder. It was believed that he would ride through storm clouds in a chariot and throw his powerful hammer Mjolnir, to create lightening.

READY FOR BATTLE
Vikings were feared around the world. They carried axes, spears and bows plus a shield for protection. The Vikings attacked fast – they'd jump out of their longships, raid your town and escape with your booty before you knew what hit you.

JOBS IN SPACE
Becoming an astronaut is the rarest job – fewer than 500 people have ever done it. Of those, only a handful – 12 – have walked on the Moon.

IF YOU WANT TO DRIVE A RACING CAR, OR BE A STAND-UP COMEDIAN, ONLINE FANTASY BROKERS WIL

IT'S A LONG DRIVE
Long-distance truck drivers perform an essential service, transporting commodities around the globe. A typical driver in Canada, James Coles, has clocked up 1.3 million mi/2.2 million km over 29 years – that's like going to the Moon and back three times.

NURSE NIGHTINGALE
Florence Nightingale is probably the most famous nurse of all time. She developed her ideas while caring for wounded and dying soldiers during the Crimean War (1853-1856). Today, much of modern nursing can be traced back to her work.

ODD JOBS
The top three occupations given in the 1880 US census were servant, farm worker and laborer. Among the more unusual jobs given were 'Good Talker', 'Bird Fancier', 'Buggy Riding' and 'Gent at Large'. One person even gave their occupation as 'Outlaw'.

YOU'RE FIRED!
In 2005, Todd Christian, a human cannonball from Britain, lost his job because he was scared of flying. He didn't mind being shot out of a cannon, but he refused to fly to a safety training course in Brazil because he was scared of the long flight.

THERE ARE SCHOOLS OF EQUINE DENTISTRY THAT TEACH PEOPLE HOW TO CLEAN HORSES' TEETH

YOU WON'T BELIEVE IT BUT...
There are pet detectives who find animals that have been lost or stolen. There are even training courses especially for the job.

A BIRD IN THE HAND
The Tower of London's Ravenmaster must make sure that there are always six ravens in the tower grounds. King Charles II declared that the Tower – a fortress originally built by William the Conqueror – would fall down if there were ever any less. The superstitious rule is still applied to this day.

YOU WON'T BELIEVE IT BUT...
The UK's oldest performing stuntman was Ron Cunningham, The Great Omani. He performed his last stunts before retirement during his 90th birthday party in 2005.

DRIVEN TO SUCCESS
Driving Formula One racing cars is another dream job, and can be one of the best-paid jobs in sport. German-born Michael Schumacher – who was seven times Formula One World Champion – has now retired, but his earnings in 2004 were reputed to be $80/£40 million.

MICROSOFT EMPLOYS 76,000 PEOPLE IN 102 COUNTRIES

YOU WON'T BELIEVE IT BUT...
A former Soviet country, Belarus, has the largest police force compared to its population.

TIMBER
The most dangerous job to have in America is lumberman – people who cut down trees for a living. Out of every 100,000 lumbermen, around 118 of them will die from accidents while working. This is 26 times more dangerous than the average US job.

CUTTING EDGE
It takes dedication to become a top surgeon. South African Christiaan Barnard was born into poverty. One of his brothers died at an early age from heart trouble and this inspired him to become a heart surgeon. In 1967, he performed the world's first heart transplant.

DANGER AT SEA
Fishing is a popular leisure pastime but, as a job, taking to the sea in search of fish is the most dangerous job there is. Commercial fishing kills more people worldwide than any other occupation – at least 24,000 a year.

TAXI DRIVERS' BRAINS GET BIGGER THE LONGER THEY'RE IN THE JOB

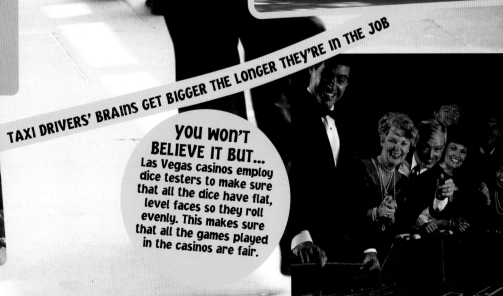

YOU WON'T BELIEVE IT BUT...
Las Vegas casinos employ dice testers to make sure that all the dice have flat, level faces so they roll evenly. This makes sure that all the games played in the casinos are fair.

IN PLACES WHERE WRITING IS READ FROM RIGHT TO LEFT, FLAGS ARE ALSO DESIGNED THAT WAY

WHO WAS UNION JACK?
The Union Jack represents Great Britain, and combines the national flags of England, Wales, Scotland and Northern Ireland. Jack isn't the name of a person – it's the name given to a flag flown by a navy to show which country it's from. No law has ever been passed making it the official British flag.

YOU WON'T BELIEVE IT BUT...
In the Harry Potter novels, the motto on the Hogwarts flag says, 'Never tickle a sleeping dragon'.

FLAG BURNING
Did you know that in some countries you can be arrested for burning the national flag? There have even been riots because of torn or defaced flags. In Denmark you are allowed to burn the Danish flag, but you can be arrested for destroying the flags of other countries.

MONSTER FLAG
The fearsome red dragon on the Welsh flag may come from the legend of King Arthur. The wizard Merlin warned the Welsh king Vortigern that his castle was built on two sleeping dragons – one red and one white. The dragons woke and fought, and the red one won.

WHAT DOES 'HALF-MAST' MEAN?
Flying a flag at half-mast, or halfway down its flagpole, is an internationally recognized symbol of mourning. Nobody knows exactly where the tradition comes from, but hundreds of years ago it was also customary after a death to leave ships looking untidy to show that the crew was too upset to tidy up.

READY, STEADY, EAT
The checkered flag is used to signal the end of a motor race. One theory of its origin is that at horse race meetings, in small towns in America, the town's ladies would cook up huge public meals. When the meal was ready, the ladies would start waving a chequered tablecloth to indicate that it was time to eat.

WHAT'S YOUR POINT?
Nepal has the only national flag in the world that isn't rectangular. It's two triangles on top of each other. It got its unusual shape after the ruling Rana dynasty split into two and their triangular pennants were stuck together to make the new flag.

YOU WON'T BELIEVE IT BUT...
The background color of pirate flags was either red or black. The red symbolized bloodshed and black symbolized death.

DOWN TOOLS
The flag of the old Soviet Union featured a hammer and a sickle to represent the factory and farm workers. With the break-up of the Soviet Union, Russia got a new flag of red, white and blue.

HARK THE HERALD
Many national flags have their roots in heraldry. This tradition comes from a time when powerful families would have their own crest, or coat of arms, to identify themselves in battle. Many of the symbols they used then, such as lions and eagles, are still in use today.

INVISIBLE FLAG
The American national anthem asks, 'Oh say, can you see?' but scientists in Texas have made an American flag that nobody can see. Using a microscopic laser beam, they created a flag 10 times thinner than a human hair. It wasn't allowed in the record books though – the judges couldn't see it.

THERE ARE SIX AMERICAN FLAGS ON THE MOON, LEFT THERE BY APOLLO ASTRONAUTS

THE PIRATE FLAG FROM THE PIRATES OF THE CARIBBEAN MOVIES WAS THE FLAG OF REAL-LIFE PIRATE CALICO JACK RACKHAM

YOU WON'T BELIEVE IT BUT...
The first true flag in Western culture was used by the Romans, who hung a usually decorated square cloth from a cross bar at the end of spears.

THE GREEN FLAG
Libya's flag is easy to remember – it's just a green rectangle. It's the only flag in the world that is one color with no design.

YOU WON'T BELIEVE IT BUT...
The historical origin of flags may date back to around 1000 BCE, when the Egyptians used primitive versions of flags – some were even made out of wood or metal.

POLE POSITION
The most popular color on the world's national flags is red, which appears on 74 percent of all flags. White comes in a close second, on 71 percent, and blue is third, appearing on 50 percent of all flags. And, in countries where people read from left to right, the flags are depicted with the pole on the left.

COMPETITION WINNER DESIGNS FLAG
Cyprus is the only country in the world to include a map of itself on its national flag. Its shape is depicted in a golden coppery color, because of the island nation's copper mines, with the olive branches of peace underneath. A competition winner designed the flag in 1960.

QUAKE ZONE
More than half of the world's volcanoes can be found in the 'Ring of Fire', a 26,000mi/40,000km long horseshoe, stretching from New Zealand, round the east coast of Asia and down the western seaboard of North and South America. Almost all earthquakes happen here.

TSUNAMI TERROR
The Asian tsunami of 2004 started with a powerful earthquake on the sea floor. This caused a huge tidal wave which was 32ft/10m high on the coast of Sumatra near the epicenter, and was still 13ft/4m when it crashed into coastal Thailand, Sri Lanka and India. Around 300,000 people were killed in just a few minutes.

THE 1980 MOUNT ST HELEN'S ERUPTION CAUSED $1 BILLION/£500 MILLION WORTH OF DAMAGE

YOU WON'T BELIEVE IT BUT...
Waves from the Asian tsunami were reported even in places such as Mexico, nearly 8,000mi/13,000km away from the earthquake's epicenter.

IT'S RAINING ASH
In 1980, Mount St Helen in the northwestern United States exploded, destroying the north face of the mountain and sending a huge cloud of ash into the atmosphere. For weeks afterwards, it rained ash in 11 states.

BURIED ALIVE
The Roman town of Pompeii was completely destroyed when Mount Vesuvius erupted in 79 BCE. Poisonous gas poured from the mountain and the entire population suffocated before their dead bodies were covered in ash. This preserved many of them and they can be seen today.

LAVA HAS BEEN KNOWN TO MOVE UP TO 6MPH/10KPH, FAST ENOUGH TO COVER NEW YORK IN TWO HOURS

YOU WON'T BELIEVE IT BUT...
The most destructive earthquake was the Shaanxi earthquake. In 1556 CE, the earthquake hit eastern China, killing an estimated 830,000 people.

BIG ERUPTION
Before the Asian tsunami, the deadliest tidal wave was caused by the eruption of the Krakatoa volcano back in 1883. The explosion destroyed most of Krakatoa Island and caused a wave 113ft/40m high. Over 36,000 people lost their lives.

QUAKE IN THE CITY
San Francisco was hit by a giant earthquake in 1906, one of the first modern cities to suffer in this way. As well as the usual devastation, the quake also broke open gas mains that caused huge fires to rage. At least 3,000 people were killed.

LAVA BOMB

An erupting volcano can create volcanic bombs – lumps of half-molten lava that cool into strange shapes as they fly through the air, and cause terrible damage when they crash to the ground. Volcanic bombs have been recorded that have looked like bread crusts, ribbons, spheres and even cow dung.

WAS THAT ISLAND THERE YESTERDAY?

A brand new island appeared off the southern coast of Iceland, the most volcanic place in Europe, in 1963. Named Surtsey, it was formed by a volcano erupting beneath the sea that produced so much lava that it grew higher than the waves.

YOU WON'T BELIEVE IT BUT...

Krakatoa exploding made the loudest noise ever. It was heard clearly in Perth, Australia – 1,926mi/3,100km away.

10 PERCENT OF THE WORLD'S POPULATION LIVES WITHIN 'DANGER RANGE' OF AN ACTIVE VOLCANO

DON'T BLOW IT!

Yellowstone Park in the western US is home to a super volcano. If it were to explode, as it did 1.3 million and 640,000 years ago, it would cause devastation and blot out the Sun for years, bringing about a new Ice Age.

BOTTOMLESS PIT

A caldera is a crater left when a volcano's magma chamber collapses after an eruption. Calderas often fill with water. An unusual example is the Deriba Crater in Darfur, Sudan. It is 3.8mi/6km across and full of water, and no one knows how deep the water goes.

YOU WON'T BELIEVE IT BUT...

The Italian city of Naples, home to over a million people, is situated close to where Pompeii stood. Since the 79 BCE eruption, Vesuvius has erupted over a hundred times – in 1631, it killed 4,000 people.

BIG GEYSER

The Poas Volcano in Costa Rica, South America, is truly unique. It's a caldera that is still an active volcano and it is also a huge lake. Because of this, experts consider it the world's largest geyser.

THERE ARE OVER 500 ACTIVE VOLCANOES ON EARTH NOT COUNTING THOSE UNDER THE SEA

GIANTS ON MARS

Our volcanoes may be big but those on other planets are far bigger. The largest volcano we know about is Olympus Mons on Mars – it's three times the height of Mount Everest. Don't worry, it won't blow up – it's extinct.

YOU WON'T BELIEVE IT BUT... Not getting any sunlight can be depressing. In winter many people get SAD (seasonal affective disorder).

QUICK FREEZE
In the icy Arctic tundra, the harsh winter temperature can drop to between -22°F/-30°C and -4°F/-20°C and can last for nine months a year. This is colder than any human being can survive prolonged exposure to.

WHY DO THE SEASONS CHANGE?
The seasons exist because the Earth's axis is tilted at an angle of 23.5°. This means that there is always a part of the planet receiving more sunshine than anywhere else. This gradually alters as the Earth revolves around the Sun. So when it's summer in one place, it's winter in another.

4AM ETERNAL
On October 24, 1876 in Connecticut, Seth E Thomas patented a clockwork alarm clock that could be set to go off at any desired time. Some 100 years earlier, a similar clock had been invented by Levi Hutchins in Concord, New Hampshire. However, his clock's alarm would only go off at 4.00am and could not be altered.

RUSSIA IS THE COUNTRY WITH THE MOST TIME ZONES – IT HAS 11

LINE 'EM UP
As soon as humans knew the dimensions of the Earth, they created some imaginary lines to help explorers work out where they were. 'Latitude' lines run from the north pole to the south pole, while 'longitude' runs in rings from east to west.

NEVER-ENDING DAY
Summer is a weird time in places like Alaska, Norway, Finland, Siberia and Antarctica because they get 24 hours of daylight. This is because they are close to the poles and so the Sun is shining on them all day long. How would you know when it was bedtime?

A KRATI IS THE SHORTEST MEASUREMENT OF TIME. THERE ARE 34,000 KRATI IN ONE SECOND

WHY GREENWICH?
The Greenwich Meridian – also called the Prime Meridian – is where you find 0° longitude. It could be anywhere, but Greenwich in Great Britain was agreed at an international conference in 1884. It was agreed as the Prime Meridian because it was already that way on two-thirds of the world's maps.

YOU WON'T BELIEVE IT BUT... If you were to stand on the equator, you would get exactly 12 hours of daylight and 12 hours of darkness every day.

THE WORLD'S FIRST CALENDARS

The Egyptians were the first people to use calendars. Nearly 5,000 years ago, they used them to predict when the River Nile would flood its banks. They also used sundials to measure time.

WET AND DRY

Countries near the equator have only two seasons, wet and dry, and their climate is warm no matter what time of year it is. For example, the monsoon season in India can last for four months and, in 2005, a record-breaking 37in/94cm of rain fell in just one day.

YOU WON'T BELIEVE IT BUT...

The longest day of the year in the northern hemisphere – when the Sun is at its most northern point in the sky – is called the summer solstice, and is on or around June 21.

CHINA IS THE LARGEST COUNTRY TO HAVE ONLY ONE TIME ZONE

BAD TIMING

Jet lag is what happens when you cross two or more time zones in a short space of time – usually by plane. Because your destination is in a different time zone to your home, your brain gets confused. Sometimes you'll be tired even though it's daylight, other times you won't be able to get to sleep at night.

ETERNAL NIGHT

Winter nights in Alaska, Norway, Finland, Siberia and Antarctica are very long because the Sun is shining on the other part of the planet, meaning the places near the poles get hardly any sunlight at all.

SOME COUNTRIES ARE FRACTIONS OF AN HOUR AHEAD OF UTC (CO-ORDINATED UNIVERSAL TIME) – MUMBAI IN INDIA IS 5 HOURS AND 30 MINUTES AHEAD

YOU WON'T BELIEVE IT BUT...

The weather is so changeable in the Australian city Melbourne, that it is known as the 'four seasons in one day' city.

FIRST OR LAST?

When the year 2000 came, all eyes were on Kiribati in the Pacific as it was the first place to celebrate the new millennium. This was because the president moved the entire nation east of the International Date Line in 1995. If he'd gone the other way, Kiribati would have been the LAST to celebrate.

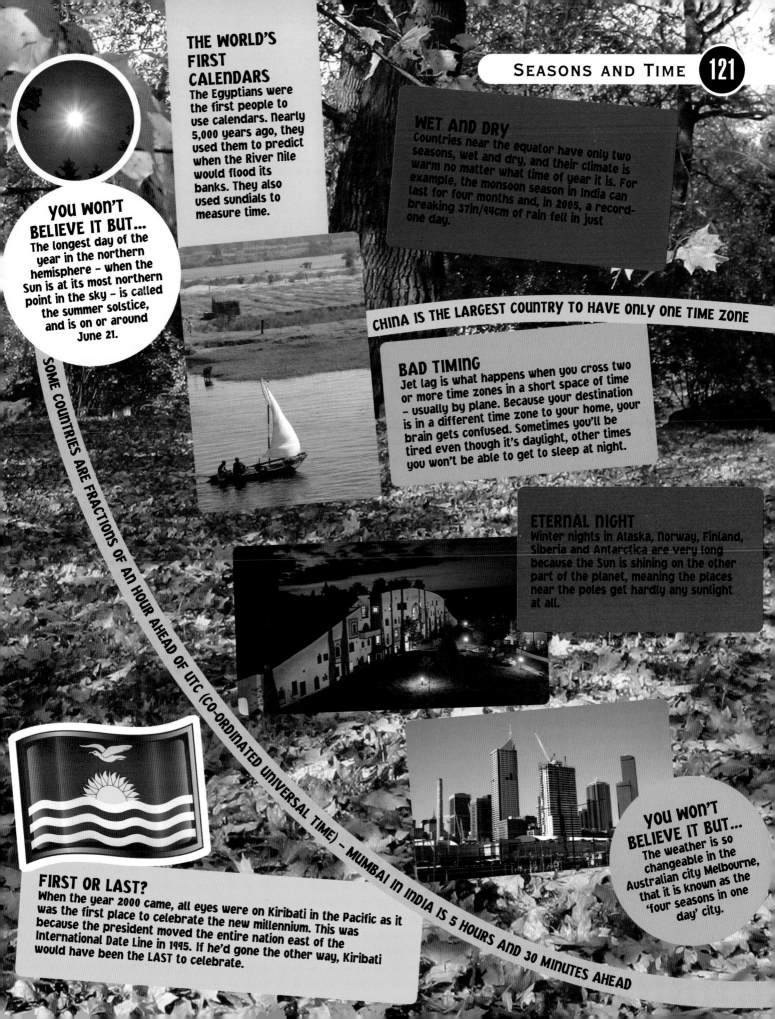

FLAMINGOS ARE THE ONLY 'FILTER-FEEDING' BIRDS, WHICH MEANS THEY FILTER THE WATER FOR FOOD

SUPERB SHOW-OFF
The male superb lyrebird likes to use a host of techniques to impress his potential mate. First of all, he prepares a display ground with a mound of earth on which he stands and calls for a female. When one appears, he then fans his large tail feathers into a bow shape and proceeds to woo her by singing a variety of songs.

YOU WON'T BELIEVE IT BUT...
The frigate bird has one of the largest wing-to-body ratios of all birds, making it an expert distance glider.

BIG BEAK
The Australian Pelican's bill is the largest in the world and can reach up to a whopping 18in/47cm. To help the pelican feed, the beak is very sensitive to make it ideal for 'feeling' for fish when pushed underwater. The pelican also has a large pouch underneath its beak which is used as a net to help catch its dinner.

PERFECT HEARING
Penguins have excellent hearing both on land and underwater. Though their ears are not visible, their sensitive ear canal allows them to pinpoint their own mate or chicks in colonies that can have over 80,000 birds.

BLUSHING, BUT NOT BASHFUL
In the spring, many herons develop bright patterns on their legs and bills – their facial skin has even been known to 'blush' slightly. The reason why is simple: they are ready to find a mate and breed, and want everyone to know it.

YOU WON'T BELIEVE IT BUT...
The marsh warbler is the bird with the most songs, with 84 different variations or mimicked sounds.

GREATER INDIAN HORNBILLS CAN LIVE UP TO 40 YEARS

NO FISHING

A BAD JOB
The oxpecker doesn't just peck oxen – it pecks any large mammal it can get near, to feed on the lice and other parasites that get caught up in the animal's fur or skin. While that might make you feel queasy, it means they always have food.

PARTY ANIMALS
Social weavers are famous for being highly sociable. They do not just build nests for themselves, but large groups co-operate to build one huge nest for the whole colony, and they sometimes share their nests with other species.

YOU WON'T BELIEVE IT BUT...
The ostrich doesn't need to worry about going thirsty – they can produce water inside themselves.

JUST FOR LAUGHS
The Helmeted Hornbill of Borneo or Sumatra has a call that sounds just like hoots of hysterical laughter.

A CANARY CAN TAKE 30 MINI-BREATHS A SECOND TO REPLENISH ITS AIR SUPPLY WHEN SINGING

ALL PUFFED UP
It is one of the more weird sights in the animal kingdom when you see a frigate bird perched on a shrub or on the ground, puffing out his large red throat like a balloon. He can stay like this for many hours as he waits, hoping to attract a female for mating.

A COLORFUL MYSTERY
The toucan bird has a very brightly colored bill, but no one quite knows why. Some believe it may help the toucan recognize other toucans. Toucans' bills are made of keratin – the same material as fingernails and hair – and are strong but light in weight.

DANCE FEVER
The common crane's mating dance is one of the most complex. Males and females each perform a series of graceful, rhythmic leaps, raising their wings in the air and bowing to each other. This display is supposed to show off the cranes' energy, fitness and suitability as mates.

YOU WON'T BELIEVE IT BUT...
Peregrine Falcons nest on broad ledges or scrapes on cliffs or quarries, but some people have found them – very rarely – perched on their window ledges.

MASSIVE ATTACK
The golden eagle has a large wingspan of over 7ft 3in/2.2m and can weigh as much as 15lbs/6.7kg when fully grown. You might think that their size would make them clumsy in the air, but you'd be wrong – they can soar with incredible grace.

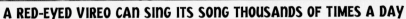
A RED-EYED VIREO CAN SING ITS SONG THOUSANDS OF TIMES A DAY

THE ROMAN NAME FOR THE SUN – SOL – WAS USED TO NAME OUR SOLAR SYSTEM

YOU WON'T BELIEVE IT BUT....
Because the Sun isn't solid like the Earth, different parts of it revolve at different speeds.

HOW BIG IS THE SUN?
Big. Compared to the Earth, anyway. In terms of stars, though, it's relatively small – if the mighty red giant Betelgeuse replaced our Sun at the center of the Solar System, its outer edge would come out as far as Jupiter, and we would not be here.

BRIGHT SPARK
Without powerful telescopes or space travel, our ancestors didn't know much about the Sun. Even so, some very clever people made good guesses. In the 3rd century BCE, the Greek scholar Eratosthenes estimated how far away the Sun was from Earth – and he may have been only 612,000mi/ 1 million km out.

THE SUN IS OVER 333,400 TIMES BIGGER THAN THE EARTH

THE SUN IS MOVING
But don't panic – we're moving with it. Just like the Earth is orbiting the Sun, so the Sun is spinning around the center of our galaxy, the Milky Way. It's 26,000 light years from the galactic center and makes a complete orbit about once every 226 million years.

SUN BLOCK
Every so often, the Moon comes between the Sun and Earth and causes a solar eclipse. For a few minutes, the day goes as dark as night.

SUN AND AIR
We wouldn't be able to breathe if it wasn't for the Sun. Plants make food out of sunlight and give off oxygen as a result, in a process called 'photosynthesis'. Some bacteria do this, too. The original oxygen in the Earth's atmosphere was created by a photochemical reaction of sunlight on water vapor.

SUN CENTRAL
Ancient peoples believed the Sun went around the Earth, because that's what it looks like. A handful of astronomers in India, Greece and the Middle East thought this might not be true but it was Nicolaus Copernicus, in the 16th century, who first proved it.

YOU WON'T BELIEVE IT BUT....
It takes a million years for the energy created at the Sun's core to reach the surface.

YOU WON'T BELIEVE IT BUT....
The Sun's temperature varies – in the 17th century, it cooled off so much that northern Europe entered into what we now call the 'Little Ice Age'.

GET SOME SUN
Vitamin D is created in the skin by sunlight. It's essential for keeping your bones, kidneys and blood healthy. Lack of Vitamin D can cause weak bones, and liver and kidney complaints.

AT THE SUN'S CORE, THE TEMPERATURE IS 27,000,000°F/15,000,000°C

EVERY SECOND, THE SUN PRODUCES FIVE MILLION TONS OF PURE ENERGY

TOP GOD
The Sun was important to many ancient cultures and was the most important god in the religions of the Romans, Greeks, Incas and Aztecs in South America, the pagan tribes of Europe and, most famously, the Ancient Egyptians, whose sun god was called Ra.

BIG FLARES
Solar flares are massive explosions, equivalent to millions of nuclear bombs, that take place within the Sun. They are caused when magnetic energy that builds up near the surface of the Sun is suddenly released. The flares can disrupt radio signals on Earth and damage orbiting satellites.

HOW FAST IS SUNLIGHT?
Like all light, sunlight is the fastest thing we know of in the Universe, traveling at 186,000mi/299,792,458m per second. Even so, the Sun is 93 million mi/150 million km from Earth meaning its light takes eight minutes to reach us.

SO LONG, SUN
The Sun makes energy by turning its hydrogen into helium. Scientists predict that in about five billion years from now, this process will be finished and the Sun will expand to become a 'red giant'. It will destroy many planets in our Solar System, including Earth.

DON'T LOOK
It might be essential for life on Earth but the Sun can be dangerous. Never look directly at the Sun – it's so bright, it can damage your eyes.

YOU WON'T BELIEVE IT BUT....
The Sun is quite young – just 4.6 billion years old – and is getting hotter. Since its birth, scientists think its output has increased by almost 40 percent.

DUST BUSTER
Dust is a huge problem in our houses and it's getting worse. One reason for this is all the electrical goods we have. They attract dust – notice how your TV is always covered in the stuff? It's important to clean regularly because dust can cause allergies, eye infections and asthma.

SMOG MONSTER
Everyone loves a roaring fire but this caused a huge problem in London. There were so many home fires that the city was often shrouded in smog – fog mixed with smoke. In 1952, London experienced its worst smog; thousands of people died and the government banned all coal burning in the city.

BED BUGS BITE
Bed bugs are creatures that like to live in mattresses. They listen to our heartbeats to work out when we are asleep and then come out to suck our blood. Their numbers are increasing throughout the US and Europe, perhaps because we don't use as many chemicals to kill insects any more.

BY THE YEAR 2015, THERE WILL BE 23 CITIES WITH MORE THAN 10 MILLION CITIZENS

SAFE AS HOUSES?
More people die in accidents in their own homes than in road traffic accidents. The room where more accidents happen than any other is the kitchen.

QUAKE CORNER
If you are in an earthquake, a house can be a dangerous place to be. The best places to shelter are under a table, in a doorway or in the corner of the room, even though they may not feel that safe. These stronger areas are the most likely to remain standing if the roof falls in.

IN 1871, TOILET PAPER IN ROLLS WAS PATENTED IN THE US BY SETH WHEELER

NO MORE BILLS?
The cost of heating and lighting a house can be very high. But in some hot countries like Australia, homeowners are switching to solar and wind power for their electricity. Not only do their bills go down, if they make more power than they use, the electricity company will pay them.

YOU WON'T BELIEVE IT BUT...
At 26ft/7m in circumference, the smallest house in the world is in Wales, UK. It is no bigger than a large closet. The rooms are too small to stand up in – and it has no bathroom.

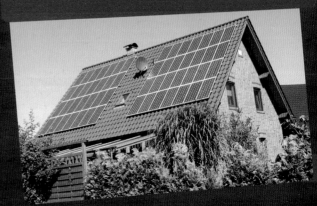

TALKING TECHNOLOGY
To help blind people in the home, scientists have started to create household appliances that can talk. The first of these is a washing machine that gives the user spoken instructions about how to use it.

TOWER IN AUSTRALIA IS THE TALLEST RESIDENTIAL BLOCK OF FLATS – NEARLY AS HIGH AS FIVE JUMBO JETS BALANCED ON TOP OF EACH OTHER

NO MORE HOUSEWORK
A woman in Oregon has invented a self-cleaning house. Her home has almost seventy housework gadgets including wardrobes that double as washing machines and a soapy spray which washes entire rooms before drying them with hot air.

FEELING FLUSH
We might take it for granted, but one of the most important inventions is the flushing toilet, invented in the latter half of the 19th century. Transporting our poo away from where we live has meant disease has dropped sharply.

IGLOO VERSUS TENT
Although 'igloo' means 'home' in the Inuit language, the Eskimo or Inuit people do not live in these ice houses all the time, and prefer a tent. Igloos are, in fact, most commonly used as temporary shelters while out on extended hunting trips.

BIG HOUSE
The Sultan of Brunei's Istana Nurul Iman Palace is the world's largest residential home. It has over 250 bathrooms, five swimming pools and covers over two million square feet – that's the size of around 35 soccer fields or 2,353 times the size of the average British house.

TREE HOUSE
It is estimated that it takes up to 44 trees to build the average house. In addition to wood, mining for the minerals and fuels needed for metals, glass, plastics, concrete and the other materials required, would create a hole in the earth equal to the size of the house itself.

YOU WON'T BELIEVE IT BUT...
Washing machines, on average, account for up to 20 percent of all the water a household uses.

IT IS TRADITIONAL IN JAPAN TO NOT WEAR SHOES INSIDE THE HOUSE, SO AS NOT TO BRING IN DIRT FROM OUTSIDE

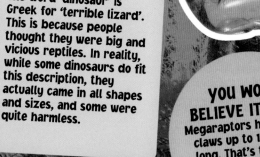

TERRIBLE LIZARDS
The word 'dinosaur' is Greek for 'terrible lizard'. This is because people thought they were big and vicious reptiles. In reality, while some dinosaurs do fit this description, they actually came in all shapes and sizes, and some were quite harmless.

YOU WON'T BELIEVE IT BUT...
Megaraptors had vicious claws up to 15in/38cm long. That's the same length as a three-year-old child's arm.

IT'S ALIVE
Some people have claimed that insects that fed on dinosaur blood might be found trapped in fossilized tree-sap with tiny drops of that blood still inside their preserved bodies. They think this could be used to clone new dinosaurs, just like in the film *Jurassic Park*. It's a great idea but, unfortunately, it's impossible, so far...

WHEN DINOSAURS RULED THE EARTH...
... Plesiosaurs ruled the seas. With a long neck and tail, a large body and four flippers, they ate fish and other sea creatures. Though they died out with the dinosaurs, some people think they are still alive, and that one might even be Scotland's Loch Ness Monster.

COMPSOGNATHUS, ONE OF THE SMALLEST DINOS, WAS ONLY THE SIZE OF A CHICKEN

THERE BE DINOSAURS...
Humans have known about dinosaur bones for thousands of years but thought they were evidence of mythical beasts like dragons and giants. It was only in 1822 when English archeologist Gideon Mantell was studying huge fossilized teeth and bones that he realized he had discovered something belonging to a giant reptile.

SO WHY DO THEY CALL YOU SPINY?
T-Rex might be famous but the biggest of the meat-eating dinosaurs was actually Spinosaurus – it measured 49.2ft/15m in length and weighed around 8.8 tons. It gets its name from the fan of spines, up to 6.6ft/2m long, that ran along its back.

SIR RICHARD OWEN CAME UP WITH THE WORD 'DINOSAUR' IN 1841

HOT STUFF
Today's reptiles – crocodiles, snakes and lizards – are cold-blooded, meaning that, without heat, they are slow-moving. Although dinosaurs were reptiles, many scientists think they may have been warm-blooded like us, as there is evidence they were faster moving than normal reptiles.

YOU WON'T BELIEVE IT BUT...
To help them digest their food, some plant-eating dinosaurs would swallow stones. The rocks would stay in their digestive system and help to grind and crush the leaves and branches swallowed by the dinosaur.

BIG BUSINESS-OSAURUS

Ever since they were discovered, dinosaurs have captured peoples' imaginations. Sir Arthur Conan Doyle wrote the novel *The Lost World* about them, and they've featured in movies since the beginning of cinema. Today, dinosaurs are big business – it is claimed the first *Jurassic Park* film made over $1 billion/£500 million from merchandising alone.

SAUROPODS HAD NOSTRILS ON TOP OF THEIR HEADS SO THEY COULD BREATHE WHILE THE REST OF THEIR BODY WAS UNDERWATER

THE LEG BONE'S CONNECTED TO THE... WHAT?

When people first started finding dinosaur bones, they weren't sure how to put them together. In the 19th century, they got the Iguanodon very wrong. Not only did they have it walking on four legs instead of two, but they thought its bony thumb was a horn on its nose.

CLEAR FOR TAKE-OFF

Pterosaurs lived at the same time as dinosaurs but were actually flying reptiles with claws and leathery wings. Unlike birds, they didn't flap their wings to fly, but glided instead. So they had to take off from somewhere high like a cliff.

YOU WON'T BELIEVE IT BUT...

Diplodocus is officially the longest dinosaur at 85ft/26m but it's likely that longer ones existed - we just haven't found them yet.

YOU WON'T BELIEVE IT BUT...

Despite what movies show, scientists think T-Rex could only run at 15mph/24kph – similar to an athlete.

BUT WHERE ARE THEY NOW?

Why the dinosaurs died out about 65 million years ago as the rulers of Earth is one of the great mysteries. All we really know is that they vanished in a relatively short period of time. One popular theory is that a huge asteroid hit the Earth, sending up a cloud of dust that blocked out the Sun.

HE IS HEAVY

The biggest dinosaurs were plant-eating sauropods, huge four-legged beasts with long tails and long necks. The largest of these are known as the Titanosaurs and include Argentinosaurus – which some scientists say weighed at least 110 tons. That's the same as 100 small cars.

DON'T BITE ME

The ferocious Tyrannosaurus Rex was one of the largest meat-eating dinosaurs. Adults were around 43ft/13m long and 16.6ft/5m tall, and walked upright on two legs. Its huge mouth was full of sharp teeth and some scientists believe T-Rex's bite is still the strongest of any creature that lived.

THE WIDEST DINOSAUR, AT 16FT/5M, WAS THE ARMORED ANKYLOSAURUS

THE ABSOLUTE TALLEST... SORT OF

If we measure from the center of the Earth, then the volcano Chimborazo in Ecuador is the tallest peak on the planet. Although only 20,561ft/6,267m above sea level, it is very close to the Equator – the fattest part of the Earth. So, it is the part of our planet that is closest to outer space.

TALLER THAN EVEREST?

There are some who say the volcano Mauna Kea in Hawaii is taller than Mount Everest. In height above sea level, it is only half Everest's height. But if you count from its base on the floor of the Pacific Ocean, its height would be well over 33,400ft/ 10,200m.

WHEN HE WASN'T CLIMBING, THE FAMOUS MOUNTAINEER EDMUND HILLARY WORKED AS A BEEKEEPER

WHAT'S IN A NAME?

The highest mountain in North America has had many names. Mount McKinley in Alaska was known as Bolshaya Gora until 1867 when the US bought the state from the Russians. But the Dena'ina people, who have lived in Alaska for thousands of years, have always called it Denali.

you won't BELIEVE IT BUT...

Litter is a problem on Mount Everest. Climbers leave behind all sorts of things, including oxygen tanks, tents and food wrappers.

you won't BELIEVE IT BUT...

Because the Earth is so much wider at the Equator, not only is Mount Chimborazo higher than Everest but, according to some so are Ecuador's beaches.

GOING STRONG

Many insist explorer George Mallory, who went missing while trying to ascend Mount Everest, was the first to reach the summit, but his son, John, is not one of them. He says: "To me, the only way you achieve a summit is to come back alive. The job is half done if you don't get down again."

HIMALAYA IS SANSKRIT FOR 'ABODE OF SNOW'

SUMMITS UP

The first two men to get up and down Mount Everest were Nepalese climber Tenzing Norgay and New Zealander Edmund Hillary in 1953. After Everest, Hillary also went to the south and north poles, the latter with Neil Armstrong, the first man on the Moon.

GOING UP

Mont Blanc is the highest mountain in western Europe. Lying in the Alps, right on the border between France and Italy, it is a major tourist attraction. So much so that there's a cable car to take tourists close to the top.

OFFICIALLY BIG
Mount Everest is officially the tallest peak on Earth, reaching 29,029ft/8,848m above sea level. It is part of the Himalayan mountain range formed when the Indian subcontinent crashed into Asia some 50 million years ago.

THE HIGHEST MOUNTAIN IN ANTARCTICA – THE VINSON MASSIF – WAS ONLY DISCOVERED IN 1957

YOU WON'T BELIEVE IT BUT...
There is no official definition separating what is considered to be a mountain from what is considered to be a hill.

THE LONG CRAWL
Touching the Void is the name of the book and documentary recounting the ordeal of mountaineer Joe Simpson. He fell and broke his leg on Peru's Siula Grande mountain. All alone, he had to crawl for three days in agony to get back to base camp.

YOU WON'T BELIEVE IT BUT...
Ben Nevis in Scotland is the highest peak in the United Kingdom but, at 4,406ft/1,344m above sea level, Everest is more than six times taller.

K2 IS KNOWN AS 'CHOGORI' BY THE LOCAL KASHMIRIS

THE HARDEST MOUNTAIN IN THE WORLD?
K2 in Kashmir is the second highest mountain above sea level. Like Everest, it is in the Himalayas, but while smaller it is much harder to climb. In the fifty years since it was first climbed, only 246 people have made it to the top. More people climb Everest every year.

FANCY A QUICK STROLL?
Africa's highest mountain is Mount Kilimanjaro, which reaches 19,340ft/ 5,895m above sea level. It is also well known because you don't have to be a trained mountaineer to climb it – you can just walk. From up there, you can even see the curvature of the Earth.

ARE THERE CLIMBERS ON MARS?
Olympus Mons on Mars is the highest mountain in the Solar System. A team led by actor Brian Blessed once pretended to climb the alien mountain for TV using Reunion Island in the Indian Ocean. They did the whole five-day climb in spacesuits.

MOUNTAIN EARTH
Mountains cover 20 percent of the world's land surface, and three quarters of the countries in the world contain at least one mountain. Some even call them home – one in ten of the world's population lives on or around mountains.

TERRIFIC HIEROGLYPHICS
Ancient Egyptians were one of the first civilizations to write, but they didn't use words like we do. They used a series of symbols and pictures called hieroglyphs. If you thought learning the alphabet was hard, then spare a thought for Egyptian children – there were over 700 hieroglyphs to remember.

YOU WON'T BELIEVE IT BUT...
Rich Egyptians would have professional mourners at their funeral. The more important they were, the more mourners they had.

ANCIENT EGYPTIANS THOUGHT DYING BY SNAKEBITE LED TO IMMORTALITY

YOU WON'T BELIEVE IT BUT...
The Pyramids of Egypt are the only one of the Great Wonders of the World to survive to this day.

VALLEY OF THE KINGS
Egyptian kings and queens were called pharaohs. Not only did they rule the country, they also owned all the land, and everything and everyone in it. They wore lots of gold, had many servants and lived in luxury. Male pharaohs had many wives, but were only allowed one queen.

RIDDLE OF THE SPHINX
The Great Sphinx at Giza is over 4,500 years old. It has a lion's body and a human's face and is one of the largest stone statues in the world. Legend has it, the Sphinx's nose was blown off by a cannonball fired by Napoleon's soldiers in the 18th century.

ANCIENT WORSHIP
The Ancient Egyptians worshipped hundreds of gods and goddesses, all of which represented different things. Many of them looked human but had the heads of animals. Ra, the sun god, had the head of a hawk, while Sobek, the god of water, had the head of a crocodile.

PHARAOH PEPI II IS THOUGHT TO HAVE BEEN IN POWER FOR 94 YEARS, LONGER THAN ANY OTHER KNOWN MONARCH

TUTANKHAMUN'S TOMB
In 1922, an archeologist discovered the underground tomb of King Tutankhamun. Inside were amazing treasures including his solid gold mask and coffin, plus precious jewels, chariots and a golden throne. Tutankhamun was only nine years old when he became a pharaoh, and he may have even been married to his sister.

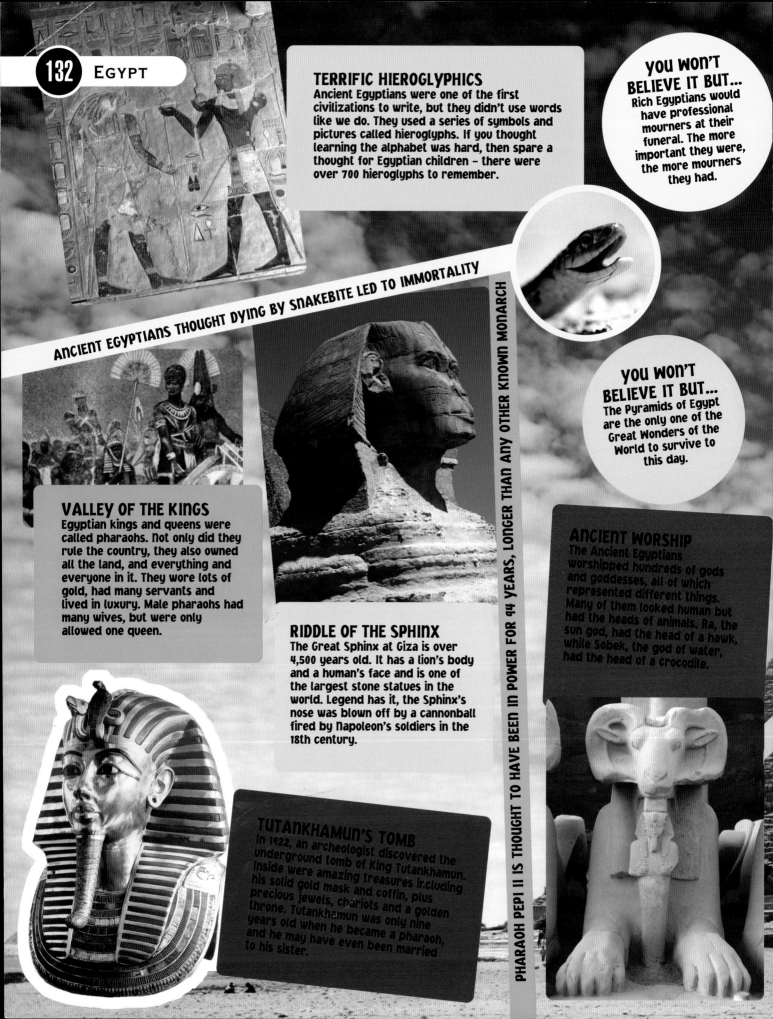

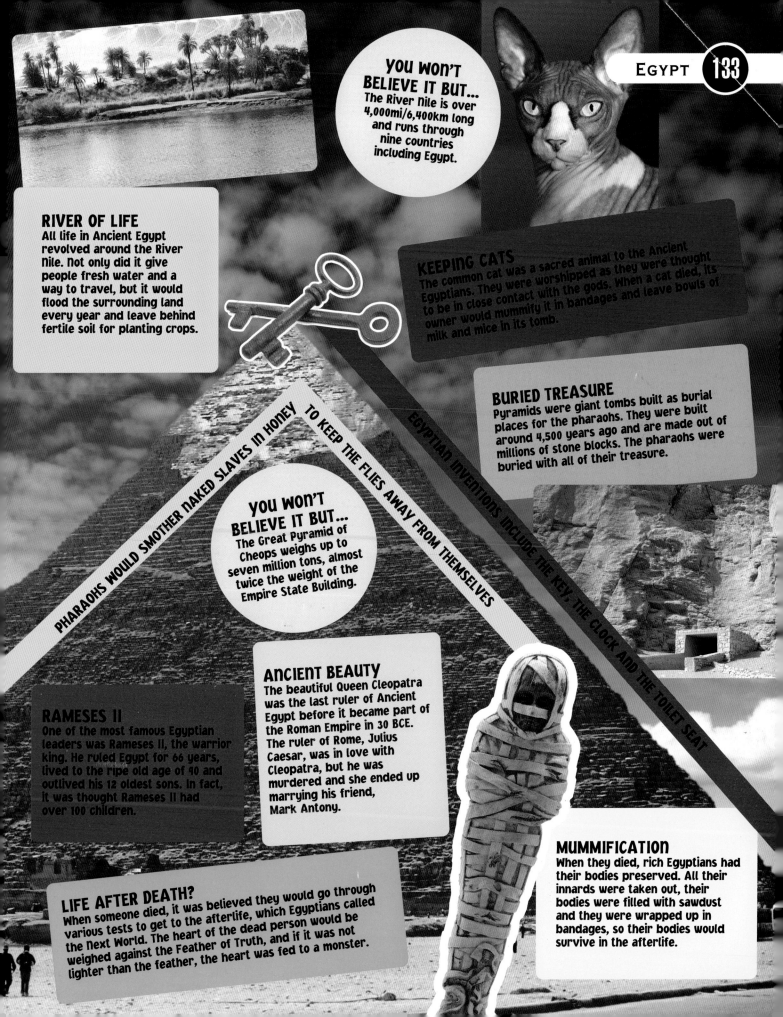

YOU WON'T BELIEVE IT BUT...
The River Nile is over 4,000mi/6,400km long and runs through nine countries including Egypt.

RIVER OF LIFE
All life in Ancient Egypt revolved around the River Nile. Not only did it give people fresh water and a way to travel, but it would flood the surrounding land every year and leave behind fertile soil for planting crops.

KEEPING CATS
The common cat was a sacred animal to the Ancient Egyptians. They were worshipped as they were thought to be in close contact with the gods. When a cat died, its owner would mummify it in bandages and leave bowls of milk and mice in its tomb.

BURIED TREASURE
Pyramids were giant tombs built as burial places for the pharaohs. They were built around 4,500 years ago and are made out of millions of stone blocks. The pharaohs were buried with all of their treasure.

PHARAOHS WOULD SMOTHER NAKED SLAVES IN HONEY TO KEEP THE FLIES AWAY FROM THEMSELVES

EGYPTIAN INVENTIONS INCLUDE THE KEY, THE CLOCK AND THE TOILET SEAT

YOU WON'T BELIEVE IT BUT...
The Great Pyramid of Cheops weighs up to seven million tons, almost twice the weight of the Empire State Building.

ANCIENT BEAUTY
The beautiful Queen Cleopatra was the last ruler of Ancient Egypt before it became part of the Roman Empire in 30 BCE. The ruler of Rome, Julius Caesar, was in love with Cleopatra, but he was murdered and she ended up marrying his friend, Mark Antony.

RAMESES II
One of the most famous Egyptian leaders was Rameses II, the warrior king. He ruled Egypt for 66 years, lived to the ripe old age of 90 and outlived his 12 oldest sons. In fact, it was thought Rameses II had over 100 children.

MUMMIFICATION
When they died, rich Egyptians had their bodies preserved. All their innards were taken out, their bodies were filled with sawdust and they were wrapped up in bandages, so their bodies would survive in the afterlife.

LIFE AFTER DEATH?
When someone died, it was believed they would go through various tests to get to the afterlife, which Egyptians called the Next World. The heart of the dead person would be weighed against the Feather of Truth, and if it was not lighter than the feather, the heart was fed to a monster.

WHAT ARE ELEMENTS?
Elements are the atoms that make up the world around us. You'll probably have heard of the more common ones, such as oxygen, hydrogen and calcium, but there are 112 known elements in all – including some that are very rare.

PLUMBING THE DEPTHS
At room temperature, lead is a soft metal with the Latin name 'plumbum'. Water pipes were often made from lead, which is how plumbers got their name. Lead can also be highly poisonous to humans, which is why it is rarely used today.

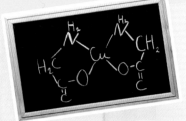

YOU WON'T BELIEVE IT BUT... Fluorine gas is one of the most volatile and poisonous elements on Earth.

YOU WON'T BELIEVE IT BUT... If you drop even a small piece of potassium in water, it will explode.

ESSENTIAL MATTER
Your body is made up of the same element as a lump of dirty old coal. That's because carbon is an essential part in the creation of all known life on Earth. But carbon can be dangerous – too much of it in the atmosphere leads to pollution.

THE SOIL ON MARS IS RED BECAUSE IT IS FILLED WITH IRON

CHEMICAL COMBINATIONS
Compounds occur when two or more elements are joined together in a chemical reaction. On their own, both sodium and chlorine are smelly and volatile. Put them together and you get something you consume every single day – sodium chloride, or common table salt.

DON'T TELL SUPERMAN, BUT KRYPTON IS THE NAME OF A GAS IN THE EARTH'S ATMOSPHERE

WHAT ARE ALLOYS?
Alloys are made when two or more elements are combined, and are often used to make metals that are stronger, lighter and able to withstand extremely high temperatures. For instance, titanium can be combined with elements such as aluminum, iron, manganese and molybdenum, and these kinds of alloys are then used in creating engines for planes.

BREATH OF LIFE
It can explode, and too much can kill you, but you're gulping down oxygen right now. Or you should be – if your lungs didn't absorb oxygen from the air, you wouldn't be able to breathe.

IS WATER AN ELEMENT?
No. Water is often referred to as an element, but it is a compound. Because the Earth is a 'closed system' (meaning that our planet rarely gains or loses extra matter), the water we use today is the same water that has been round for millions of years.

WHERE DO ELEMENTS COME FROM?

Most elements occur naturally on the Earth. They can be found in the ground or in the air, and can be solids, liquids or gases depending on the temperature. New elements are occasionally discovered or created during nuclear reactions.

PARTY BALLOONS FLOAT BECAUSE THEY ARE FILLED WITH HELIUM, WHICH IS LIGHTER THAN AIR

HYDROGEN
FLAMMABLE GAS
NO SMOKING
NO OPEN FLAME

YOU WON'T BELIEVE IT BUT...

If you collected together all the gold that has ever been mined, you'd still only have enough to fill an average-sized house.

HEAPS OF HYDROGEN

Hydrogen is the simplest and most common element, and one of the essential elements in both air and water. In fact, it's so common that it is claimed that over 90 percent of the atoms in the entire universe are hydrogen. For something so common in our lives, it is difficult to spot – it's odorless, tasteless and colorless.

MAGNIFICENT MAGNESIUM

Magnesium is a very light metal with one very exciting property. Unlike heavier metals, magnesium can be set alight very easily, and it burns with a brilliant white flare. You'll already have seen it in action as it's used for making fireworks.

KEEP UP YOUR STRENGTH

You've probably been told lots of times that milk makes your bones stronger, and it's calcium you can thank for this. But, at normal room temperature, it appears as a silvery metal.

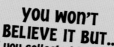

YOU WON'T BELIEVE IT BUT...

Astatine, a radioactive element, is one of the rarest elements with less than 0.0035oz/100mg occurring naturally in the world and is highly unstable.

MIND THE GAP

When Russian scientist Dmitri Mendeleev compiled the first periodic table in 1869, he left gaps for new elements that he thought other scientists would discover. Over a hundred years later, all these spaces have been filled.

FISH BREATHE OXYGEN, JUST LIKE HUMANS, BUT THEIR BODIES EXTRACT IT FROM WATER RATHER THAN AIR

THE FIRST EUROPEANS
Although cavemen lived in Europe several million years ago, modern man didn't settle there until around 7,000 BCE. The first European people who could read and write were the Minoans from the island of Crete, in around 2,000 BCE. Approximately 3,000 tablets have been discovered with Minoan writing on them.

ALL ROADS LEAD TO ROME
Over many centuries, the Romans built and ran an empire that completely dominated western Europe and beyond. At the Roman Empire's territorial peak, it controled approximately 2,300,000 sq mi/5,400,000 sq km of land. The Western Roman Empire fell apart though after the invasion by barbarian tribes in the fifth century CE.

RENAISSANCE MEN
The Renaissance was a period between the 14th and 17th centuries during which culture and science flourished thanks to the brilliance of the people living in Italy and the rest of Europe. Renaissance era inventions included portable clocks, the flush toilet and the submarine.

YOU WON'T BELIEVE IT BUT...
The Russian city of Volgograd was renamed Stalingrad during Joseph Stalin's reign. It was changed back in 1961.

SOME SCIENTISTS BELIEVE THE MINOAN CIVILIZATION WAS DESTROYED BY A TSUNAMI

SHIP SHAPE
King Philip of Spain wanted Queen Elizabeth's throne so he sent the Spanish Armada to seize it in 1588. This huge fleet consisted of 130 ships packed with 8,000 sailors and 18,000 soldiers. A fierce battle with the English fleet ensued. The Spanish were defeated and its empire soon went into decline.

YOU WON'T BELIEVE IT BUT...
Over 317 million people now use the single European currency of the Euro.

VIVE LA REVOLUTION
The French people were tired of being treated badly by their monarchy, so they rose up against it at the end of the 18th century in what became known as the French Revolution. They stormed the Bastille, a notorious French prison, and eventually had their Queen, Marie Antoinette, beheaded for treason in 1793 at the young age of 37.

DISNEYLAND PARIS OPENED ON APRIL 12, 1992

EXPANDING YOUR HORIZONS
From the 15th century, European countries started to take over the world – they expanded and colonized many lands. Spain led the way by discovering the Americas, Britain followed suit by taking Australia plus parts of India, while France colonized parts of Canada and Africa. This period was called the Age of Discovery.

THE MACHINE AGE
From the late 18th century, Britain was home to the Industrial Revolution. Expensive and time-consuming manual labor was gradually replaced by machines in factories that could do the same job faster and cheaper. The Industrial Revolution swept across Europe and changed society for ever.

EUROPE COVERS JUST TWO PERCENT OF THE EARTH'S SURFACE

BIRTH OF EUROPE
The European Union was created in 1957 but was known back then as the European Economic Community. The EU has always tried to take steps to bring European countries closer together, like launching the single European currency in 2002. In 2007, Bulgaria and Romania were inducted to the EU, bringing the union total to 27 nations so far.

EUROMILLIONS
There are more Euros in circulation than any other currency. As of 2007, 14.25 billion Euro notes, worth a total of E462 billion/£876 billion, have been printed since its launch in 2002. If placed end to end, they would reach the Moon and back five times. In addition, 50 billion Euro coins have been minted, to a value of E15.7 billion/$21 billion. Altogether, they would weigh 240,000 tons – that's the same as 24,000 big trucks.

YOU WON'T BELIEVE IT BUT...
As of 2007, Turkey is still waiting to join the EU. It has had the longest application process of any EU applicant country – it formally applied to join in 1987.

WORLD AT WAR
World War Two wasn't strictly a world war, because some countries such as Sweden, Switzerland, Republic of Ireland, Lichtenstein, Monaco, Andorra, Afganistan, Yemen and Portugal, remained neutral.

THE CHANNEL TUNNEL BETWEEN ENGLAND AND FRANCE COST $20/£10 BILLION

YOU WON'T BELIEVE IT BUT...
During World War One, British and German troops called a ceasefire on Christmas Day in 1914 to exchange gifts, sing carols, and play soccer.

GERMANY REUNITED
After World War Two, Germany was divided into two countries by the Berlin wall: East and West. West Germany became a functioning part of Europe and Russia controlled East Germany. Construction on the Berlin wall began on August 13, 1961, and the official demolition began on June 13, 1990. Pieces of the wall can now be bought in many tourist shops in Germany.

SING-STRUCK
British singer Engelbert Humperdinck has the largest fan club in the world. There are eight million of his 'Englettes' in 250 divisions across the globe. Few, however, have met Humperdinck – he maintains a 'mysterious image' by disappearing after live shows, often sneaking out of bathroom windows.

WHO WAS ST VALENTINE?
Although no one knows for sure, St Valentine may have been an early Christian priest who was publicly beheaded by the Romans for marrying couples in secret. In 496 CE, Pope Gelasius decreed that February 14 was St Valentine's Day.

TIGERS WERE VOTED THE WORLD'S FAVORITE ANIMAL IN A RECENT POLL

YOU WON'T BELIEVE IT BUT...
Worldwide, the best-loved toys of the past hundred years have included Crayola crayons, the Cabbage Patch Kids, electric train sets, Play-Doh and Barbies.

VANILLA HIT
Everybody loves ice cream and, according to the International Ice Cream Association, just under 30 percent of ice cream sold worldwide is vanilla. The next most popular flavor is chocolate, which accounts for just under four percent of sales. They attribute vanilla's popularity to the fact that it goes well with other flavors.

SAVE THE CATSUP
People love some very strange objects. The Collinsville water tower, built in 1949 to look like a bottle of Brooks Old Original Catsup, has its own fan club. In 1995, the 170ft/52m tower was going to be demolished, but the Catsup Bottle Preservation Group was formed to save it – and succeeded.

OWN GOOOOAAAL
Brazilian people love soccer so much that whenever the national team plays they will skip work to watch. To avoid this, many companies set up TVs at work. Brazilians call their country 'o país do futebol' ('the football country') – and the Brazil's best-selling car is the Volkswagen Gol, named after the Brazilian Portuguese word for 'goal'.

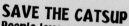
A BILLION VALENTINE'S DAY CARDS ARE SENT EACH YEAR

THE MOST HATED INVENTION IN AMERICA...
... is the cellphone. Although most people also admitted they couldn't live without it.

EVERYONE HATES HOMEWORK...
... and the most frequent excuse for not doing it seems to be, "The dog ate it".

KOREA CRAZE

Everyone loves cartoon characters, but while some are international, a lot of countries have their own beloved creations. Korea's best-loved cartoon character, created in 1983, is a green-and-white dinosaur called Dooly. In local polls, the character regularly comes top, beating such international favorites as Mickey and Minnie Mouse.

YOU WON'T BELIEVE IT BUT...
Worldwide, the most popular sport to play is soccer – an amazing 240 million people in more than 200 countries enjoy playing the game.

BLOG-BUSTER

More people love reading Xu Jinglei's blog than any other – it has had in excess of 100 million hits. The Chinese singer, actress and director was hailed as the world's most widely-read blogger in July 2007. She started her blog in 2005 and it follows her day-to-day life and career.

BEST BAR NONE

The Snickers bar is the most-loved candy bar in the world. Sales of the bar, which consists of nougat, peanuts and caramel, covered in chocolate, began in 1930. In 2006, more than $2/£1 billion worth of them were sold worldwide – more than any other chocolate bar. Manufactured by Mars Inc, it was originally named after a horse.

IT IS CLAIMED THE LONGEST KISS EVER LASTED 417 HOURS

WIKI-ED

According to Alexa, the web-statistics company, people love the video sharing website YouTube, the social networking site Myspace and the online encyclopaedia Wikipedia, more than any other non-search-engine websites. In any one week, an average of 12 percent of all internet users visited YouTube, 5 percent visited MySpace and 6 percent visited Wikipedia.

YOU WON'T BELIEVE IT BUT...
France is the most popular holiday destination. Every year around 75 million tourists visit – 10 million more people than actually live there.

YOU WON'T BELIEVE IT BUT...
The reason other people talking on cellphones irritates us so much is because we're nosy – we want to listen in on both sides of the conversation.

THE MOST HATED FOOD IN THE UK...
... is tripe – the stomach lining from a cow. It's followed closely by snails, which are among France's favorite foods.

THE MOST HATED HOUSEHOLD CHORE...
... is ironing.

GET A MOVE ON
Work on the Sagrada Familia cathedral in Barcelona began in around 1882, and it still isn't finished. Its architect, Gaudi, was run over by a tram in 1926 and he left no written plans behind, so there has been a lot of disagreement about how the finished cathedral should look.

YOU WON'T BELIEVE IT BUT...
It is commonly thought that the Vatican's Swiss Guard still wears a uniform designed by Michelangelo in the early 16th century.

FULL HOUSE
Europe is home to around 720 million people in total – that's 10 percent of all the humans on the entire planet. The average European family now has 1.37 children.

THERE ARE 23 OFFICIAL LANGUAGES IN THE EUROPEAN UNION

IS ANYBODY THERE?
The largest European country, and the largest country in the world, is Russia. It stretches for thousands of miles, from Norway in northern Europe to Asia and the Japan Sea. Despite its enormous size, there are only 100 million people living there – a little over double the population of Britain.

SINGING WINNERS
The Eurovision Song Contest is Europe's biggest television event, watched annually by over 100 million people. When the contest began in 1956, just seven countries took part; in 2007, there were 42 countries.

COVERING 3.9 MILLION SQUARE MILES, EUROPE IS THE WORLD'S SMALLEST CONTINENT AFTER AUSTRALIA

DIVINE PRESENTS
Europe may take its name from Europa, a character in Greek mythology whose name means 'broad-browed'. Zeus, king of the gods, disguised himself as a bull, carried her away to the island of Crete and gave her a bronze robot called Talos and a javelin that never missed.

YOU WON'T BELIEVE IT BUT...
The Aland Islands, Finland, are home to only 26,000 people, making them one of the smallest European nations.

LET'S STICK TOGETHER
The European Union is the name given to a group of European countries that together make important decisions about money, security and trade. Most EU members now use a single currency called the Euro.

YOU WON'T BELIEVE IT BUT...
The phrase 'all roads lead to Rome' relates to when the Roman Empire introduced paved roads to Europe.

MULTILINGUAL
Many European citizens can speak several languages. Switzerland, for instance, has four common languages spoken within its borders. German, French and Italian are all spoken frequently, but the official local language is the little-used Romansh.

CYCLING HEROES
The Tour de France is perhaps Europe's most famous sporting event. In 2007, there were 189 riders who covered over 2,845mi/4,000km in 22 days over 20 stages.

SWEDEN CONTAINS OVER 100,000 LAKES

THE REALLY OLDEN DAYS
The oldest European ruins were found underground in Germany, Austria and Slovakia in 2005. These ancient temples were built over 6,000 years ago, making them older than the legendary pyramids of Egypt.

GONDOLIER GRADUATE
In order to pilot one of Venice's famous gondolas, you have to be born in Venice. It usually takes a 10-year apprenticeship and gondoliers work 12-hour days during the summer tourist season. However, they do get the winters off, and most retire at 50.

EUROPE, ONLY SMALLER
The Mini-Europe park in Heysel, Belgium, contains scale models of Europe's most famous buildings such as the Eiffel Tower. The accurate models can take a long time to create – the model of the Spanish Cathedral of Santiago de Compostela took 24,000 hours to build. It would take one person 13 years to make.

THE AVERAGE ADULT MALE IN HOLLAND IS OVER 6FT/2M TALL, MAKING THE DUTCH THE WORLD'S TALLEST PEOPLE

SPORTING SUMMIT
Mont Blanc, situated between France and Italy, is western Europe's highest mountain, standing 15,774ft/4,808m tall. It was first climbed in 1786 by Jacques Balmat and Dr Michel-Gabriel Paccard, an achievement that helped create the sport of mountaineering.

YOU WON'T BELIEVE IT BUT...
From Ashford to Calais is 32 minutes by the Eurostar train, of which 21 are spent in the Channel Tunnel.

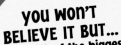

YOU WON'T BELIEVE IT BUT...
The mouth of the biggest shark – the plankton-eating whale shark – can be as wide as 4.9ft/1.5m.

WHO SAID THAT?
As its name suggests, the pygmy shark is the smallest of the shark family. It lives in warm seas throughout the world and only reaches up to 10in/26.5cm in length – a great white shark is more than 20 times bigger.

A FISH OUT OF WATER
The thresher shark has an unusually long tail that makes up to half its body length. It's used as a weapon to stun prey – usually fish or squid. They are athletic, too, being one of the few sharks able to jump fully out of the water.

SHARK INTELLECT
By fish standards, sharks are highly intelligent and have brains almost equal to those of many mammals, when compared to their body size. Scientists are still studying them, but it is thought they have good problem-solving skills and good memories.

WHAT'S ON THE MENU?
Tiger sharks will eat almost anything, including seals, turtles, jellyfish, seabirds, fish, sea snakes, crabs, other sharks and even human garbage. They have been found with boat cushions, alarm clocks and license plates in their stomachs.

MEGA MARINER
The largest meat-eating shark to have ever lived was the megalodon. Fossils of this enormous beast show it could reach up to 52ft/16m in length – almost three times the size of a great white. Scientists think the megalodon used to eat whales.

ARE YOU FEELING SLEEPY?
Nobody knows how sharks sleep. They've been seen resting on the bottom in shallow seas, but they have their eyes open and are still aware of their surroundings.

YOU WON'T BELIEVE IT BUT...
Sharks were called 'sea dogs' until the 16th century. The word 'shark' may come from the indigenous people of the Caribbean.

OPEN WIDE
The basking shark is a huge eating-machine that lives in the colder oceans, where you might not expect to find big sharks. Don't worry, though – it eats plankton. It just opens its mouth wide and its dinner floats in.

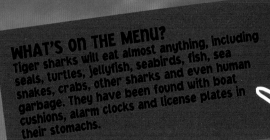

HUMANS KILL MILLIONS OF SHARKS EVERY YEAR

SHARK EGGS ARE KNOWN AS MERMAID'S PURSES

DOWN IN ONE
The great white shark is the most feared shark. While few people are attacked by sharks, if they are it's probably a great white doing the attacking. With several rows of diamond-sharp teeth, they can bite you in half.

A STRANGE LOOKER
The bizarre-looking hammerhead shark is a ferocious meat-eater but is of little danger to humans because its mouth is suited to feeding off the seabed. Each end of its distinctive shaped head houses an eye and nostril.

YOU WON'T BELIEVE IT BUT...
In ancient Hawaii, the people worshipped all sorts of shark gods.

THE WHOLE TOOTH
A shark will never run out of teeth. If a tooth gets broken or lost, another one moves forward from the rows and rows of spare teeth behind. An adult shark can get through over 20,000 teeth in its lifetime.

YOU WON'T BELIEVE IT BUT...
The swell shark, found in New Zealand, barks like a dog when taken out of the water.

THE WORLD'S OCEANS ARE 70 PERCENT SHARK-FREE

MOST SHARKS GIVE BIRTH TO LIVE YOUNG

SWALLOWED ALIVE
In early 2007, diver Eric Nerhus had a brush with death when a shark attacked him off the coast of Australia. The creature tried to swallow him head-first but Nerhus dug his fingers into its eyes and it spat him out – but only after his head had been inside the shark for two minutes.

GREAT SENSE OF SMELL
Sharks have an amazing sense of smell – some species can tell if there is just a tiny drop of blood in the ocean around where they are swimming. They also like the smell of poo, so they can often be found where human sewage is pumped into the sea.

MARINE MONSTERS
Many creatures are believed in without having ever been found. One of the most famous is the Loch Ness Monster, who was first seen, or so the tale goes, by St Columba in 565CE. Another lake monster, the Swedish Storsjöodjuret, first made its appearance 400 years ago – and was protected by law from 1986 to 2004.

UPSIDE DOWN LEAVES
Farmers are among the world's most superstitious people. Some believe that bad weather is coming if flowers close up, the leaves on trees turn upside down, or cats wash behind their ears. In Britain, it's believed that if it rains on St Swithin's Day, July 15, then it will then rain for 40 days.

UNLUCKY FOR SOME
The number 13 is widely considered unlucky, but some people are so scared they suffer from a condition called triskaidekaphobia – a fear of the number 13. The US president Franklin Roosevelt was a sufferer. This strange superstition comes from the Bible's Last Supper – which was attended by 13 people.

IN RUSSIA, CHILDREN BELIEVE THAT WASHING THEIR HANDS CAN WASH OUT KNOWLEDGE NEEDED FOR EXAMS

THE LOST CITY
Atlantis is one of the world's greatest myths. The great Greek philosopher Plato first described a lost civilization that had explored the world by sea nearly 10,000 years ago – before earthquakes and floods sank their island. Geologists and enthusiasts have looked all over the Atlantic for Atlantis – but with no luck so far.

YOU WON'T BELIEVE IT BUT...
If you cut a child's fingernails with scissors, they'll grow up to be a thief – or so they say in Orkney.

IN THE MIDDLE AGES, PEOPLE FOUND GUILTY OF WITCHCRAFT WERE BURNT ALIVE

DINING WITH THE DEAD
Mexicans celebrate the 'Day of the Dead' every November. Families give each other sugar skulls and skeletons and cook a special 'bread of the dead'. Some, however, believe the dead return to visit their families. Determined to be good hosts, these people leave a feast ready for their unearthly visitors.

YOU WON'T BELIEVE IT BUT...
A horseshoe nailed to the door with the prongs pointing up is lucky – if hung the wrong way, luck flows out.

ONE, TWO, THREE... FIVE?
In China, Japan and Korea, the number four is considered extremely unlucky. The reason is simple – in their languages the word for 'death' sounds almost the same as the word for 'four'. Cellphone numbers with a 'four' in them sell for less, and many buildings miss out the fourth floor altogether.

YOU WON'T BELIEVE IT BUT...
During a plague outbreak in the sixth century, the Pope proclaimed that people should say "God bless you" after someone sneezed, a superstition still practiced today.

TAINTED TOMB
When archeologist Howard Carter opened Tutankhamun's tomb in the 1920s, he was said to have unleashed an ancient curse. Several members of his team did die but Carter himself lived until 1939. One explanation for the deaths may be a fungus in the tomb that was breathed in by the archeologists.

NO MORE NOSTRADAMUS
The 16th century French mystic Nostradamus claimed he could see the future and wrote his predictions down as poems. Skeptics, however, say his poems are nonsense. He did get one thing right – on the evening of July 1, 1566, he told a friend, "You will not find me alive at sunrise." He died that night.

THE MEANING OF MAGPIES
No one is sure why, but magpies are connected with superstitions all over the world. In Scotland, a magpie on a house means someone inside is going to die and, in Sweden, they are the pets of evil witches. But, in China, magpies are a sign of happiness.

TRAVELERS TALES
For hundreds of years, Christians considered St Christopher to be the patron saint of travel, because he carried Jesus over a river – or so it is believed. Thousands of people buy St Christopher's medals each year. However, Christopher's story is fatally flawed – because the Catholic Church says he probably didn't exist.

FOUR IN 10 AMERICANS BELIEVE IN MIND READING

YOU WON'T BELIEVE IT BUT...
Black cats were considered good luck but this changed when they became associated with witchcraft and people started hunting witches.

SOME NATIVE PEOPLE BELIEVE THAT PHOTOS CAN CAPTURE PART OF SOMEONE'S SOUL

COUNT ON ME
Count Dracula was a real person – a Transylvanian king known as Vlad the Impaler, whose nickname, Draculea, means 'son of the Devil'. Though he was a barbaric man, rumors that he drank blood probably aren't true – but that didn't stop Bram Stoker, who used him for his 1897 novel *Dracula*.

THERE AND BACK AGAIN
The space shuttle is only designed to travel a few hundred miles way from Earth and back again. It can't carry enough fuel to fly all the way to the Moon, and it wouldn't be able to land because it needs a flat runway.

IN THE 1940S, SCI-FI WRITER ARTHUR C CLARKE PREDICTED HUMANS WOULD REACH THE MOON – BY THE YEAR 2000

ON MAY 5 1961...
... Alan Shepard became the first American in space, although he never went into orbit. That honor fell to John Glenn on February 20, 1962. However, Shepard did get to walk – and play golf – on the Moon in 1971.

THE PRICE OF SPACE
Space shuttles are an expensive way to travel, as it can cost around $450/£225 million for each launch. They're even more expensive to make – the newest shuttle, Endeavor, cost $1.7 billion/£850 million to build back in 1987.

YOU WON'T BELIEVE IT BUT...
The word 'astronaut' literally means 'star sailor'. It comes from the Greek words 'astra' meaning 'star', and 'nauta' meaning 'sailor'.

YOU WON'T BELIEVE IT BUT...
Russian cosmonaut Valentina Tereshkova was the first woman in space. She orbited the earth 48 times back in 1963 as part of the Vostok 5 mission.

WHAT'S A SPUTNIK?
One of the most important dates in history is October 4, 1957, when the first human-made object was sent into space. In a rocket designed by Sergey Korolyov, the satellite Sputnik was put into orbit.

MAN IN SPACE
On April 12, 1961, Russian Cosmonaut Yuri Gagarin became the first human being in space. He orbited the Earth for 108 minutes in the Vostok 1 spacecraft.

SHOOTING FOR THE STARS
In 2000, Russian movie producers planned to shoot the very first film in space. An actor called Vladimir Steklov was even trained as an astronaut so he could be filmed on the real Russian space station, Mir. Sadly, they ran out of money before they could blast off.

FUEL FOR THOUGHT
Dr Robert H Goddard's first rocket flight in Massachusetts lasted less than three seconds, and landed in a cabbage patch, but his 1926 experiment showed that rockets could be launched using liquid fuel. His discovery paved the way for modern space exploration.

ONLY 12 PEOPLE HAVE EVER WALKED ON THE MOON

YOU WON'T BELIEVE IT BUT...
Moon rocks are very valuable. In 1993 at Sotheby's auction house in New York, three fragments weighing less than one gram were sold for $442,500/£221,250.

WHO WAS FIRST TO THE MOON?
Luna (or Lunik) was the name of the Soviet Union's lunar program. In 1959, the Luna 2 probe became the first object to travel from the Earth to the Moon.

EMBARRASSING END
The US's first attempt to launch a satellite into orbit had a dramatic end in 1957. America already had a rocket, but it was being used by the miltary. So President Eisenhower ordered his scientists to make the Vanguard using the technology. They did, but it blew up on

ROUGHLY 1,000 TONS OF SPACE DUST FLOATS DOWN TO EARTH EVERY YEAR

ROCKET MEN
The three pioneers of rocket development are Konstantin Tsiolkovsky, Robert Goddard and Hermann Oberth. Although they lived in different countries and worked separately, all were inspired by science fiction, in particular, *From Earth To The Moon* by Jules Verne and HG Wells' *War Of The Worlds*.

A GIANT LEAP
"One small step for man, one giant leap for mankind." These were the words spoken by US astronaut Neil Armstrong on July 20, 1969, as he became the first human to set foot on the Moon.

YOU WON'T BELIEVE IT BUT...
The first astronauts on the Moon were able to smell moondust from inside their landing craft when they removed their helmets. Neil Armstrong described the smell as "wet ashes in a fireplace".

YOU WON'T BELIEVE IT BUT...
Bridgeville, in California, was the first town to be auctioned on eBay – it eventually sold for $700,000/£350,000.

GIANT GREENHOUSES
The Eden Project is a huge environmental enterprise in Cornwall, England. It boasts two huge greenhouses of which one, the Tropical Biome, is the biggest in the world. Eleven double-decker buses could be stacked inside. The other giant greenhouse recreates a temperate ecosystem. Between them, they contain 100,000 plants.

HOW DID SOCIETY START?
Before humans settled down to grow crops, domesticate animals and build houses, they were hunter-gatherers. One person roaming the land in search of animals and plants for food would probably die. By forming themselves into a tribe, all of them could help, and be helped by, the others – the first society.

ARREST THAT MAN
Police are an essential part of society but the first police force wasn't an immediate success. Sir Robert Peel set it up in London, England in 1829 but most of the new recruits were terrible and had to be sacked. The first policeman was fired after just four hours – for being drunk

HORSE-DRAWN BUS
The first city public transport system in the world was an omnibus service – a horse-drawn bus – in Nantes, France. Stanislas Baudry founded the service in 1826. Although it was a useful innovation, the first omnibuses only carried 14 passengers – modern buses can manage up to 140.

MONGOLIA HAS THE LOWEST POPULATION DENSITY IN THE WORLD WITH ABOUT FOUR PEOPLE PER SQUARE MILE

WHAT A STATE
The idea for the 'welfare state' – medical treatment, accommodation and unemployment benefit for all who need it – is an idea that was adopted by a lot of countries after World War Two. Before that, most societies looked after their poor and needy through charity – which wasn't always as reliable.

THE WORLD'S LARGEST CITIES ARE SHANGHAI IN CHINA AND MUMBAI IN INDIA

YOU WON'T BELIEVE IT BUT...
Some countries don't take any tax from their citizens. These include Saudi Arabia, the United Arab Emirates and Monaco.

WORK OF A LIFETIME
It is exceptionally hard for people to get citizenship in the tiny country of Andorra in western Europe. Even people who have lived there for 20 years cannot claim this privilege – they must have lived there for at least 25. Out of a population of approximately 70,000, only around 15,000 have citizenship.

YOU WON'T BELIEVE IT BUT...
America has the highest populations of dogs and cats in the world. However, the pet fish is most popular – there are almost 169 million of them.

ON THE MOVE
Nomadic people usually live in desert regions and move from place to place about six times a year – rather than settling down in one area. By keeping moving, they make sure that their animals do not over-graze single areas.

MONACO HAS THE WORLD'S OLDEST POPULATION – 22 PERCENT ARE OVER 65

LICENSED TO DRIVE
You have to have a driving license to prove that you are a competent driver on the road, but this wasn't always the case. In the US, driving tests and licenses were first introduced in 1910 in New York after the number of accidents sky-rocketed. But these were only for professional chauffeurs.

A GUIDE TO LONG LIFE?
The average world life expectancy is currently 67 years, but a hundred years ago it was just 30. How long you can expect to live depends on a number of things – pollution, stress, healthcare and availability of food. Andorra's citizens have the highest life expectancy – they live on average 83.51 years.

JERICHO IS THE OLDEST CONTINUOUSLY INHABITED CITY IN THE WORLD

FUNNY MONEY
Most societies use either paper notes or metal currency, but hundreds of years ago things like spices could be used to buy goods and services. Even today, in the Solomon Islands, 'shell money', made from carefully shaped sea-shells, and 'feather money', made from glued bird feathers, are both acceptable currency.

PERFECT CITY?
Which city is the best to live in? According to *The Economist* magazine the answer is Vancouver, Canada, which was voted top a record four times running – in 2002, 2003, 2004 and 2005. Cities were ranked on their infrastructure, health care, safety and access to goods and services.

YOU WON'T BELIEVE IT BUT...
More than half of the US's population, estimated at 301,140,000, live in just nine states: California, Texas, New York, Florida, Illinois, Pennsylvania, Ohio, Michigan and Georgia.

WHO FOUND AMERICA FIRST?
Christopher Columbus was thought to have discovered North America in 1492. However, some believe that wood carvings and ancient legends show that the Vikings reached Canada hundreds of years before Columbus. They called it Vinland, or vine land, because of the grapes that grew there.

YOU WON'T BELIEVE IT BUT...
Sir Martin Frobisher, the Elizabethan explorer was, between 1555 and 1575, a legalized pirate. Frobisher was a 'privateer,' a sailor authorized by the British government to attack the treasure ships of enemy countries.

RANGING ROVER
Sir Walter Raleigh was an English adventurer who traveled to the Americas in the 16th century and was very popular with Queen Elizabeth I. Raleigh also helped introduce potatoes to Britain.

SIR FRANCIS DRAKE, THE BRITISH EXPLORER, WAS CONSIDERED TO BE A PIRATE BY THE SPANISH

TOMB RAIDER
Howard Carter was one of the most famous explorers of the 20th century but he didn't actually discover a new country – he uncovered the tomb of the pharaoh Tutankhamen in Egypt in 1922 and, more importantly, the pharaoh's solid gold coffin.

POLES APART
Norwegian explorer Roald Amundsen won the race to reach the south pole in Antarctica, beating British rival Robert Falcon Scott. Not only did Scott come second but he and his men got stuck in a storm and died on the ice before they could return to base.

NO ONE HAS SET FOOT ON THE MOON SINCE 1972

TALES OF THE ORIENT
Venetian explorer Marco Polo set out for China in 1271 and didn't return for 24 years. He was one of the first Europeans to travel the Silk Road to the East.

YOU WON'T BELIEVE IT BUT...
A popular myth is that Queen Isabella of Spain sold her crown jewels to pay for Columbus' voyage. She did not – the voyage was paid for by several wealthy investors.

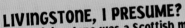

MAGELLAN GOES GLOBAL

Ferdinand Magellan was a Portuguese explorer whose expedition was the first to sail around the world. He named the Pacific Ocean and discovered a short cut through the tip of South America to the Atlantic. Sometimes he spent so long on the ocean, he had to eat boiled leather and rats.

MISTAKEN IDENTITY

Juan Ponce de Léon, a Spanish nobleman of the early 1500s, heard that the Fountain of Youth existed on an island north of Cuba. Determined to find the island, he paid for his own ships to search for it. He never did discover the fountain, but on March 27, 1513, he did discover Florida.

WHAT A WRECK

In 1985, Dr Robert Ballard and his crew discovered the wreck of the Titanic on the ocean floor. With a submarine and camera, he showed the world ghoulish images of the biggest ship ever made, split in half and rusted beyond recognition.

LIVINGSTONE, I PRESUME?

David Livingstone was a Scottish missionary who dedicated his life to exploring Africa. He loved Africa even though a lion attacked him shortly after arriving. He disappeared for a while and was presumed to be dead, until a journalist found him alive and well in East Africa.

LIFE ON MARS?

Mankind continues to explore the stars in the hope of one day finding life on other planets. The Mars Exploration Rover mission has produced incredible pictures of the red planet.

A LONG WAY FROM HOME

A British explorer, navigator and map-maker, Captain James Cook was the first European to claim Australia on behalf of his country.

YOU WON'T BELIEVE IT BUT...

Meriwether Lewis and William Clark were the first people to cross North America, making their trek between 1804 and 1806. They traveled an amazing 3,700mi/5,454km from the Missouri River to the Columbia River.

DOCTOR WHO?
Hippocrates was a physician in Ancient Greece. He is often called the Father of Medicine. He was one of the first people to realize that diseases were not caused by supernatural forces, and could be treated and cured. Even today, when becoming a doctor, people take the Hippocratic Oath, promising to care for their patients.

AN INTERESTING MIX
In ancient times, it was believed the human body was made up of four elements – blood, yellow bile, black bile and phlegm. Medicine was based around the idea that, if you felt ill, it was because you had too much, or not enough, of one of these substances.

YOU WON'T BELIEVE IT BUT...
Vomiting is good for you. It's your body's way of getting rid of things in your stomach that are making you sick.

WHAT WAS THE BLACK DEATH?
Black Death was the name given to the bubonic plague, a very nasty disease that spread through Europe in the 14th century. Victims would cough up blood, and millions died. Although a few cases still occur, it is now extremely rare.

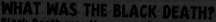
IF YOU SUFFER FROM A GELASTIC SEIZURE, YOU WON'T BE ABLE TO STOP LAUGHING

GUT FEELING
Claudius Galen of Pergamum was a Greek medical pioneer. He worked as a doctor in the gladiatorial arenas and used gladiators' wounds to study their guts while they were still alive. He used this knowledge of anatomy in his later work.

YOU WON'T BELIEVE IT BUT...
Before anesthetics, patients were sedated with opium or made drunk with alcohol before surgery.

THE DARK AGES
After the fall of the Roman Empire, Europe entered the Dark Ages, the early part of the Middle Ages. But enormous medical advances continued in the Islamic world. Rhazes (ar-Razi) was a Persian scientist who wrote about measles and correctly realized that high fever was a symptom, not the disease.

SUCK IT UP
Early doctors were taught that certain ailments could be cured by draining the patient's blood. If you were lucky, the doctor just cut your arm. If you were unlucky, he would place slimy leeches on your flesh and let them suck your blood until you felt better.

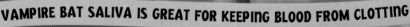
VAMPIRE BAT SALIVA IS GREAT FOR KEEPING BLOOD FROM CLOTTING

ARE GERMS ALIVE?
Yes, they are. Germs are tiny organisms that can make us ill. Germs come in two types: viruses and bacteria. Each type needs to be treated differently. Some bacteria, such as the ones in yogurt, can also be good for you.

THE SOUND OF MOO-SICK
Smallpox is a contagious disease that used to kill many people. Edward Jenner realized that milkmaids who caught a disease called cowpox would not catch smallpox. He extracted some of the fluid from cowpox sores and turned it into a vaccine that protected people from smallpox.

A CLOSE SHAVE
In the days before hospitals became widespread, minor ailments would be dealt with by... the barber. For a fee, the barber would slice off warts, pull out teeth and drain the pus from boils – often using the same scissors and razors used to cut your hair.

YOU WON'T BELIEVE IT BUT...
People used to believe that you could cure a headache by pressing a hangman's rope to your forehead.

SPLITTING HEADACHE?
If you had a headache in days gone by, it was probably a good idea to keep quiet. It was common practice then to drill holes in the skull to relieve pressure, or to allow 'evil spirits' to escape. Archeologists have found gruesome holes in skulls.

YOU WON'T BELIEVE IT BUT...
A number of medical procedures, including anesthesia and the treatment of several diseases, were discovered by doctors experimenting on themselves.

HEALTHY HEART
William Harvey, a 17th-century English doctor, was the first to claim that the heart pumps the same blood around the body, cleaning it as it goes. Before this, it was believed the liver was constantly turning food and drink into new blood, which was then used up by our body.

FLYING CHAIRS
Magnetic resonance imaging (MRI) uses magnetic fields to let doctors see inside patients. The only thing to remember is not to take anything metal into the same room because the strong magnetic forces will attract the object – whether it is a watch or a metal chair.

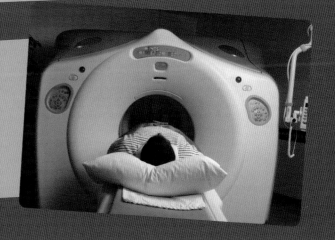

PUBLIC SERVICE
In 1851, George Jennings, an engineer, installed public toilets for the Great Exhibition held in London. Over 827,000 of the 6.2 million visitors paid to use them. Realizing how beneficial they were, the government had toilets installed throughout London.

RULING THE WORLD
In the 18th and 19th centuries, it was claimed that "the Sun never sets" on the British Empire. This was because it owned so many colonies around the world, it was always daytime somewhere in the empire. At its peak, the British Empire controlled around one quarter of the globe.

OVER 250 LANGUAGES ARE SPOKEN IN LONDON

THE ANIMAL KINGDOM
In Wales, a country famous for its countryside and farming, there are more sheep than people. With 11 million sheep, they outnumber their human owners by nearly four to one.

YOU WON'T BELIEVE IT BUT...
Heathrow airport, just outside London, has almost 200,000 passengers passing through it every day.

BRITAIN'S FAVORITE FOOD
The most popular meal in Britain is not roast beef or fish and chips but the curry dish, chicken tikka masala, created by the Asian community in Britain specifically to appeal to Western tastes.

THE QUEEN
The British queen is a constitutional monarch, so she carries out ceremonial duties, opens Parliament, oversees the Trooping of the Colour and visits British territories overseas. All the laws that are passed by Parliament still have to be signed by Her Majesty. But the Queen has no power to change them.

TAKE THE TUBE
The London Underground, also known as 'the Tube', is the world's oldest underground railway system. It covers 287 stations over more than 250 miles of track. Despite what the name might suggest, more than half of the Underground is actually above the ground.

YOU WON'T BELIEVE IT BUT...
Some of the most famous kings of England, such as Richard the Lionheart, spent so much time in France that they had trouble speaking English.

YOU WON'T BELIEVE IT BUT...
The French are world famous for their cheeses. However, with over 700 regional varieties, Britain has more.

TRIPLE CHALLENGE
Britain's three highest mountains are Ben Nevis in Scotland, Snowdon in Wales and Scafell Pike in England. Many people raise money for charity by attempting to walk and climb all three in just one day – the Three Peak Challenge – a task that involves over 26mi/41km of climbing, and 500mi/800km of driving in between.

AT 22 LETTERS, MUCKANAGHEDERDAUHAULIA IS THE LONGEST PLACE NAME IN IRELAND

A GOOD DEAL
Scotland's Orkney Islands were once part of Norway. In 1469, King Christian I of Norway, Denmark and Sweden said that he would offer the Orkney Islands as security against the payment of his daughter Princess Margaret's dowry for her marriage to Scotland's King James III. Christian never came up with the dowry, so Scotland kept the islands.

HIT OR MYTH?
England's patron saint is Saint George, who famously killed a dragon. However, legend has it that George was a Roman soldier, born in Turkey, who never even visited England. The story of his fight with a dragon may have been borrowed from a Libyan legend after the Crusades.

SCOTLAND'S MOTTO
The Royal motto of Scotland is 'Nemo me impune lacessit', which means 'Nobody attacks me with impunity'. Or, to put it another way, 'If you attack me, I will fight back'. It is believed that the motto refers to the thistle, the Scottish national flower, whose spiky leaves would deter bare-footed bandits in days gone by.

PARDON ME
In 1671, an Irish adventurer called Colonel Thomas Blood stole the British Crown Jewels from the Tower of London. He didn't get far, however, as he was soon caught while trying to exchange one of the stolen items for ale in a tavern. Luckily for Blood, King Charles II was so entertained by his story, he gave Blood a full pardon and an estate to live in.

NATURAL WONDER
The Giant's Causeway, in Ireland, is a huge formation of hexagonal stone columns stretching into the sea. They were naturally formed by volcanic activity, but local legend says a giant called Finn McCool, who wanted to build a path over the water to fight a Scottish giant, threw them into the sea.

YOU WON'T BELIEVE IT BUT...
There are almost 21,000 licensed taxis in London, although the famous 'black cabs' now come in 12 colors.

I'M NOT LAZY

Just because it's got a shuffly walk and likes sleeping during the day, the sloth bear has a reputation for laziness. When it comes out at night, it can run faster than humans. Native to Bangladesh, India, Sri Lanka and Nepal, it has special claws for digging out its favorite food – ants.

MALE LIONS' MANES GROW LONGER IN ZOOS IN COLD COUNTRIES

WHO'S THE BIGGEST BEAR?

The Kodiak bear is a huge type of brown bear that lives exclusively on Kodiak and neighboring islands off the cost of Alaska. Adult males stand over 10ft/3m tall on their hind legs and can weigh up to 1,500lbs/700kg – the same as a small car.

TONGUES OUT

The giant anteater of South America has an amazingly long and sticky tongue. After ripping open insect nests with its huge claws, it uses its 2ft/60cm tongue to scoop up dinner. Cunningly, the anteater always leaves some insects alive to rebuild their nest and provide it with another meal.

CHEETAH-ED OUT FOOD

While the cheetah may be the fastest land creature – doing 62mph/100kph at full speed – they can be too slow when it matters. While they kill their prey efficiently, cheetahs are often so tired after the chase that scavengers are known to step in and steal their catch.

THE COLLECTIVE noun FOR A GROUP OF BEARS IS A SLEUTH OR SLOTH

MY, WHAT SHARP TEETH

Because it is known as the saber-toothed tiger, many people think prehistoric cat smilodon was an ancestor of today's tiger. In fact, it wasn't related to any modern big cats. Its fearsome fangs could be up to 8in/20cm, like the blade of a hunting knife.

YOU WON'T BELIEVE IT BUT...

There are only around 5,000-7,500 tigers left in the wild.

FEED ME

Cats chose to live with humans. No one knows why for sure, but experts think wild cats recognized the benefits to be gained from adopting humans – mainly free food. They have been pets for at least 3,500 years and maybe longer. In return, they keep our homes free of rats and mice.

WHAT A PONG
The civet is named after the strong-smelling substance it produces in glands near its tail. Although the cat-like civet uses this to scare off predators, humans use it as a minor ingredient in perfume. It costs around $3,000/£1,500 for only 1lb/0.45kg, so is only used in the most expensive concoctions.

POUNCING PUSSY-CAT
The African serval has the most incredible pounce of any wild cat. It can leap up to 13ft/4m to land on top of its prey – usually rats and other rodents – and can spring more than 3.25ft/1m straight up to snatch birds out of the air.

SAVE THE LION
While the African lion is classified as a 'vulnerable' species, its Asian cousin is on the verge of disappearing completely. There are only 200-300 Asiatic lions left, all living in the Gir Forest National Park in Gujarat, north western India. There are plans to release them in other jungles in India.

THERE ARE OVER 400 BREEDS OF DOMESTIC DOG

YOU WON'T BELIEVE IT BUT...
The story of Mowgli in *The Jungle Book* is based on legends that sometimes children lost in the wild are brought up by wolves.

ONCE A WOLF...
... always a wolf. Dogs might be domesticated but they cannot hide their wolf origins. Like the wolf, they howl, are highly sociable, and think about food pretty much all the time.

IN ANCIENT EGYPT, THE PUNISHMENT FOR KILLING A CAT WAS DEATH

YOU WON'T BELIEVE IT BUT...
Pandas are the most expensive animal in the zoo, because they all belong to China, whose government charges Western zoos $2/£1 million rent a year per panda.

YOU WON'T BELIEVE IT BUT...
Hyenas have some of the strongest jaws in the animal kingdom – they can crunch up tin cans and tires.

WRAPPED UP WARM
Sea otters can float so well because they have the thickest fur of all animals (up to 1 million hairs per sq in/150,000 hairs per sq cm), making them completely waterproof.

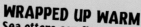

PERMANENCE OF POLES

It is impossible to make any sort of permanent research base at the north pole. This is because there is no actual land there to build on, just ice that is constantly shifting.

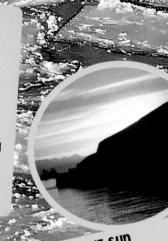

MEANWHILE, DOWN SOUTH...

The south pole is the Earth's southernmost point, located in the middle of the continent of Antarctica. America, Britain, France, Australia and lots of other countries have scientists working at the south pole. In 1959, an agreement was made that all Antarctic research must be for peaceful purposes only.

YOU WON'T BELIEVE IT BUT...

In places, the ice that covers 99 percent of the Antarctica is more than 3 mi/5km thick.

THE POLES ARE SO COLD BECAUSE THEY ARE THE PARTS OF THE EARTH THAT ARE ALWAYS FURTHEST FROM THE SUN

YOU WON'T BELIEVE IT BUT...

Antarctica is such an enormous continent, the UK could fit into it more than 50 times over.

DUE SOUTH

Explorers needn't worry about having a compass once they are standing at the magnetic north pole – whatever direction they walk in, it will be south.

YOUNGEST TRAVELER

The youngest person to visit both the north and south poles is American Jonathan Silverman. He visited the north pole at the age of nine on a Russian icebreaker, and the south pole in 2002, aged 11, traveling by aircraft from Chile.

FREQUENT FLIERS

Arctic terns breed in the Arctic but fly to Antarctica on the other side of the world and then back again each year. The journey is more than 12,000mi/19,000km, making it the longest migration in the animal kingdom.

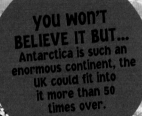

WHO GOT TO THE NORTH POLE FIRST?

Robert Peary, his partner Matthew Henson, and four Inuit guides are generally credited with being the first to reach the north pole on April 9th 1909. However, some people think they missed the actual pole by a few miles. So we are still not really sure.

SEEING DOUBLE
There are two north poles. One is the geographic pole, at the most northern point of the planet. The other is the magnetic pole, where compasses point. The magnetic north pole is actually a few hundred miles away from the geographic pole.

YOU WON'T BELIEVE IT BUT...
Antarctica is completely surrounded by the vast Southern Ocean, half of which freezes in winter.

THAT'S (NOT) HOT
The north pole is much warmer than the south pole. This is because it is at sea level and in the middle of the ocean, while the south pole is at a higher level and in the middle of land. However, both are still very cold by any normal standard.

IS ATLANTIS UNDER THE ICE?
Some people believe the fabled lost civilization of Atlantis is buried under the Antarctic ice. An ancient map shows Atlantis south of both Africa and South America. Its shape on the map even looks like the land mass that is under the ice.

POLAR BEARS CAN'T EAT PENGUINS – THEY LIVE AT OPPOSITE ENDS OF THE PLANET

FROZEN SOLID
The top of the Arctic sea is frozen solid. In winter, that frozen crust of ice covers a larger area than the US, although it shrinks in the summer. Anyone falling into the water would freeze to death in minutes.

YOU WON'T BELIEVE IT BUT...
Scientists have determined that the north magnetic pole moves approximately 25mi/40km each year.

THERE IS A TOWN IN ALASKA CALLED NORTH POLE WHERE CHRISTMAS DECORATIONS STAY UP ALL YEAR AROUND

IS IT MORNING YET?
Because the Earth rotates around the center, and the poles are at the top and bottom, days and nights are very strange at the north pole. It gets six months of constant daylight, followed by six months of darkness.

ANYONE SEEN A POLAR BEAR?
Despite the cold, the north pole is home to a variety of wildlife. The most famous is the polar bear, which snacks on unlucky seals. Scientists have even seen polar bears covering their black noses to help them creep up on their lunch.

ABANDON AIRSHIP
The Empire State Building is one of the best-known buildings in New York. At one time, it was the tallest in the world. The mast at the top was originally going to be used as a docking station for flying airships, but the idea was considered too dangerous.

EGYPTIAN MYSTERY
Nobody knows for sure how the ancient Egyptians built their enormous pyramids. They were constructed as monuments to the dead kings who were buried inside. The largest is the Great Pyramid of Giza, which was built over 4,000 years ago.

COMFY CRUISING
The Freedom Ship is a concept for a cruise liner that is so large, it is referred to as a floating city. The idea is that passengers could buy homes on it and live on board. Along with shops, offices, banks and schools, the designers have even included an airport on the top deck.

FURNITURE STORE IKEA SELLS FLAT-PACKED HOUSES THAT YOU BUILD YOURSELF

STRAIGHT UP
Taipei 101 was the world's tallest building when it was completed in 2004, measuring 1,669ft/509m. The building got its name because it is in the city of Taipei, Taiwan, and has 101 floors. It also features the world's fastest elevators, rushing visitors to the top in under 37 seconds.

CAN YOU DIG IT?
The idea of building a tunnel under the sea between Britain and France was first suggested 200 years ago. Construction finally began in 1987 and the Eurotunnel was officially opened in 1994. It is 31mi/50km long, and runs 150ft/46m under the sea.

YOU WON'T BELIEVE IT BUT...
The world's largest toyshop is Toys 'R' Us, in New York's Times Square. It contains a full size Ferris wheel.

YOU WON'T BELIEVE IT BUT...
Yokohama Marine Tower is one of the world's tallest lighthouses, standing 324ft/106m tall.

THE PANAMA CANAL CUTS JOURNEYS BETWEEN THE PACIFIC AND ATLANTIC OCEANS BY 7,000MI/11,250 KM

WHERE IS THE WORLD'S LONGEST BRIDGE?
The world's longest suspension bridge is the Akashi Kaikyo Bridge in Japan. Measuring over 1mi/1.6km in length, it carries six lanes of traffic. An even longer two-mile bridge was designed in Italy in 2006, but it was never built because of the danger from earthquakes.

WHY ARE THERE TWO LONDON BRIDGES?
'London Bridge is falling down'. That's what the rhyme says, but the famous bridge has actually been pulled down and rebuilt many times. In 1962, an American millionaire bought the old bridge and shipped it to Arizona, where he rebuilt it as a tourist attraction.

YOU WON'T BELIEVE IT BUT...
The Steel Dragon 2000 rollercoaster in Japan is over 1.5m/2.4km long. It takes just under four minutes to ride.

AS WELL AS HIS FAMOUS TOWER, GUSTAV EIFFEL ALSO DESIGNED THE SUPPORT STRUCTURE FOR THE STATUE OF LIBERTY

LEAVE THE LEAN
In 1999, engineers were able to raise the Leaning Tower of Pisa by over 17in/45cm but the people of Pisa did not want their famous tower completely straightened. In 1995, a previous attempt to support the tower went wrong, and it nearly collapsed.

MAGNIFICENT SEVEN
The Seven Wonders of the World were all ancient monuments. Only one, the Pyramids of Giza, is still standing today. Others included a huge Greek temple, the elaborate gardens of a palace in Babylon, and the Colossus of Rhodes, an enormous statue that may have inspired the Statue of Liberty.

TRAGIC TAJ
The Taj Mahal was built in India over 350 years ago and is considered one of the most romantic buildings in the world. It was built by the emperor Shah Jahan in honor of his dead wife.

YOU WON'T BELIEVE IT BUT...
The tallest dam in the world is located on the Vakhsh River in Tajikistan. It is 1099ft/335m tall.

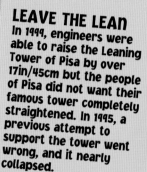

FAMOUS TOWER
The Eiffel Tower in Paris is the most famous landmark in France. It was built by Gustave Eiffel in 1889. The landmark is such a popular tourist attraction that it takes two tons of paper every year just to print all the tickets.

SMALL CITY
Vatican City in Italy is home to the world's largest religious buildings, and is the center of the Catholic Church. It is also where the Pope lives. It has under 900 residents, but Vatican City has its own army and is officially the world's smallest country.

BUCKLE UP
The world's most dangerous road is between La Paz and Coroico in Bolivia. The narrow track has a rock wall on one side and a 3,600ft/1,040m drop on the other. That's three times higher than the Empire State Building.

MAKING A SPLASH
If you drove your car into a lake, you'd expect it to be ruined. And it would be, unless you were driving an amphibious vehicle – cars that can drive on land as well as water.

YOU WON'T BELIEVE IT BUT...
The first ever powered flight, made by the Wright Brothers in North Carolina, 1903, lasted only twelve seconds. Their plane traveled just 120ft/36m.

A REAL REDEYE FLIGHT
During his record-breaking solo flight across the Atlantic in 1927, Charles Lindbergh had to stay wide awake for over 33 hours. To stop himself falling asleep and crashing, he pinched himself and opened the plane's window to let in blasts of ice-cold air.

WILD PASSENGERS
The first passengers to ever fly in a hot air balloon were a sheep, cockerel and duck. They went on their airborne journey thanks to the Montgolfier brothers in France, 1783. Later that same year, the brothers successfully launched a balloon with human passengers.

THE FIRST EVER MOTORCYCLE, INVENTED IN AMERICA IN THE 1860S, RAN ON STEAM

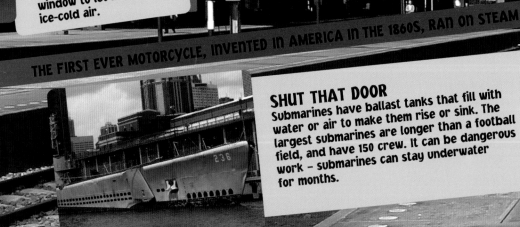

YOU WON'T BELIEVE IT BUT...
The most money ever paid for a car was $8.7/£4.35 million in 1987 for a 1931 Bugatti Royale Kellner Coupe.

SHUT THAT DOOR
Submarines have ballast tanks that fill with water or air to make them rise or sink. The largest submarines are longer than a football field, and have 150 crew. It can be dangerous work – submarines can stay underwater for months.

LIGHT AS A FEATHER
Formula One racing cars are carefully designed to be as fast as possible, and that means being aerodynamic – and very light. In fact, the average Formula One racing car weighs only 1,334lbs/605kg, less than half the typical family car, and that's including the driver and fuel.

NOW THAT'S FAST...
The Bugatti Veyron is the fastest car that is legal to drive on public streets. It can go faster than 250mph/400kph, and can go from 0–60mph/0–100kph in just over two seconds.

SUPER-HOT YACHTS
Stylish and speedy, it's no wonder every millionaire has to own a luxury yacht – or maybe even two. One of the world's most expensive yachts is the Annaliesse, which has space for 36 guests and a diving center to keep them entertained. At $103/£50 million, the boat costs more than 500 Rolls Royce cars.

THE AMAZING SPIDER-BOAT
Standing above the water like a weird insect, the WAM-V is an experimental boat designed by American engineers. It balances on flexible skis which bend to match the shape of the waves. Passengers get a smoother ride as the ship glides over the waves.

AMERICAN ENGINEER RICK HERRON HAS BUILT A WORKING JET PACK THAT ALLOWS HIM TO FLY FOR FIVE MINUTES

YOU WON'T BELIEVE IT BUT...
In 1900, there were around 8,000 cars in the USA. 100 years later, that number jumped up to 600 million in the world.

FUEL FOR THOUGHT?
Using petrol in our cars is expensive and causes pollution, so scientists are looking for new ways to power vehicles. Electric cars have been produced, but other forms of alternative fuel include solar energy and compressed air. One scientist even made a car run on pig poo.

THE WORD 'HELICOPTER' COMES FROM THE GREEK WORDS 'HELIX' ('SPIRAL') AND 'PTERON' ('WING')

BEAM ME UP
The crew of the Starship Enterprise in *Star Trek* can zip from planet to planet using teleporters, but such technology is science fiction... isn't it? In 2002, scientists in Australia were able to teleport tiny sub-atomic particles from one place to another.

HOW'S THAT FOR JETLAG?
The Concorde, which last flew in 2003, was the world's only supersonic passenger plane, able to fly at twice the speed of sound. Because of the five-hour time difference, this meant that when Concorde flew from London to New York, it landed earlier than when it took off.

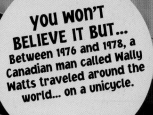

YOU WON'T BELIEVE IT BUT...
Between 1976 and 1978, a Canadian man called Wally Watts traveled around the world... on a unicycle.

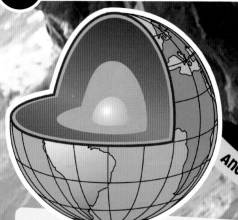

YOU WON'T BELIEVE IT BUT...
Scientists now believe the Earth's oceanic crust is split up into 52 plates – 14 large ones and 38 that are much smaller.

BREAKING UP
Pangaea is the name given to a theoretical super-continent that scientists think broke up into the seven separate continents about 200 million years ago. Initially, most of the land in the northern hemisphere was still together in a huge continent called Laurasia. The southern landmasses were called Gondwana.

ANOTHER NAME FOR THE EARTH'S CRUST AND UPPER MANTLE IS 'LITHOSPHERE'

MOVING MANTLE
In 1924, the British geologist Arthur Holmes came up with the idea that the continents were moving because the mantle – the super-hot magma under the Earth's crust – was moving. He said it was bubbling away under the surface and this would cause the continents to move.

KNOW YOUR BOUNDARIES
Earthquakes happen where the plates meet – known as a 'plate boundary' – which is why some countries are always being hit by large quakes and others, like the United Kingdom, only ever get very small ones.

THE BIGGEST JIGSAW
If you look at a map of the world and then imagine that the Atlantic Ocean isn't there, you'll suddenly notice that Africa and South America fit into each other. That's because they were once one huge landmass, along with all the other continents.

MIND THE GAP
A 'divergent' plate boundary is where the plates are moving apart. Over time they form huge, flat-bottomed 'rift valleys' such as the Great Rift Valley that stretches across Africa to the Middle East. They move apart at the same speed as your fingernails grow.

PANGAEA IS GREEK FOR 'ALL THE EARTH'

CRACKING UP
In the 1960s, scientists realized that the Earth's crust below the continents – known as the 'oceanic crust' – was also split up into what they called 'plates'. It is in the places where these plates meet that boiling magma comes up from below to propel the continents on their way.

YOU WON'T BELIEVE IT BUT...
Mountains vary in size because they were all formed at different times through continental collisions and then worn down over time by the weather.

DRIFT THEORY
'Continental drift' is the name given to the idea that the continents move about over time. It was first put forward by Alfred Wegener (1880-1930), although he had no idea what was making the continents shift around.

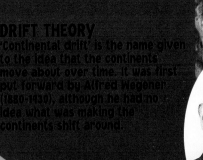

MOVE ALONG PLEASE
Iceland is right on the boundary of the North American and Eurasian plates, and the island's Álfagjá rift valley is still growing as these move slowly apart. It's 60ft/18m wide now, but in 100 years it will be 4.9ft/1.5m wider. A bridge has been built across the rift, meaning you can walk from Europe to North America in one minute.

INDIA WAS A SEPARATE CONTINENT BUT JOINED WITH ASIA AROUND 40 MILLION YEARS AGO

GROWING PAINS
In an average year, Mount Everest grows by about 0.02in/4mm because of the movement of two tectonic plates – the Indian and Eurasian. Although these plates collided millions of years ago to form the Himalayas, they continue to press against each other – making these already enormous mountains even bigger.

YOU WON'T BELIEVE IT BUT...
Earth is the only planet in the Solar System with a warm enough middle to have plate tectonics.

DID YOU HEAR A BANG?
Probably not if you were listening for the sound that two plates make when they crash into each other. This is because the collision happens so slowly. Even so, the effect is still dramatic over time – the two plates push against each other for millions of years and slowly create mountains.

THE LARGEST PLATE IS THE PACIFIC PLATE

PULL OF THE MOON
A new study recently came up with another reason why the plates and continents are moving – it's the Moon. According to this theory, the Moon's gravitational pull is dragging everything westwards around the planet, meaning Britain will one day be where Iceland is now.

SMASHING PLATES
There are three different kinds of plate boundary. A convergent boundary, also known as 'destructive', is where two or more plates are moving into each other. One plate slips beneath other and melts, giving rise to many volcanoes — and a lot of fiery action.

VOLCANIC BOUNDARY
Volcanoes mostly occur on, or very near, the edges of continental plates. This is because the magma escapes and rushes up, forming a volcano. The existence of volcanoes on plate edges is related to the existence of magma 'hot spots'. Extinct volcanoes occur when plates move and transport them away from the magma source.

YOU WON'T BELIEVE IT BUT...
The Great Rift Valley, caused by a 'divergent' plate boundary, stretches around 3,700mi/6,000km from Lebanon in the Middle East to Mozambique in Africa.

IT'S A GIANT
The world's largest amphibian is the Chinese giant salamander, which can grow up to 5ft 11in/1.8m in length. They feed on fish and crustaceans and can live, we think, for 55 years.

CROC KILLER TOAD
The giant cane toad is so huge and poisonous it can even kill crocodiles. Native to Central and South America, it was introduced to Australia in the 1930s to eat beetles ruining sugar-cane crops. It is now a huge pest itself, its lethal poison killing many animals.

SMALL BUT DEADLY
Poison dart frogs are so-called because, in the South American jungles where they live, the native hunters use the frogs' venom to poison the tips of their darts, which they then use to kill animals for food.

THE FIRE-BELLIED FROG SMELLS OF GARLIC

YOU WON'T BELIEVE IT BUT...
The biggest cane toad, caught in Australia in 2007, weighed 2lbs/0.9kg and its body was 8in/20cm long.

YOU WON'T BELIEVE IT BUT...
Fire salamanders can squirt poison at predators up to 6.5ft/2m away.

YOU'RE FIRED
The fire salamander gets its name because people once thought the salamanders were born from fire. This may be because they live in trees and often found themselves mixed up in people's firewood. When the fire got hot, the salamander would scamper out, and give everyone a fright.

NO MICROPHONE NEEDED
The croaking of some frogs is so loud that it travels for miles. Luckily for frogs, their hearing is specially designed to avoid being damaged by loud noises. The trick is that their ears are connected to their lungs – which channel away some of the pressure caused by vibrations.

THERE ARE AROUND 6,000 SPECIES OF AMPHIBIAN

KITTEN FOR TEA
The West African goliath frog is the biggest frog of all. It measures 11.2in/30cm from nose to tail and weighs 7.2lbs/3.3kg. It will eat anything it can fit in its mouth, and has been known to eat rats, small dogs and even kittens.

FLOOD FOSSIL
In 1726, the Swiss physician Johann Jakob Scheuchzer stated that he had found a human who had been killed by Noah's flood – it turned out to be the fossil of a large prehistoric salamander.

YOU WON'T BELIEVE IT BUT...
Poison dart frogs stop being so poisonous when they are in captivity – this is because they get their venom from the food of their jungle homes.

FROGS DO HAVE TEETH, BUT ONLY ON THEIR TOP JAW

RIBBIT... RIBBIT...
Many frogs have loud mating calls and their croaking can fill the night. No one knows which is the loudest in the world as there are so many different types, all making a racket. The loudest in Europe is the European tree frog.

WARTS AND ALL
Because toads have bumpy skin, people used to think witches caught their warts from touching the toads they put into their cauldrons when making spells. Even today, many people still think you can catch warts from toads. You can't.

FOOLED YOU
Certain cunning frogs have come up with a great plan to foil predators – they have a stripe down their center that 'splits' them in two. From above they don't appear to have the outline of a typical frog and they can blend into the background with greater ease.

YOU WON'T BELIEVE IT BUT...
In India, frogs were thought to embody thunder – the Sanskrit words for 'frog' and 'cloud' are the same.

IT'S RAINING FROGS
Tales of thousands of frogs dropping from the sky sound far-fetched – but it actually happens. Storms passing across a lake teeming with frogs can pick the creatures up and carry them through the sky for many, many miles before dropping them.

SUPER-SIZE

For centuries, the Earth battled the bulge round its center successfully, but satellite data suggests that it is getting fat. Scientists think that melting glaciers and ice caps have caused the sea-level to rise – and this is most obvious at the equator.

YOU WON'T BELIEVE IT BUT...

The Moon is moving slowly away from the Earth – about 13ft/4m a century.

AN ESTIMATED 1,000 TONS OF ROCK FALL TO EARTH FROM SPACE EVERY YEAR

ICE TO SEE YOU

Most scientists think the Earth formed around 4.57 billion years ago, at the same time as the other planets in the Solar System. It is likely it was a barren rock for many millions of years until chemical reactions created the atmosphere and water. However, some think that ice from comets bombarding the Earth, melted and created the oceans.

A WONDERFUL WORLD

Because of the insistence of some scientists that there must be life on other planets, we sometimes forget that not only is Earth the only planet known in the Universe to support life, but it is also the only planet known to have liquid water on its surface.

YOU WON'T BELIEVE IT BUT...

Three-quarters of the mass of Earth's atmosphere is within 6mi/11km of the planet's surface.

THE FIERY FIRST AGE OF THE EARTH IS CALLED THE HADEAN ERA – AFTER HADES, THE GREEK GOD OF THE UNDERWORLD

MAKE ROOM

Extinction is normal. The life on Earth today only represents a tiny fraction of all the species to have existed. Scientists estimate that 99.9 percent of all of the planet's species have already died.

POCKET-SIZE PLANET

It is easy to think that the Earth is very, very big – and it certainly is if you are human – but I would be a planet like Jupiter than the Earth – think you could fit our planet inside Jupiter more than 1,300 times.

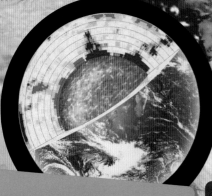

YOU WON'T BELIEVE IT BUT...
Because of humans, many experts think half of the species living today will be extinct by the end of the century.

SUPER HEAT
The closer you get to the Earth's core, the hotter it gets. Near the very center, it is thought to be a blistering 7,000°F/3,870°C. A planet can only lose heat at its surface, so it is very hard for heat buried in the Earth's core to escape.

FOSSILS INTO FUEL
Hundreds of millions years ago, the Earth was covered in lush forests and its waters were full of microscopic life forms. When these died, they became buried and, over many years, were squeezed and transformed into oil, gas and coal. These ancient dead trees and aquatic organisms now help power our cars and light our homes.

THE WIND CARRIES 100 MILLION TONS OF SAND AROUND THE EARTH EVERY YEAR

DRILLING WITH DIAMONDS
Diamond is the hardest substance found in the Earth and can be used to make drills that can bore through almost anything. It is more famous, however, for being made into long-lasting jewelry. Talc, in contrast, is the softest mineral and is used to make baby powder.

HAVE YOU SEEN MY ATMOSPHERE?
The Earth's magnetic field is incredibly important as it keeps us safe from the harmful radiation from the Sun's solar wind, while its gravity stops our atmosphere drifting off into space. The planet Mars has much lower gravity, making its atmosphere incredibly thin.

TAKE A DEEP BREATH...
What's inside your lungs isn't just the oxygen we need to live but lots of other gases, plus – depending where you are – a certain amount of pollution. Air is 78% nitrogen, 21% oxygen, 0.9% argon, and 0.03% carbon dioxide. The air also contains water vapor in varying concentrations.

YOU WON'T BELIEVE IT BUT...
Oil has been used for thousands of years – among others, it was used by the ancient Egyptians, the Sumerians and Native Americans.

ZIRCON, THE OLDEST KIND OF ROCK ON EARTH, IS 4.4 BILLION YEARS OLD

STRAIGHT TO THE CORE
If you journey from the surface to the center of the Earth, you will travel about 3,963mi/6,378km – although only a tiny amount of that will be spent burrowing through solids. If the Earth were the size of an apple, then the Earth's crust would be thinner than the apple skin.

AROUND AND AROUND
At the equator, the Earth's circumference is 24,901.55mi/40,075km. But when measured around the north and south poles, it is just 24,859mi/40,008km. This is because Earth is not a perfect sphere, but is a little fatter around its middle.

SUPER, SUPER BOWL

Generally played on the first Sunday of February, the Super Bowl is the biggest event in American football. It's an enormous entertainment spectacle that, along with the football being played, features pop stars performing before the game and during halftime. Super Bowl watchers manage to munch their way through 14,500 tons of potato chips.

READY FOR ACTION?

Ping pong is one of the fastest sports around. In 1993, Jackie Bellinger and Lisa Lomas set a world record by hitting the ball back and forth across the table 173 times in 60 seconds. Players often stand a long way back from the table so they have time to react.

YOU WON'T BELIEVE IT BUT...

A sumo wrestler called Takamisugi was known for his ability to eat 65 bowls of stew, containing 29lbs/13kg of beef, in one sitting.

BATTER UP

Baseball pitchers have used a gross trick called a spitball to beat their opponents. Spitting on the ball before they threw it would cause the ball to wobble instead of traveling in a straight line. Spitballs were banned in 1920, when a player called Ray Chapman was killed after he was hit in the head with one.

IN 2003, TWO GERMAN TENNIS PLAYERS PLAYED A SINGLE MATCH FOR MORE THAN 25 HOURS

CALL THAT TRAINING?

Unlike other athletes, sumo wrestlers must be very fat so it's harder to push them around. They have no breakfast, but enjoy a huge lunch of rice, fish, vegetables and meat, all washed down by lots of beer. After their feast, they have a long nap so they don't use up any of those precious calories.

SNOWBOARDING WAS INTRODUCED AS AN OLYMPIC SPORT IN 1998

YOU WON'T BELIEVE IT BUT...

Athletes at the Ancient Greek Olympics used to believe that eating lizard meat made you run faster.

YOU RAN HOW FAR?

The marathon is a race of more than 26mi/41km. In 490 BCE, a soldier called Pheidippides ran all the way from Marathon to Athens to deliver news of a victory in battle, and the modern race honors his bravery and stamina. It usually takes runners four or five hours to finish.

BASEBALL'S FINEST
Babe Ruth was born in 1895 and grew up to become one of baseball's most famous and talented players. He hit 714 home runs during his career, and was so fast that scientists studied him to find out how he did it. They discovered that his brain, eyes and ears all worked faster than normal.

SHORTS AND SWEATY
A famous tennis player called Don Budge made a useful discovery. He weighed his pants before and after a game and discovered they had gained weight during the match. 7lbs/3kg of sweat, in fact. Ever since then, tennis players have worn light clothing.

SOME WEIGHTLIFTERS CAN LIFT AS MUCH AS 580.9LBS/263.5KG. THAT'S ABOUT THE WEIGHT OF YOU AND FIVE FRIENDS

YOU WON'T BELIEVE IT BUT...
Cross-country skiing is considered the best aerobic fitness activity in the world – it uses every major muscle group.

AN INSPIRATIONAL TRIUMPH
Jesse Owens was a black athlete who inspired the whole world. A gifted sprinter, he represented the US at the 1936 Olympics, held in Germany. The German nazi leader, Adolf Hitler, wanted to prove that white people were superior but Jesse Owens won four gold medals and showed the world that Hitler was wrong.

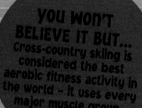

POLE POSITION
The Six Meters Club is the nickname given to pole vaulters who have managed to clear the 20ft/6m height. That's like vaulting over a two-story house. Sergei Bubka was the first person to achieve this feat in 1985, and fewer than 20 athletes have been able to match it since.

SPORT FOR ALL
Disabled athletes are becoming more and more popular and successful. The Paralympics is an event dedicated to disabled sporting achievement. It started in 1948 as a competition for British pilots who had been injured in the war. More countries joined in and, in 1960, the first international Paralympics were held.

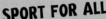

A GAME OF ENDURANCE
Lacrosse is considered to be the oldest American sport. It was originally played by Native Americans and in its early form the games could last for two or three days – as tribes competed against each other.

YOU WON'T BELIEVE IT BUT...
Tiger Woods started playing golf at the age of 2 and became the youngest winner of The Masters in 1997 at the age of 21.

SHAME ON YOU
In some cultures, feeling guilty or ashamed can be a serious business. In Imperial Japan, for instance, warriors who had dishonored themselves would commit ritual suicide – seppuku – by cutting open their own bellies.

YOU WON'T BELIEVE IT BUT...
When someone gets embarassed and blushes, their red cheeks are actually the result of an increase in blood flow to the face.

BE AFRAID
An irrational fear is known as a phobia. People are scared of all sorts of things but top of the list is arachnophobia, or fear of spiders. Other creepy-crawlies aren't popular, either – scientists believe this is because our ancient ancestors had to look out for poisonous bugs.

DO CLOWNS MAKE YOU CRY?
This is probably will if you suffer from coulrophobia – a pathological fear of clowns. The most likely explanation for this phobia is the fact the you're smiling while a clown in make-up looks sad.

FEAR MAKES YOUR MOUTH DRY BY SHUTTING DOWN YOUR DIGESTIVE SYSTEM

CHEER UP
Although it can be a little difficult to keep happy and smiling, research has shown that 72% of people think that cheerful men and women who smile frequently are more confident and successful.

GO ON – GIGGLE
Laughter is incredibly good for you. It releases endorphins, which are chemicals from the brain that make you feel good, and it also exercises muscles all over your body – a belly laugh is called that for a reason.

YOU WON'T BELIEVE IT BUT...
If you get really, really angry, you can become stronger. Being in a rage causes an adrenaline rush, which increases physical strength.

FOOLISH PRIDE
Pride does come before a fall – a study at Princeton University in New Jersey, USA, got 200 people to play a war game. Before, everyone was asked how well they thought they would do. The more confident people tended to lose – they were so sure they were going to win they didn't concentrate.

THAT'S SHOCKING
In 1938, Italian psychiatrist Ugo Cerletti came up with the idea of treating mentally ill people by electrocuting the brain – known as 'electroshock'. However, it was sometimes found to make patients worse, so today it is only used when it will really do some good.

YOU WON'T BELIEVE IT BUT...
Laughter is the best medicine, so when you're feeling down, get the joke book out, or the latest comedy show on – because laughter is an excellent medicine.

UNLUCKY FOR SOME
Many people are superstitious about the number 13, but for a few people it's a full-blown phobia, called triskaidekaphobia. A fear of Friday 13th is known as friggatriskaidekaphobia.

FISH UPON A STAR
Hollywood hero Brad Pitt might be one of the coolest men on the planet, but put him in a fish shop and he'll probably start crying. He's one of the thousands of people who have ichthyophobia – a fear of fish.

SAD TEARS HAVE A DIFFERENT CHEMICAL COMPOSITION TO JOYFUL TEARS

YOU WON'T BELIEVE IT BUT...
Laughter has been proven to relieve pain.

THAT'S NOT FUNNY...
It doesn't seem fair, but people who are scared of long words are said to suffer from Hippopotomonstrosesquippedaliophobia. This started as a joke, but is now so well known, it's kind of true. Another name for this phobia is almost as long – it's Sesquipedalophobia.

WHAT A GEM
The Cullinan is the world's largest diamond. Discovered in South Africa in 1905, it weighed 2.2lbs/almost 1kg. After it was found, it was cut up into the Great Star of Africa, the Lesser Star of Africa, and around 100 smaller diamonds, which now form part of the British crown jewels.

SOMALIA IS THE ONLY COUNTRY IN THE WORLD WHERE ALL THE CITIZENS SPEAK ONE LANGUAGE, SOMALI

YOU WON'T BELIEVE IT BUT...
The Nile crocodile is found all over the continent and lives underground to hide from extreme temperatures.

A DEADLY SPORT
Hunting in Africa was so popular in the last century that many species of animals were completely wiped out. Even today, there are endangered animals in Africa that are on the verge of extinction. For instance, there are only around 600 mountain gorillas still living in the wild.

THINK SPHINX
The Sphinx is one of Egypt's most famous attractions. Nobody is sure who built it, or why, but it's the largest surviving statue from the ancient world. It has the face of a human and the body of a lion and has been swallowed by the desert sand many times, but it always gets uncovered.

YOU WON'T BELIEVE IT BUT...
The African elephant is the largest living land mammal and can weigh up to nine tons.

DAZZLING DIALECTS
There are around 800 different African dialects and languages in use across the continent. But only about 10 of these languages are widely spoken, and most African languages are used by less than 10,000 people.

VERY FISHY
Lake Malawi is the third largest lake in Africa. Scientists believe it is over 40,000 years old, and it contains the largest number of fish species of any lake in the world. It's over 2,300ft/700m deep at its deepest point and there are over 500 types of fish swimming about down there.

VALUABLE RESOURCES
Some countries like South Africa and Nigeria have valuable minerals such as diamonds, gold or oil. But others depend entirely on one crop, such as coffee or cocoa. If there is a water shortage, or if people stop buying their crops, these countries can run out of food.

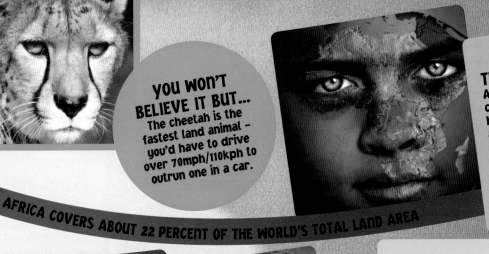

YOU WON'T BELIEVE IT BUT...
The cheetah is the fastest land animal – you'd have to drive over 70mph/110kph to outrun one in a car.

THE BIG COUNTRY
Africa might look like one big country but in fact it's the second biggest continent in the world, after Asia, with an estimated population of 770 million people, including the tropical islands of Mauritius, the Seychelles and Madagascar. In total, there are 53 different African countries.

AFRICA COVERS ABOUT 22 PERCENT OF THE WORLD'S TOTAL LAND AREA

HOP TO IT
The world's largest frog comes from Africa. Called the goliath frog, it can grow to 1ft/0.33m in length – twice the size of the largest common bullfrog. Despite their size, they don't have a croak to match. In fact, they don't croak at all – they're completely silent.

HOORAY FOR... NOLLYWOOD?
Nigeria is Africa's largest producer of movies. Only America and India produce more films each year, and the local film business is often referred to as Nollywood.

DON'T FALL IN
The Nile is the world's longest river, and it runs almost all the way across Africa. Starting below the equator and flowing up to the Mediterranean, it's over 4,000mi/6,400km long.

THE NAMIB DESERT IS THE OLDEST DESERT IN THE WORLD

THE CRADLE OF LIFE?
The oldest human fossils ever discovered were found in Ethiopia in 2003. The three skeletons were around 160,000 years old, and were found with ancient axes and animal bones. It's because of discoveries like this that many scientists believe that Africa was the birthplace of the human race.

YOU WON'T BELIEVE IT BUT...
A giraffe's tongue can be as long as 17in/45cm, and they are already almost 6ft/2m tall when they're born.

FEROCIOUS FIGHTERS
Africa is famous for its large animals, and hunters still go on safari trips to find and shoot some of the most dangerous creatures on the planet. Hunters call the most deadly animals - buffalos, rhinos, elephants, lions and leopards - the Big Five, because of how ferociously they fight back if cornered.

THE BODY ELECTRIC
Your nerves are like cables and contain hundreds of neurons, some of which are a few feet long. These are stringy fibers that transport billions of electrical signals all over your body from head to toe, incessantly.

YOU WON'T BELIEVE IT BUT...
RSI, or repetitive strain injury, can occur in your wrist when you're on the computer keyboard too long.

KNEECAPS BECOME FULLY FORMED BETWEEN AGES TWO AND FOUR

FOOTBALL CRAZY
Of all the 206 bones in the adult human body, it seems that soccer players are prone to breaking just one group: the metatarsals. It's not all that surprising. These are five long, thin, relatively vulnerable bones in the foot. But they also heal quite quickly.

SPEAKING IN TONGUES
Your tongue is more flexible than any other part of you. It contains a number of strong muscles in a clever bundle that can twist and turn in almost any direction you choose.

YOU WON'T BELIEVE IT BUT...
Most people blink around 15 times per minute. The average blink lasts approximately 100-150 milliseconds.

YOUR BODY'S WEIGHT IS ABOUT 40 TIMES THAT OF YOUR BRAIN

THE ARMOR INSIDE
Your skeleton is a bone framework that gives your body its shape and protects your delicate bits. If you think a blow to the ribs hurts, imagine how much your lungs and heart would hurt if someone thumped you and the ribcage wasn't there.

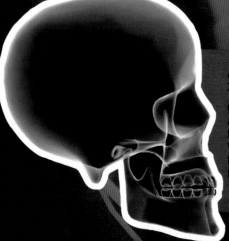

SKULL'S OUT
There are four shapes of bones: flat, like your shoulder blades; short, like wrists and ankles; long, like fingers; and irregular, like the awkward-shaped ones in your back. Your skull is eight flat plates joined together to shield your brain. It's called the cranial vault.

DO I CONTROL ALL MY MUSCLES?
Muscles are made of elastic tissue and enable movement. The bigger ones wrap around bones, and are tied in place by little strings called tendons. You can control about 640 'voluntary' muscles, but there are many more 'involuntary' ones. So the answer is no.

SPEEDY MUSCLES
The fastest muscles in your whole body are those in your eyelids. They cause you to blink about once every two or three seconds, which moistens the eyes. If you did not do this, your eyes would dry out.

BREAKING NEWS
Bones may look solid as rock, but they're made up of living cells surrounded by minerals. They have hollow spaces inside to carry nerves and blood vessels. When a bone breaks, new tissue arrives to plug the cracks.

YOU WON'T BELIEVE IT BUT...
The thigh bone, or femur, is the longest – and strongest – bone in the body.

WHY DON'T I FORGET TO BREATHE?
Some of your actions are voluntary, some not. For example, it's voluntary when you kick a ball. However breathing, circulation and digestion are managed for you by your nervous system, without you having to constantly remember to do them.

HOW STRONG IS YOUR HEART?
Your heart is mostly made up of involuntary muscles, which all have incredible stamina. These cardiac muscles, made of Y-shaped fibers, push and pull the blood in and out of your heart.

RACING NERVES
Your nervous system sends messages to your brain at a speed of 186mph/300kph. If you could run at that speed, you would complete a marathon in well under 10 minutes.

YOU WON'T BELIEVE IT BUT...
Shivering is your muscles contracting and relaxing quicker than usual to try to heat up the body.

THAT'S AN ORDER
Your nervous system is like a network of cables carrying information to and from your brain, which enables you to react quickly to anything that happens. It sends out messages to your body, saying, for example, "run", "stand up" or "laugh".

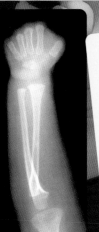
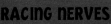
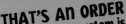

YOU WON'T BELIEVE IT BUT...
It takes the venus flytrap 10 days to digest an average-sized insect.

WHAT A STINKER
You'd hardly know the rafflesia, found in the jungles of Southeast Asia, was there. It attaches itself to the vines of other plants and grows entirely inside them. The only parts visible are its large, red flowers, which smell like rotting meat to attract insects.

THE RAFFLESIA FLOWER CAN MEASURE 39IN/100CM IN DIAMETER AND WEIGH UP TO 22LBS/10KG

YOU WON'T BELIEVE IT BUT...
Mistletoe might be poisonous but it forms the basis of many medicines for treating heart and breathing problems.

DROWNED AND DIGESTED
Pitcher plants are so-called because they are shaped like a pitcher for carrying water. But it isn't water inside the plant's leaves – it's a horrible substance that drowns the insects and then slowly dissolves their bodies.

GETTING CAUGHT
The best-known carnivorous plant is the ferocious-looking venus flytrap. Yet its sharp teeth don't munch any flesh, unlike in the movies. They act as prison bars once the plant's 'mouth' has snapped shut and trap the insect inside.

PAINFUL PROGRESS
One of the slowest growing cacti is the Saguaro cactus of the Arizona Desert, which grows less than an inch in its first ten years. A fully-grown Saguaro can reach 12 to 20ft/3.7m to 6m tall, but will take between 75 and 100 years to get there.

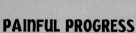
ORCHIDS HAVE AROUND 25,00 DIFFERENT SPECIES – MORE THAN ANY OTHER FLOWERING PLANT

TRIGGERING THE TRAPDOOR
Bladderworts are as remarkable as they are unpleasant. They pump air from a bladder to create a vacuum inside. The plant is covered in little spines and when an insect touches them it triggers a trapdoor to the vacuum. The bug is then sucked inside, where it suffocates.

FAST-PACED PLANTS
Bamboo and duckweed's claims to fame are that they are thought to be the fastest growing plants in the world. Certain types of bamboo are capable of growing by almost 3ft/1m a day – an astonishing feat – whilst duckweed will spread and can double its size in 10 days.

WAITING GAME
The seeds of the broomrape flower can lie dormant for many years but sense when another plant nearby is starting to grow. The seed then sends out a shoot, which attaches to the new plant and starts robbing it of nutrients.

STICKY CUSTOMERS
Flypaper traps are a type of carnivorous plant that catch insects by trapping them in their gooey outer coating, just as their name suggests. To attract bugs, the plants use all sorts of tricks – they give off a smell or pretend to be female insects.

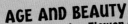

TAKING LESS THAN A SECOND TO CLOSE ITS 'MOUTH', THE VENUS FLYTRAP HAS REMARKABLY SPEEDY MOVEMENT

AGE AND BEAUTY
A Sacred Lotus Flower seed, around 1,288 years old, is the oldest to have ever been successfully planted and grown. The Beijing Institute of Botany handed seven ancient seeds to a plant specialist in Los Angeles – and the sprightliest went on to grow a flower that lived for nine months.

YOU WON'T BELIEVE IT BUT...
The Western Australian Christmas tree is so aggressive that it attacks underground power cables, thinking that they are roots.

THERE ARE AROUND 400 SPECIES OF CARNIVOROUS PLANTS

KILLER IN THE WATER
The waterwheel plant is similar to the venus flytrap, only it grows in freshwater and eats waterborne insects. It has no roots, but floats on the surface of the water.

FLOWER POWER
In the 1630s, the newly introduced tulip flower was such a must-have status symbol in Germany and the Netherlands that it was worth a fortune – anything from $17,000/£11,500 to $76,000/£37,000 in today's money. It was so in demand that it wound up being listed on the stock exchange.

TERRIBLE TRIFFID
Flesh-eating plants have inspired many writers over the years but the most famous was John Wyndham, whose fictional creation – the Triffid – has come to mean any freakish and large plant. The Triffids kill humans by stinging, and then slowly eat them. Worse – they can walk.

YOU WON'T BELIEVE IT BUT...
Most carnivorous plants grow in poor or hostile conditions, which is why they have developed the ability to get nutrients from insects.

CHUTE TO SAFETY
Frenchman Jean Pierre Blanchard is believed to be the first person to use a parachute in an emergency. In 1793, he claimed the device saved his life after jumping from an exploding hot air balloon.

YOU WON'T BELIEVE IT BUT...
A bicycle made in 1817 by German Baron Karl Drais didn't have any pedals – you had to push it along yourself.

NASA IS ALREADY PLANNING A SYSTEM TO CONTROL SKY TRAFFIC FOR FLYING CARS

FASTER THAN A SPEEDING BULLET
The Japanese 'bullet train' first opened in 1964 and was originally able to travel at around 130mph/209kph. Thanks to advances in design, the trains now travel at over 180mph/290kph.

THE FIRST HELICOPTER
In 1907, Paul Cornu, a French bicycle-maker carried a man into the air for 40 seconds in the world's first manned helicopter flight. However, the flying machine had to be held by four men holding sticks to keep it stable.

MONSTER PLANE
The world's largest aircraft is the An-225 Mriya, a Ukrainian military transport. It weighs 1.3 million lbs/600,000kg, more than 170 adult elephants. Its wings are so large that 40 tall men could lie end to end across them. Once in the air, it can travel at 530mph/850kph.

PEDAL POWER
Greek cycle champion Kanellos Kanellopoulos made the longest man-powered flight in April 1988, when he flew almost 120km/75 miles across the Aegean sea. The flight took four hours, during which he had to keep pedalling to stay in the air.

A BOEING 747 PASSENGER JET IS HELD TOGETHER BY AROUND THREE MILLION RIVETS

YOU WON'T BELIEVE IT BUT...
A Mercedes car, built in 1957, drove almost 2 million mi/3.2 million km in 21 years.

IN THE 1930s PEOPLE USED TO TRAVEL IN GIANT BALLOONS CALLED ZEPPELINS, FULL OF EXPLOSIVE GAS

SAFETY FIRST
In the early days of the car, a man walked in front waving a flag to warn people out of the way. The first pedestrian killed by a car on a public road is believed to be Bridget Driscoll, who was run over in London in 1896. The car was traveling at just 4mph/6.5kph.

YOU WON'T BELIEVE IT BUT...
For a time, early Ford cars were only available in black, had two forward gears and one reverse gear.

A LOT OF HOT AIR
Hot air balloons fly because the air inside them is heated by a burner. Hot air rises and so the balloon, and anyone in the basket, is carried into the sky. There is no way to steer, but the balloon can go up and down by raising or lowering the heat.

PENNY FOR YOUR BIKE?
The penny-farthing was one of the first commercial bicycles, and was almost as tall as an adult. Its name refers to the front wheel being much larger than the back, like the penny and farthing coins used in England at the time.

IS IT A PLANE, OR A HOVERCRAFT?
Hovercrafts can travel over land or sea, thanks to a large cushion of air underneath the vehicle that means that it floats above the surface it is traveling over. Because of this, hovercraft drivers are actually trained as pilots.

LONG RIDE HOME
A Californian mechanic has built a limousine that is 100ft/30m long – that's the equivalent of five giraffes lying end to end. If you were lucky enough to be a passenger you could take a dip in its swimming pool – complete with diving board.

ARE CARS ELECTRIC?
Modern scientists are trying to find fuels that cause less pollution, but did you know that most of the earliest motor vehicles were powered by electricity or steam, and it wasn't until 1910 that the petrol engine became so popular?

HARRY'S MAGIC
JK Rowling came up with the idea for Harry Potter while stuck on a train for four hours. She wrote a lot of the first book in a café in Edinburgh. The seven-book series has now sold over 300 million copies around the world, and has been translated into 63 languages.

PLATFORM 9¾

KING OF HORROR
Stephen King is one of the world's best-selling writers. His stories usually involve monsters, ghosts and fantasy. He has published more than 50 books, and around 40 short stories. Many of his stories have been turned into films, such as *The Shining* and *The Shawshank Redemption*.

YOU WON'T BELIEVE IT BUT...
Detective author Arthur Conan Doyle wrote a novel called *The Lost World* in which dinosaurs are found living in modern times.

SOME BOOKS LET YOU TURN TO DIFFERENT PAGES TO CHOOSE THE WAY THE STORY ENDS

FACTORY FACT
Charles Dickens was one of Victorian England's most celebrated authors but he started out in life working in a factory as a child.

BOND, JAMES BOND
The character of James Bond comes from a series of books by Ian Fleming. The famous James Bond films are often very different to the original stories. Fleming worked in military intelligence during World War Two, so his spy stories were based on actual experience.

YOU WON'T BELIEVE IT BUT...
Mary Shelley wrote her most famous book, *Frankenstein*, as her entry to a ghost story competition set by Lord Byron.

IN RUSSIA, WINNIE THE POOH IS CALLED VINNIE POOKH

TALES OF OZ
The film *Wizard of Oz* was based on a book, and was just one of 14 adventures in Oz written by Frank Baum. The land of Oz was so popular that even after his death in 1919, other writers set their stories in the same world after Baum's wife, Maud, gave her permission for the series to continue.

YOU WON'T BELIEVE IT BUT...
The fantasy story *Eragon*, in which a young hero becomes a Dragon Rider, was written by Christopher Paolini, who was just 15 when he started writing.

THE LORD OF THE RINGS

JRR Tolkien was a professor at Oxford University who was very fond of the English language and mythology. He wrote books telling stories from a huge and complex fantasy world called Middle-earth. *The Lord of the Rings* is his most famous, and it took him 12 years to write.

FAMOUS FAIRY TALES

During the 1800s, Hans Christian Andersen wrote many classic fairy tales and children's stories, which at first he regarded as being 'bagatelle' – unimportant and insignificant. He nearly stopped writing them altogether, but came to believe that fairy tales were a form of poetry. His best-known stories include *Thumbelina*, *The Emperor's New Clothes* and *The Little Mermaid*.

THE GREATEST STORYTELLERS OF ALL TIME?

During the 19th century, Jacob and Wilhelm Grimm were two German brothers who collected and retold popular stories known as folk tales, including famous scary tales such as *Hansel and Gretel*, *Little Red Riding Hood* and *Rapunzel*. Their stories inspired Walt Disney, who went on to make the animated classics based on their stories, *Snow White and the Seven Dwarves* and *Cinderella*.

TIME AND SPACE

HG Wells is often referred to as one of the first science fiction authors. His stories included ideas like space travel many decades before they were possible. He also used aliens and time travel to make people think about how modern society behaved.

SOME AUTHORS USE A FAKE NAME CALLED A PSEUDONYM, OR PEN NAME, WHEN WRITING

AUTHOR AND ARTIST

Victor Hugo was a famous 19th century French author who wrote the classic *The Hunchback of Notre Dame*, which tells the story of a deformed bell-ringer who falls in love with a gypsy girl and rescues her. When not writing, Hugo was a keen artist and produced 4,000 drawings in his lifetime.

WHERE'S ALICE?

Lewis Carroll was the pen name used by the 19th century writer Charles Dodgson. He made up stories for a girl called Alice, who was the daughter of one of his friends. She begged him to write them down, and the result was the beloved children's book *Alice in Wonderland*.

YOU WON'T BELIEVE IT BUT...

Daniel Radcliffe, the actor who plays Harry Potter in the films, had to read all the books to go on file to find out how they ended.

THE FIRST ICE CREAM

The Chinese invented ice cream around 750 CE, hundreds of years before it came to Europe. They would mix buffalo, cow and goat milk, and then flavor it with camphor, an insect repellent.

THE CHINESE HAVE USED ACUPUNCTURE FOR OVER 2,000 YEARS

CHINA'S REAL NAME

Chinese people call their country Zhong Guo, or 'middle kingdom'. The name comes from the ancient Chinese belief that theirs was a civilized country in the center of a ring of undeveloped countries.

YOU WON'T BELIEVE IT BUT...

China has over 500 million pigs – almost one for every two people. Unsurprisingly, over half the pork in the world is eaten there.

STRINGS ATTACHED

Chinese coins had holes in the middle and would be kept on pieces of string. Because these strings were heavy to carry, merchants started to use paper exchange certificates to pay for their goods. This is where the idea of paper money originated.

MONGOL INVASION

Genghis Khan was a fearsome warrior who united scattered wandering tribes into the Mongol Empire. His grandson, Kublai Khan, led the Mongols to invade China to the south and took control of large parts of the country and central Asia in the 13th century.

YOU WON'T BELIEVE IT BUT...

In Chinese mythology, the dragon is considered to control the power of water, rather than the power of fire.

GOING OUT IN STYLE

China's first emperor, Qin Shi Huang (246-221 BCE) spent much of his reign overseeing the building of his tomb. It took 700,000 people nearly 40 years to build the underground mausoleum, which is around 23 sq mi/60 sq km in size. When it was rediscovered by accident in 1974, it contained over 8,000 life-sized soldier statues.

PEOPLE'S PIONEERS
Ancient China gave the world many exotic and important inventions that had never been seen before in the West. The Chinese invented paper and printing, the compass, umbrellas, porcelain and the game of chess.

EVERYBODY'S TALKING
Over 200 different languages are spoken in China, but the official language is Mandarin – the world's most popular language, with over a billion people round the world using it as their first language.

WHEN LIU LONG BECAME EMPEROR OF CHINA IN 105 CE, HE WAS THREE MONTHS OLD

WHO WAS CONFUCIUS?
Confucius was one of the most important thinkers in Chinese history. Over six million people still worship him. Confucianism has no god, just a set of teachings about how to lead a good life. In Taiwan, Confucius' birthday (September 28) used to be celebrated by sharing the hair of a sacrificial cow. It was believed that receiving the hair would make you smarter.

YOU WON'T BELIEVE IT BUT...
Emperor Qin Shi Huang was so scared of being assassinated that legend has it that he slept in a different palace every night.

THE CHILD EMPEROR
In 1848, Emperor Guangxu was imprisoned by his aunt, the Empress Dowager, who then took charge of the country. He died the day before her in 1908. She had chosen her three-year-old nephew Pu Yi as China's new emperor, leaving a tiny toddler running the country.

GREAT WALL OF CHINA
In around 214 BCE, Qin Shi Huang ordered the building of a huge wall to protect China from invasion. The Great Wall of China was 4200mi/6700km long, 30ft/9m high and took 10 years to build.

YOU WON'T BELIEVE IT BUT...
More than a million people helped build the Grand Canal, an artificial waterway that runs south from Beijing for over 1,000mi/1,700km.

THE FIRST KNOWN STORY OF CINDERELLA COMES FROM NINTH CENTURY CHINA

THE DIVIDING LINE
China and India have never agreed the border between their two countries. The area called Arunachal Pradesh is run by India, but China claims it belongs to them. In May 2007, some Indian officials from the area applied for permission to visit China, but were told they didn't need it because they were already considered to be Chinese.

EXPLOSIVE ATMOSPHERE

Since the Earth first came into being, volcanoes have played a huge part in creating its atmosphere. There are some who argue that recent eruptions, such as Mount St Helen's in 1980, have blasted gas and ash into the air, contributing to the 'Greenhouse Effect', and also have a haze effect which reduces temperatures.

WORLD WITHOUT ICE

The polar ice caps contain most of the fresh water on the Earth. They are already melting, as are the huge glaciers in the world's mountain ranges. This is pouring into the oceans, causing the sea level to rise and threatening some life on land.

YOU WON'T BELIEVE IT BUT...

The ice caps melting won't just cause a sea level rise – the ice reflects 80 percent of the Sun's heat back into space. Without them, global warming will get faster.

MANY SPECIES OF JUNGLE FROG HAVE ALREADY DIED OUT DUE TO GLOBAL WARMING

IS IT ME, OR IS IT HOT IN HERE?

The 'Greenhouse Effect' is the name given to explain why we think the Earth is getting hotter. 'Greenhouse gases' like methane, carbon dioxide and carbon monoxide trap the Sun's rays on Earth and don't let them escape back out to space.

HEAT IS ON

An increase of 3.6°F/2°C in temperature will be enough to have a bad effect. Droughts will ravage parts of the world and deserts will get bigger. Also, complicated eco-systems in tropical places such as the Amazon rainforest will start to fail, and coral reefs, finding the oceans too warm, will die.

YOU WON'T BELIEVE IT BUT...

Over its lifetime, one tree can absorb one ton of global warming-causing carbon dioxide.

YOU WON'T BELIEVE IT BUT...

The last time the Earth was 10.8°F/6°C hotter than today was 251 million years ago, and then 90 percent of all life on Earth became extinct.

UP TO A THIRD OF THE WORLD'S CARBON DIOXIDE COMES F...

DIM AND DIMMER
Global dimming is a theory held by scientists that says, while greenhouse gases have been causing global warming, other factors have been lowering the temperature. These include volcanic ash and gases from aerosols that put a hole in the ozone layer. Without this, the Earth might be even hotter.

COULD IT BE THE SUN?
Scientists know the Sun sometimes goes through periods when it is hotter than usual, which has caused global warming in the past. However, if the Sun were currently going through one of these phases, the upper atmosphere would also be warmer. It isn't.

IF THE ICE AT THE NORTH POLE MELTS, POLAR BEARS WILL BECOME EXTINCT IN THE WILD

IT'S GETTING HOTTER
A rise of 5.4–7.2°F/3–4°C in temperature will be terrible – most of the US will be a desert. Because the sea will have risen so much, many low-lying countries will disappear under water.

HOW HOT IS IT GOING TO GET?
No one knows. Scientists think it could be 2–11.5°F/1.1–6.4°C hotter in 100 years, depending on whether we stop producing greenhouse gases. Most scientists agree that, even if we stop producing greenhouse gases now, it's too late to stop the temperature going up by 1.8°F/1°C.

IS THERE HOPE?
Environmental groups are already pressuring governments to lower greenhouse gas emissions. Fossil fuels are one of the worst offenders and we can all help by cutting down. Walk instead of driving, buy food locally and switch off electric lights when you're not using them.

TO STOP A 3.6°F/2°C INCREASE IN THE EARTH'S TEMPERATURE, WE NEED TO CUT OUR GREENHOUSE GAS OUTPUT BY 80 PERCENT BY 2050

SHIFTING SEAS
Our planet is constantly changing. Since the glaciers started to melt, towards the end of the last Ice Age 18,000 years ago, the oceans have risen by 430ft/130m. The difference between this and recent rises in sea level is that now it's happening more quickly.

COW CONTRIBUTION
Cows may be a contributor to global warming. When they break wind, they give off methane, which traps 23 times the heat that carbon dioxide does. Experts believe that the world's 1.5 billion cows may be responsible for up to 18 percent of the planet's greenhouse gas problems.

IT IS AGAINST THE LAW TO KISS ON A RAILWAY IN FRANCE

THE HUMAN SPACE
According to recent estimates, there are 6,602,224,175 people in the world – so they need a lot of room. If all of these people were to hold hands and form a line, it would wrap around the entire planet over 200 times, or reach to the Moon and back more than 12 times.

YOU WON'T BELIEVE IT BUT...
It's not unusual for countries to change their name. For instance, Persia became Iran, and Siam is now called Thailand.

ALBION IS THE OLDEST KNOWN NAME FOR ENGLAND

LOVE   JOY   PEACE

HOW MUCH LAND DO YOU USE?
Your global footprint is the amount of workable land required to sustain your lifestyle. In America, the average person uses up resources equal to over 24 acres (9 hectares) of land. In a less developed country like Mozambique in Africa, people use just 1.5 acres (0.6 hectares).

NOW YOU'RE TALKING
There are nearly 7,000 languages spoken around the world, of which over 2,000 are from Asia. Papua New Guinea, despite only having four million citizens, has over 800 languages. Amazingly, over 4,000 of the world's languages can only be spoken, not written.

YOU WON'T BELIEVE IT BUT...
Since 1990, around 30 new countries have been created. Most of them used to be part of the USSR or Yugoslavia.

A TIME FOR PEACE
The 20th century saw over 150 wars between countries. However, some of the countries that have been involved in the most wars are now among the most peaceful – European countries such as England, France and Spain spent hundreds of years fighting each other before making peace.

WORLD'S WEALTHIEST
The country with the highest income per person is Luxembourg, a tiny European country with only one city. People in Luxembourg have an average income of $66,000/£33,000 each.

THE COUNTRY THAT'S SMALLER THAN A TOWN
At less than one square mile, Vatican City, the home of the Catholic Church, is officially the world's smallest country. The whole of Vatican City could fit into Russia, the world's largest country, nearly 40 million times over.

THIS LAND IS MY LAND
In 1967, former Army Major and radio DJ, Paddy Roy Bates, settled on an abandoned Navy platform off the coast of England and declared that it was his own country. Calling it Sealand, he made himself a prince and even went on to produce his own stamps and coins. The 'country' still exists today.

SEEN IT ALL
In 2003, Charles Veley, from San Francisco, claimed to have become the world's most traveled man. In just a few years, he spent over $1 million/ £500,000 visiting more than 90 percent of the world's countries – 618 in all. That means he's seen more of the planet than some of history's greatest explorers.

CAN YOU CHANGE A MILLION DOLLAR NOTE?
There are around 200 currencies in use in the world today, with some countries accepting several different kinds of money.

YOU WON'T BELIEVE IT BUT...
Because an ice shelf collasped due to global warming, a new island has appeared near Greenland. Scientists have called it Warming Island.

TV SPIN-OFF
The country suffix of the tiny island of Tuvalu's internet domain name is .tv – which it uses to make money. In 2000, the country signed a deal with a company called DotTV to sell the domain name to TV stations and television production companies around the world, and it expects to make around $100 million/£50 million from the deal. Ironically, Tuvalu itself doesn't have any TV stations of its own.

STUCK IN THE MIDDLE
When a country is completely surrounded by another country, and it is impossible leave without passing through the surrounding nation, it's called an enclave. There are only three enclaves in the world. Vatican City and San Marino are both in Italy, while Lesotho is in South Africa.

THE WORLD'S NEWEST COUNTRY, MONTENEGRO, IN EUROPE, ONLY BECAME INDEPENDENT IN 2006

MAKE SOME ROOM
The tiny European state of Monaco is the most crowded country – it has over 32,000 people squeezed into less than one square mile. The world's least densely populated country is Mongolia, in Asia, with just under five people per square mile.

YOU WON'T BELIEVE IT BUT...
The Land of the Midnight Sun is an area in the north of Europe where, in summer, the Sun never sets. This is because it's so far north that it always faces towards the Sun.

ACCORDING TO A 2006 UK SURVEY, DENMARK IS THE WORLD'S HAPPIEST COUNTRY

HOW MUCH TO THE MOON?
America's Moon landings were a terrific success but they were very expensive. Worried about the cost, the US government decided to design a re-usable spacecraft that could land like a plane and, in 1981, the first space shuttle, Columbia, blasted off from Cape Canaveral.

CHALLENGER EXPLODES
A blow to modern space exploration came in 1986 when space shuttle Challenger blew up just after launch. On board were seven astronauts, including Christa McAuliffe, who was to be the first teacher in space.

A NUMBER OF SPACE TOURISM COMPANIES ARE BEING SET UP, SO YOU COULD TAKE TO THE STARS ONE DAY

BEAM ME UP...
The name Enterprise was chosen for the first shuttle after *Star Trek* viewers wrote hundreds of letters to the White House, suggesting that the shuttle be named after Captain Kirk's starship in the famous science fiction TV series.

WHY DID THE SKYLAB FALL?
After just six years in space, the US space station Skylab came to a dramatic end in 1979. Increased solar activity from the Sun caused Skylab to fall out of orbit. It burned up in the atmosphere and pieces landed all over the Earth – one falling part hit and killed a cow. Luckily, nobody was on board.

VIKINGS ON MARS
Two space probes, Viking 1 and 2, visited Mars in 1976. As well as orbiting the planet, they both sent down 'landers' to the surface of the Red Planet. But even though the Vikings landed, they did not find any life any Mars.

THE RUSSIANS PUT THE FIRST LIVING CREATURE INTO SPACE IN 1957 – A DOG CALLED LAIKA

YOU WON'T BELIEVE IT BUT...
The Japanese are the third nation to put an object into orbit around the Moon, but a little later than the US or Russia. It was 1990.

YOU WON'T BELIEVE IT BUT...
Although many astronauts have played musical instruments while in space, their instruments would have been completely silent outside the spaceship because there is no atmosphere for sound to travel through.

PLANETARY PICS
It took seven years for the Cassini-Huygens mission to reach Saturn. It entered into orbit around Saturn and then sent the Huygens probe off on its own mission. It sent back 350 remarkable photographs before it landed on the surface of Saturn's moon, Titan.

A COMPANY ONCE PROMISED A FREE TACO FOR EVERY AMERICAN, IF A PIECE OF A FALLING SPACE STATION HIT THEIR TARGET IN THE SEA. IT MISSED

YOU WON'T BELIEVE IT BUT...
The space shuttle Columbia exploded re-entering the atmosphere in 2003, returning from its 28th mission. All seven crew perished.

IS THERE ANYBODY THERE?
One of the great unanswered questions of space exploration is whether we will find life on other worlds and, if we do, whether it will be intelligent. Scientists argue that our universe is so big that there must be someone – or something – out there.

VOYAGER FAR AWAY
Space exploration isn't just about astronauts. Most of what we know about space comes from unmanned probes. Voyager 1 visited Jupiter and Saturn after launch in 1997, before leaving our Solar System forever. It is the furthest human-made object from the Earth – 9.3 billion mi/ 15 billion km from the Sun and counting.

LOST IN SPACE?
A Russian cosmonaut Valeri Polyakov holds the record for spending the most continuous time in space. He sat staring out the window of the Soviet Union's Mir space station for nearly 438 days – that's over a year.

YOU WON'T BELIEVE IT BUT...
During his 438 days in space, Russian cosmonaut Polyakov orbited the Earth over 7,000 times and traveled 402 million mi/ 250 million km.

AT ITS CURRENT DISTANCE, SIGNALS FROM VOYAGER 1 TAKE 13 HOURS TO REACH EARTH

THE $20 MILLION TICKET
In 2001, American Dennis Tito became the first space tourist when he paid Russian company MirCorp to fly him up to the Soyuz Space Station. Several other tourists have followed. Tickets are available – at $20/£10 million. Despite the price, MirCorp is fully booked until 2009.

AFTER THE MOON, WHERE?
The space shuttle program will end by 2010, NASA says. It will be replaced by Orion, a spacecraft currently being developed, which will carry a crew of six astronauts. The plan is to put people back on the Moon and then, eventually, to head for Mars.

NATURALLY HOT
Although Reykjavik in Iceland has a cold climate, heating your home is surprisingly cheap – because of underground hot springs. For generations, Icelanders used surface springs to provide hot water for baths and laundry, but in about 1430 they developed a system for harnessing the underground springs. Today, around 90 percent of the population has geothermal heating.

PEOPLE IN FINLAND, NORTHERN EUROPE, MAKE A TYPE OF IGLOO

THAT YURT
The nomadic tribes of Mongolia have perfected the art of tent dwelling with the yurt. These can be huge and consist of a circular frame covered in about 30 sheep fleeces. It is believed that Genghis Khan had many yurts (known as 'gers' in Mongolia) mounted on carts, each pulled by 22 bulls.

DID YOU KNIT THAT YOURSELF?
The Uros tribe are descendants of an ancient people who live on Lake Titicaca in Peru, South America, the highest navigable lake in the world. They have made their home on a huge floating island they made by weaving reeds together.

YOU WON'T BELIEVE IT BUT...
In La Paz, Bolivia, the world's highest capital city, the air is so thin that there's not even enough oxygen to feed fires.

TALES FROM THE TREE HOUSE
Have you ever wanted to live in a tree house? The Korowai and Kombai people who live in the jungles of Papua, Indonesia, do just that. Two or three families share a treetop hut, which is built at a height of 26–164ft/8–50m. The huts let them escape from heat, flooding – and from other tribes.

THE MOST EXPENSIVE HOUSE EVER IS A MONTANA MANSION THAT COST $155/£77 MILLION IN 2007

MOVE TO MARS
There are orbiting space stations that are home to astronauts and, perhaps one day, we will join them in space – there are plans to establish permanent colonies on the Moon and, one day, Mars and beyond.

YOU WON'T BELIEVE THIS BUT...
If you want to get away from it all then consider buying your own private island – depending on how big and where the island is, prices can range from $200,000/£100,000 to $40/£20 million.

PREDICTING THE FUTURE
In 1957, the Monsanto House of the Future opened at Disneyland in California. It was intended to showcase objects that homes would have in decades to come. Some predictions were correct – we do use microwave ovens, electric toothbrushes and plastic chairs. Others, like the nuclear-powered refrigerator, were not quite so accurate.

YOU WON'T BELIEVE IT BUT...
Shanghai's Huangpu River may soon be home to the world's first modern floating city – dreamed up by Dutch designers.

WIGWAM OR TEEPEE?
Aren't they the same thing? No. A teepee is a cone-shaped tent made from animal skins draped over 10 or 20 saplings and used as a home by some Native American tribes. Wigwams were also made by Native Americans, but were dome-shaped.

YOUR HOME IN A BOX
Between 1908 and 1940, you could mail order a do-it-yourself house-building kit. The American Sears catalogue offered a total of 447 different varieties to suit all budgets and tastes – from mansions to basic holiday cottages. Sears sold more than 10,000 houses and some still survive today.

BUCKINGHAM PALACE HAS 775 ROOMS

GO WITH THE FLOW
Feng Shui is the ancient Chinese concept of arranging space and objects to direct the flow of energy, or 'chi', through a home. If the space is arranged in a certain way, then it can enhance the well-being of those who live there. For instance, mirrors can be used to reflect in a beautiful view from the outside to help bring nature into your home.

IT'S TENT TIME
The fastest home to put up is a Bedouin tent. These nomads, who travel throughout North Africa and the Arabian desert, can assemble one of their enormous tents in just half an hour.

YOU WON'T BELIEVE IT BUT...
British engineers have created a building block made out of waste such as sewage and recycled glass – the blocks are six times stronger than concrete blocks, but are no more expensive to produce.

THE MOST EXPENSIVE CITY TO LIVE IN IS MOSCOW IN RUSSIA

HOW MUCH FOR YOUR TRAILER?
Seven percent of US citizens live in mobile homes, known as trailers. Though these began life as a cheap housing option, some mobile homes in California – where housing is incredibly expensive – have been selling for $1/£0.5 million and more.

UNDERGROUND LIVING
Montreal, Canada, has the world's biggest 'underground city'. Approximately 20mi/32km of tunnels take you between more than 60 apartments, buildings, shops and offices. In downtown Montreal alone, the tunnels connect 80 percent of offices. At least 0.5 million people use the network daily – to escape the city's chilly winters and baking hot summers.

WHY DO I COUGH AND SNEEZE?
Air contains dirt and germs, and coughing and sneezing get rid of these irritants after your mucus has trapped them. Pollen, pepper, dust and cold air can also make you sneeze. It's your body's way of throwing out unwanted guests.

YOU WON'T BELIEVE IT BUT...
At birth, you have over 350 bones in your body, but as an adult you will have 206, because some fuse together.

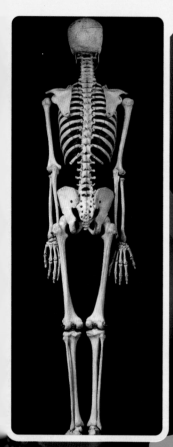

MOST PEOPLE PRODUCE ENOUGH URINE TO FILL 500 BATHS OVER THEIR LIFETIME

BLINK OF AN EYE
Blinking spreads tears across the eye, keeping it clean. Each blink lasts around 0.3 of a second and the average person blinks every 2.8 seconds. In a single day, you blink around 11,500 times – and in a year, you will blink approximately 4.2 million times.

WHAT'S IN BLOOD?
A single drop of blood contains half a drop of plasma, five million red blood cells, 10,000 white blood cells and 100,000 platelets. Platelets help stop bleeding, red cells carry oxygen and carbon dioxide, and white cells help fight germs.

THE HUMAN BODY CONTAINS ABOUT 30 TRILLION RED BLOOD CELLS

YOU WON'T BELIEVE IT BUT...
There is a theory that we yawn because our brain senses we're not taking in enough oxygen, and it sends a message to draw it deep into the lungs.

WHAT IS A HICCUP?
That's when your diaphragm moves in an odd way, perhaps because you ate too quickly, and you suddenly breathe in. The unexpected air hits your vocal cords and takes them by surprise, and they make that funny noise.

WHAT'S IN A HEARTBEAT?
The heart pumps blood around your body through your blood vessels. The blood carries nutrients, water, oxygen and waste to their destinations. Every minute, 1–2gal/4–7l of blood pump through your heart.

SKIN DEEP
The average adult has over 20 sq ft/6 sq m of skin. Your skin is constantly renewing itself – in an average minute, you shed between 30,000 and 40,000 dead skin cells.

TOUGH TO SWALLOW
The average person produces around 4pt/2l of saliva every day, which means we swallow around 105,668pt/50,000l of our own spit during our lifetime.

YOUR LEFT LUNG IS A TOUCH SMALLER YOUR RIGHT. THE SUBSEQUENT SPACE LEAVES ROOM FOR YOUR HEART – WHICH IS RATHER IMPORTANT

BABY BOOMER
In the 238 days before a baby is born, its weight increases around five million times. The average baby weighs around 7.5lbs/3.5kg and measures about 20in/50cm when it is born.

LOVE YOUR HEART
A muscle about the size of your fist, the heart beats about three billion times in a lifetime.

YOU WON'T BELIEVE IT BUT...
You breathe in and out over 20,000 times each day, about 7.3 million times a year.

IT IS ESTIMATED THAT A BABY IS BORN SOMEWHERE ON EARTH EVERY SEVEN SECONDS

WHAT DO LUNGS DO?
Think of a mail sorting office, but handling gas instead of letters. Oxygen is needed, and is delivered around your body after entering through the lungs. Carbon dioxide isn't, so it's picked up by the blood, and then expelled by your lungs when you exhale.

YOU WON'T BELIEVE IT BUT...
If you stretched out all 600 million alveoli (air sacs) in your lungs, they'd cover a tennis court.

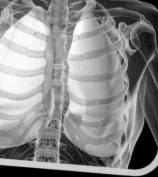

VEINS ROUND THE WORLD
Blood vessels, such as veins, arteries and capillaries, carry blood to and from the heart. If all the blood vessels from a human body were laid end-to-end, they would stretch around the Earth twice.

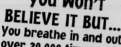

ON STILTS

When a tree falls to the rainforest floor, it destroys many of the plants that grow there. However, the amazing stilt palm grows stilt-like roots and 'walks' away from the debris, moving towards the light.

SPEED OF FIRE

Forest fires can burn at a rate of 10mph/15kph, but some trees with extremely thick bark, such as pines and sequoias, are protected from the worst of its ravages – their bark is scarred by the fire, but the wood remains undamaged.

RARE BREEDS

The mountain rainforests of Central America, known as cloud forests, are home to many rare birds with strange names, including Emerald Toucanets, Three-wattled Bellbirds and the Resplendent Quetzal, a sacred bird to the Mayans and Aztecs.

YOU WON'T BELIEVE IT BUT...

Thousands of years ago, forests covered 48 percent of the Earth's surface, but now half of them are gone and just one-fifth of the Earth's original forests remain completely undisturbed.

STANDING TALL

The Sequoia National Park, Califorinia, is where the first giant Sequoia tree was found. This tree is thought to have orginated 100 million years ago, and some have survived for 2,000-3,000 years. They can grow up to 2ft/60cm each year.

EONS OLD

The strangest forest in the world can be found at Curio Bay in New Zealand, where a fossilized forest stretches 8mi/13km along the coast. The trees stand between 50-100ft/15-30m tall, and are up to 180 million years old.

AROUND ONE PERCENT OF SUNLIGHT REACHES THE AMAZON RAINFOREST FLOOR

MORE THAN HALF OF ALL THE SPECIES ON EARTH LIVE IN THE RAINFORESTS

FAKE FOREST

The bamboo forests of southwest China are known as treeless forests. Bamboo, which grows over 60ft/18m high and provides food for giant pandas, is a grass, not a tree. It is one of the fastest-growing plants on the planet, sometimes growing over 3ft/1m in 24 hours.

YOU WON'T BELIEVE IT BUT...

The Amazon rainforest encompasses 2.8 million sq mi/7 million sq km, about the size of the US mainland.

THERE ARE APPROXIMATELY 1.5 ACRES/0.6 HA OF FOREST FOR EVERY PERSON LIVING ON THE PLANET

A FOREST FIRE IN BORNEO BURNED NON-STOP FOR 10 MONTHS IN 1982-3

SWAMP LOVER
Mangrove forests grow in the swampy land where tropical rivers join the sea. The trees have long, tangled roots that grip the mud to stop them being washed away and other roots that poke out of the water, sucking in oxygen so the trees can breathe.

AMAZON ADVENTURE
In 1744, the French explorer Jean Godin set off through the Amazon rainforest from Peru, leaving behind his pregnant wife Isabela. Unfortunately, Jean got trapped on the other side of the forest and they weren't reunited until 20 years later – when Isabela grew tired of waiting and began her own perilous journey to find him.

AMAZING AMAZONIA
The Amazon rainforest is the biggest forest in the world. Spread over nine countries, it contains more species of animal than anywhere else – it's home to a massive number of insect varieties and thousands of different species of mammals, reptiles and birds. But scientists are still finding more.

DOC TREE
Rainforests provide us with many of our medicinal plants. Cough syrup is made with tree resin; aspirin and quinine, which is used to combat malaria, are made from tree bark. The Rosy Periwinkle plant is used to treat leukemia.

THE HIGH LIFE
The world's highest forest is found in the Andes, over 13,100ft/4,000m above sea level. Its trees have evolved to survive in the harsh conditions, protecting themselves from the biting wind and sun with small, thick leaves that grow waxy hairs.

PUT THAT OUT
Forest fires are a real danger. The worst in recent years was in northeast China in 1987. The blaze lasted for a month, destroying 2.5 million acres/1 million hectares of forest. About 50,000 people were left homeless, 213 killed and 226 injured.

YOU WON'T BELIEVE IT BUT...
Over 60 years, an average tree sheds approximately 3,600lbs/1,630kg of leaves – returning 70 percent of the nutrients to the soil.

ODD JOB
Many American presidents had unusual careers before entering the White House. Jimmy Carter, the 39th president, was a peanut farmer, and Abraham Lincoln, the 16th president, once worked chopping wood and making rails for fences.

YOU WON'T BELIEVE IT BUT...
New York's Statue of Liberty was created by sculptor Auguste Bartholdi and a team of 100 workers in France. They worked every day of the week for nine years, finishing the statue in 1884 and delivering it to the US in 350 pieces.

SOLD OUT
When the USA introduced Prohibition (the banning of alcohol) in 1919, some towns were so convinced that alcohol caused almost all crime, that they sold their jails because they didn't think they would need them any more once the ban came into effect.

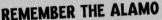

REMEMBER THE ALAMO
In 1836, holed up in a Texan chapel called the Alamo, fewer than 150 US volunteer troops fought off thousands of Mexican soldiers for nearly two weeks. Their victory spurred on the rest of Texas, who went on to defeat the Mexican invaders.

YOU WON'T BELIEVE IT BUT...
Thomas Jefferson's face was originally carved on the left side of George Washington's at Mount Rushmore (as you look at the sculpture). It was moved to the right because of flaws in the rock.

FORMER US PRESIDENT RONALD REAGAN USED TO BE A FILM ACTOR

LOSER AND LOSER
Henry Clay ran for US president five times, in 1824, 1832, 1840, 1844 and 1848, and lost every time. In 1920, Eugene V Debs made a fifth unsuccessful bid for the presidency while serving a 10-year sentence for violation of the Espionage Act. The winner of the losers though is the persistent Norman Thomas, who ran six times and received no electoral votes.

THE NEAR WHITE HOUSE
Before Theodore Roosevelt, the 26th US president, came to office, the White House wasn't even called the White House. It was called the President's Palace, President's House, and the Executive Mansion. Roosevelt officially named it the White House in 1901.

THE US FLAG'S 13 STRIPES REPRESENT THE FIRST 13 COLONIES THAT REBELED AGAINST THE BRITISH

GOLD HUNT
In 1848, news began spreading that gold had been discovered in California. During the Gold Rush that followed, the population of San Francisco grew from under 600 to over 40,000 in just two years. By 1854, over 300,000 people had flooded into California to seek their fortunes.

PET SURPRISE

Theodore Roosevelt, the 26th US president (1901–1909), was famous for his many pets. When Roosevelt's son Archie got the measles, Quentin, another of Roosevelt's sons, thought a visit from the family pony might cheer Archie up. So Quentin put the animal on the White House elevator and brought him upstairs to Archie's room.

BOONE AT THE FRONTIER

Famed frontiersman Daniel Boone never wore the coonskin cap he is usually depicted as wearing. As a Quaker, he wore a wide-brimmed black felt hat, as shown in the portraits painted of him. The reason for the coonskin cap is because in the 1923 film *In The Days Of Daniel Boone*, he is depicted as wearing the cap, and the image stuck.

ON JULY 20, 1969, PRESIDENT RICHARD NIXON WAS THE FIRST TO PLACE A PHONE CALL TO THE MOON

YOU WON'T BELIEVE IT BUT...

There is a tiny spider hidden in the upper-right corner of the artwork on the back of the American dollar bill.

FIRST (REAL) LADY

In 1916, Jeannette Rankin became the first woman ever elected to the House of Representatives. She was elected as a Republican from Montana. Strangely, although she had a vote in Congress, many states did not allow women to vote until a change to the US Constitution in 1920.

GUMMED UP

Chicago is home to the William Wrigley Jr Company, the world's largest chewing-gum manufacturer, which was established there in 1891, originally making household products. One year later, it started offering packs of chewing gum as free gifts with its other products, but the gum soon became more popular than all the other products. Wrigley currently produces 20 million packets of gum a day.

YOU WON'T BELIEVE IT BUT...

US forces used Native American languages as code during the World War Two – they were never broken.

REGULAR MISTAKE

Paul Revere, a Boston silversmith, became famous for his messenger ride during the night of April 18, 1775, during the American Civil War, when he brought news of the advancing British troops to Kentucky by uttering the famous line: "The British are coming!" But he didn't say this – most people in America considered themselves British too at that time so what he actually said was: "The Regulars are coming out!" 'The Regulars' was the name for the King's army.

FRIES TO CHIPS

The potato chip was invented in 1853 by George Crum, a chef in New York. French fries were popular at the restaurant where he worked, but one day a diner complained that the fries were too thick. Crum made a thinner batch but the customer was still unsatisfied, so he finally made fries that were too thin to eat with a fork, hoping to annoy the fussy customer. However, the customer was happy – and potato chips were invented.

THE CURRENT POPULATION OF THE US IS ESTIMATED AT OVER 300 MILLION

YUMMY GUM
At the end of the rainy season, the African Senegal Gum Acacia oozes sap, which is collected to make a gooey substance called 'Gum Arabic'. This has a wide range of uses, from medicines to treat sore throats, coughs, diarrhea and dysentery through to helping make fireworks and watercolor paint.

AROUND FOUR PERCENT OF ALL PLANT SPECIES ON EARTH ARE MOSSES

YOU WON'T BELIEVE IT BUT...
Some ferns grow amazingly quickly. Azolla, for instance, can double its size in just three days.

THE GRASS IS GREENER
Grass is great at protecting land from harmful erosion. A thick lawn is six times more effective than a wheat field, and four times more effective than a hayfield, at absorbing erosion-causing rainfall. Bermuda Grass has probably saved millions of acres of farmland from erosion – although it was once regarded as a pest.

SLOW STARTER
It takes up to 400 million years for peat moss to become coal. When the moss is covered with sediment and remains undisturbed, all moisture is crushed out and it hardens – turning into lignite, coal's softest form.

DOUBLE DEFENSE
Some plants use poison as a defense, but milkweed's toxicity makes it more likely to be eaten. Found in Canada and North and South America, it is eaten by insects, such as the Monarch butterfly, that have learnt about the effects of the poison. The insect retains a level of toxicity after digesting milkweed and, if birds then eat the insect, the bird will become sick.

YOU WON'T BELIEVE IT BUT...
Sphagnum moss was used for treating wounded soldiers in World War One because of its antiseptic qualities and for its sponge-like ability to soak up blood.

CUNNING DESIGN
Tumbleweeds have a unique way of spreading their seeds in the American desert. Most plants, weeds and grasses rely on birds or the wind to carry their seeds away, but when tumbleweed becomes fully grown, it breaks off at the base and tumbles over and over in the wind – spreading its seeds.

FUR FOR THOUGHT

The Jumping Cholla desert plant is also known as the Teddy Bear Cholla. Its short, furry-looking branches resemble teddy bear limbs. However, this 'fur' is actually made up of spines, which will stick firmly to you, given half a chance. It was the plant's ability to 'jump' at people that inspired its first name.

FOOLING FIRE

Buffalo grass is one of the hardiest varieties of grass. It has evolved to protect itself against flames, because its habitat is susceptible to wildfires caused by lightning strikes. The fires move quickly, destroying everything flammable above earth level – so Buffalo grass keeps safely underground the parts of it that grow.

THERE IS A CALIFORNIAN CREOSOTE BUSH THAT IS ESTIMATED TO BE 12,000 YEARS OLD

YOU WON'T BELIEVE IT BUT...

The front lawn of an average-sized house has the cooling effect of just less than 9 tons/8,165kg of air conditioning.

POWER FOOD

Caribou Moss (or Reindeer Lichen), found in Arctic regions, is a great superfood because it comprises 94 percent carbohydrates. However, only caribou (reindeer) can exploit this, because they have special micro-organisms in their stomach which allow them to digest it. Other animals find the moss too acidic.

NO LOSS FOR MOSS

Mosses can go for long periods of time with very few nutrients – in fact, they generally spend half the year dormant. During the summer months, when there is little rainfall, their metabolism slows to a virtual standstill – and does so again in the winter, when it's too cold for photosynthesis.

HUNDREDS OF YEARS AGO, CARPET MOSS WAS USED IN BEDS TO PROMOTE GOOD-QUALITY SLEEP

YOU WON'T BELIEVE IT BUT...

A 0.4 sq in/2.5 sq cm patch of lawn contains six grass plants – so a typical house lawn will be home to over a million plants.

CLEVER CREOSOTE

For years, the Creosote Bush mystified scientists because of the regularity of spacing between wild bushes. They looked as if they had been planted deliberately. However, researchers have found that the bush's root system is so good at absorbing water that no other plant can grow within a certain radius.

DOUBLE AGENT

The shrub Oleander has been used as a component of medicines for almost 4,000 years. More recently, it has proved useful in the treatment of cancer and heart failure patients. However, in its natural form, Oleander is one of the world's most toxic plants – consuming a single raw leaf could kill you.

MIGHTY AMAZON
Even if the Nile is longer, the Amazon is still a record-holder. As it winds through the rainforest, it gets very deep and wide, and holds the highest volume of water of any river, discharging on average 28 billion gallons/127 billion liters of water into the sea every minute.

YOU WON'T BELIEVE IT BUT...
Lake Superior, the largest freshwater lake in the world, and the largest of the Great Lakes, contains just under 3,000 cu mi/12,000 cu km of water. That's far more than all the other Great Lakes put together.

SO, WHICH IS LONGEST?
There is still disagreement over which is the world's longest river. It is generally agreed that the Nile is the longest at over 4100mi/6600km – that's as long as 132,000 Olympic-sized swimming pools laid end to end. The Amazon is said to be slightly shorter at 4000mi/6400km – but no one can agree where it actually starts.

THAT SINKING FEELING
In 1904, during the Russo-Japanese War, the Russian army was blocked by Lake Baikal. The army needed to get troops and supplies to Siberia quickly and, because the lake had a thick blanket of ice, they decided the ice was thick enough for them to run tracks over it. It wasn't, and the train broke through and sank.

LAKE BIWA, JAPAN, IS HOME TO OVER 50 ANIMAL SPECIES, INCLUDING 38 DIFFERENT MOLLUSKS, THAT ARE FOUND NOWHERE ELSE

FLUSHED AWAY
All lakes have a 'flushing rate'. This is the length of time it takes for the water in the lake to be completely renewed. Water leaves the lake through run-offs, evaporation and drainage. Depending on the lake, new water enters via rainfall, tributaries, rivers and streams or melting ice. Flushing can take a very, very long time though – Lake Superior's flushing rate is between 400 and 500 years.

THE SHALLOWEST LAKE IN THE WORLD IS LAKE RUKWA IN SOUTHWEST TANZANIA – IT'S JUST 23FT/7M DEEP

THE GREATEST LAKES
Lake Superior, Lake Michigan, Lake Huron, Lake Erie and Lake Ontario are referred to as the Great Lakes. These five interconnected North American and Canadian lakes are the biggest group of freshwater lakes in the world, and contain 20 percent of the planet's fresh water – 86.34 quadrillion gallons/22.81 quadrillion liters. That's enough water to cover all of America to a depth of just under 10ft/3m.

YOU WON'T BELIEVE IT BUT...

So much water flows from the Amazon into the ocean, that early sailors could drink fresh water straight from the sea even before they were in sight of land.

SEAL RIDDLE

The Nerpa or Baikal Seal is a unique species of seal that is found only in Russia's Lake Baikal. The seal is so special because it is the only type that lives in fresh water. Scientists still can't work out how the seals originally got into the lake, as it is hundreds of miles from any seas or oceans. The most popular theory is that thousands of years ago, the lake may have been joined to the Arctic Ocean and the seals' ancestors got in through there.

LAKE OR SEA?

The title of the biggest lake in the world is actually a sea – the Caspian Sea. It covers 143,244 sq mi/230,528 sq km and is located between the Russian Federation and Iran. The Caspian is referred to as a sea mainly because, millions of year ago, it was connected to both the Atlantic and Pacific Oceans. Now, its water has only about one-third of the saltiness of most sea water. The largest freshwater lake is Lake Superior, which covers 31,000 sq mi/49,890 sq km.

CAN YOU TOUCH THE BOTTOM?

Lake Baikal in Siberia, Russia, is the deepest and oldest lake in the world. Situated in a rift valley between two tectonic plates, it was formed 25–30 million years ago. At its deepest point, it measures 5,370ft/1,637m – so deep that four Empire State Buildings stacked on top of each other would still not break the surface.

IN THE DRY SEASON, THE AMAZON MEASURES 6.8MI/11KM AT ITS WIDEST POINT

PRESIDENTIAL WATERS

Lyndon B Johnson and Theodore Roosevelt are the only two American presidents to have lakes named after them. Lake Lyndon B Johnson is a man-made reservoir, built in Texas in 1950. Initially called Lake Granite Shoals, its name was changed in 1965. Theodore Roosevelt Lake is also man-made, and is located in Arizona. It was opened in 1911 with a ceremony at which Roosevelt was present.

SWIMMING FOR PEACE

"Swim for peace, friendship and clean water," says Martin Strel, a record-breaking swimmer who likes to swim the lengths of whole rivers. In 2004, he swam the filthy Yangtze to highlight its hideous pollution. He was sick for 10 days afterwards.

COLOSSAL COAST

The overall coastline of the five Great Lakes adds up to 10,900mi/17,549km. This is equal to around 44 percent of the Earth's circumference. In Michigan alone, the coastline adds up to 3,288mi/5,294km. This means that, even though it does not border an ocean, Michigan has more coastline than any state except Alaska.

YOU WON'T BELIEVE IT BUT...

An easy way to remember the names of the five Great Lakes, in west-to-east order, is to memorize the phrase 'Super Man Helps Every One' – Superior, Michigan, Huron, Erie and Ontario.

LAKE BAIKAL CONTAINS ONE-FIFTH OF T

YOU WON'T BELIEVE IT BUT...
The smallest painting is believed to be *The Harvest* by Filipino miniaturist Norris Castillo. Created in the 1970s, it is an oil-on-canvas painting smaller than the average postage stamp.

POP STAR
Andy Warhol, a central figure of the 1960s Pop Art movement, was famed for his colorful paintings of everyday objects. One of his most famous paintings was of a can of Campbell's Tomato Soup.

GOGH, GOING, GONE
Vincent Van Gogh is now one of the world's most famous painters, but was almost unknown during his lifetime. He sold just one painting when he was alive, but his work now attracts many buyers. In 1987, nearly 100 years after his death, one of his paintings, *Irises*, sold at auction for $54/£27 million.

ART WITH A SPLAT
In contrast to traditional painting using a brush and palette, 'action painting' involves laying a canvas on the floor and splattering it with paint. It was popularized in the 1940s by artist Jackson Pollock, who would pour paint on to the canvas and move it around with sticks, trowels and knives, even throwing on sand and broken glass.

CLAUDE MONET PAINTED HIS FAMOUS *WATER LILIES*, DESPITE SUFFERING FROM FAILING EYESIGHT

WHAT'S SHE SMILING ABOUT?
Now on display in the Louvre gallery, Paris, the *Mona Lisa* is probably the most famous painting in the world. It was painted by Leonardo da Vinci in 1506 and has intrigued historians for centuries as they have tried to work out who the woman is, and why she has such a strange smile.

CLAIM TO FAME
Tiziano Vecelli was one of the leading painters in 16th century Venice. Known by a single name, Titian, he was also famous for being the only artist to actually have a color named after him. Titian is a shade of burnt orange-brown and was used in many of the artist's paintings.

YOU WON'T BELIEVE IT BUT...
Pablo Picasso is the only artist to have a car named after him – the Citroen Picasso. Citroen paid Picasso's descendants to use his name, but the deal was criticized by art fans who were worried that Picasso would become more known for the car than for his art.

IT TOOK MICHELANGELO FOUR YEARS TO PAINT THE CEILING OF THE SISTINE CHAPEL

PRICE OF ART
The most money ever paid for a painting is thought to be $140 million/£70 million for *Number 5* by Jackson Pollock. Pollock painted it in 1948, and it was bought by a Mexican called David Martinez in 2006. The exact price has never been confirmed though – indeed, the prices paid for all of the 10 most expensive pieces of art have never been revealed officially.

MONKEY BUSINESS
Congo the chimpanzee was a new artistic sensation who swung onto the art scene in the 1950s. A careful painter, he knew when his paintings were finished and would refuse to work on them again once completed. Famous human artists, Picasso and Miró, both owned some of his masterpieces. Three of his paintings made a total of $26,000/£15,000 when sold in 2005.

IT'S A MAD WORLD
Salvador Dali, a famous surrealist painter of the 20th century, often used optical illusions and other tricks in his work. His best-known painting, *The Persistence of Memory*, features giant melting watches. However, many fake Dalis are thought to exist, as it's believed that during the last years of his life, Dali signed over 40,000 blank sheets of paper.

THERE IS AN ART GALLERY ON THE INTERNET DEDICATED TO PAINTINGS MADE BY ELEPHANTS

BUT IS IT ART?
In the early 1960s, pop artist Roy Lichtenstein took panels from comic books and enlarged them. One of his most popular paintings, *Wham!* – a giant cartoon explosion – was created using stencils with rows of over-sized dots.

YOU WON'T BELIEVE IT BUT...
Pointillism is a style of painting that uses very small dots of color to fool your eyes into seeing a single image.

ART EXPERTS CAN IDENTIFY THE WORK OF AN ARTIST JUST BY LOOKING AT THEIR BRUSH STROKES

YOU WON'T BELIEVE IT BUT...
Escher was a 20th-century artist who specialized in impossible optical illusions. His most famous is a waterfall that flows into itself.

INTERNATIONAL MAN OF MYSTERY
British graffiti artist Banksy is something of a mystery. It is believed that his real name is Robert Banks, but nobody knows for sure. Banksy paints graffiti pictures on buildings and walls all over the world, without telling anyone where or when. His 'art stunts' have included sneaking into the penguin enclosure at London Zoo and painting "We're bored of fish" on the wall.

THE BIG PICTURE
The largest painting ever created on an easel is a huge replica of Vincent Van Gogh's painting *Sunflowers*. It was created by Cameron Cross, a teacher and artist, in 1998 and can still be seen in Altona, Canada. It stands 76.6ft/23.3m tall (more than three times as tall as the tallest giraffe) and was painted on 24 sheets of plywood, fixed together using 17gal/64l of paint.

TINY TALENT
Salvador Dali made several surrealist films that were just as strange as his paintings. In 1929, at the Paris premiere of one of them, *Un Chien Andalou (A Dog From Andalusia)* the director Luis Bunuel, who had co-written the film with Dali, hid behind the screen with stones in his pockets because he was afraid the audience would find the film so confusing that they might attack him.

A LUXURY LOAF?

Before the Industrial Revolution, it was very expensive to produce white bread. Grain-refining had to be done by hand, so white bread was a luxury – most people made do with rough brown. However, brown bread contains both the husk and the inner part of the grain so is far more nutritious.

YOU WON'T BELIEVE IT BUT...

If the total water in an adult's body decreases by 10 percent due to excessive vomiting or diarrhoea, doctors get seriously worried.

THE MOST NUTRITIOUS FRUITS AND VEGETABLES ARE DARKER IN COLOR

YOU WON'T BELIEVE IT BUT...

You could stand on your head and the muscles in your esophagus would still pull food into your stomach.

NO EXCUSE FOR A SWEET TOOTH

If you never ate any sugar again, you would be none the worse – providing you had an otherwise balanced diet. Food probably wouldn't taste as good though. Sugar itself has no nutritional value, and simply provides energy because it is a carbohydrate.

AN ORANGE A DAY

Humans cannot manufacture their own vitamin C. Most animals produce this vitamin in their livers, but primates, humans, guinea pigs and some bats have lost this ability. One of the enzymes needed to synthesize vitamin C is simply not present, so they need to consume vitamin C from external sources.

BRAND NEW BELLY

Your stomach produces a new lining every three days. This is to stop it from digesting itself while it produces the acid necessary for breaking down food. It has to do this pretty quickly because new food and chemicals enter it every day.

THE FOUNTAIN OF LIFE

Water is an incredibly important nutrient – between 50 and 70 percent of an adult body is made up of water. Blood is 80 percent water and even muscles are 70 percent water. Water also cools the body, carries heat out through the surface of the skin via sweat, and lubricates joints and skin.

ALMOST $20/£10 BILLION IS SPENT YEARLY ON DIET PRODUCTS IMITATING FATS AND SUGARS

SUPERFOOD

Eggs are often referred to as 'the perfect food'. They contain all eight of the essential amino acids needed to make protein, which is vital for your body to grow and heal. However, to get your entire necessary protein intake from just eggs, you would need to eat eight every day – which is not recommended.

YOU WON'T BELIEVE IT BUT...
You put more pressure on your spine by laughing and coughing than by walking.

CHOCOLATE CAN HELP PREVENT HEART DISEASE AND CANCER

BAD FAT, GOOD FAT
Fats are split into two different kinds – saturated fats and unsaturated fats. Saturated fats have been linked to heart diseases, while unsaturated fats are better for you. Olive oil, sunflower oil and soybean oil are the lowest in saturated fats – coconut oil is the highest with 92 percent saturated fat.

LITTLE AND OFTEN
Many dieticians believe that we might be better off eating five or six smaller meals a day. When you eat only three, you go without food for four or five hours in between meals. Your body may run out of nutrients, making you hungry enough to eat more than your body can absorb at once.

A CRUNCHY DIET
It is estimated that humans deliberately eat 2,000 different insects – including caterpillars and termites in Africa and grasshoppers and bee larvae in Japan. Many of these are considered delicacies – and they're also good for you, containing more protein, fats and carbohydrates than the same amounts of either fish or beef.

YOU WON'T BELIEVE IT BUT...
Asparagus makes some people's pee smell strange. This change in smell can start as soon as 15 minutes after eating asparagus.

NUTTY ABOUT NUTS
Humans have been eating nuts since history began, because they are extremely healthy, nutritious – and very tasty. Almonds are the most nutritious of all – they have the highest fiber content of any nut or seed and only 10 percent of their fat is saturated.

FABULOUS FRUIT
According to a US Department of Agriculture study, guavas are the world's healthiest fruit, containing five times as much vitamin C as oranges. Believed to originate in Mexico or Brazil, guavas have been cultivated for over 3,000 years and were favorites of both the Aztecs and Incas.

THE SWEET POTATO, OR YAM, IS OFTEN RANKED AS THE MOST NUTRITIOUS VEGETABLE

YOU WON'T BELIEVE IT BUT...
The purest energy source in your body is... fat.

ACCIDENTAL INVENTION

Brothers Dr John Harvey Kellogg and Will Keith Kellogg accidentally left some cooked wheat aside for too long, and it became stale. The wheat was supposed to be turned into a big sheet of dough by feeding it through rollers. They decided to push stale wheat through the rollers anyway, and it broke up into flakes. After tasting them, they decided to market the flakes as a new cereal, Kellogg's Cornflakes, which then became the mainstay of their business.

YOU WON'T BELIEVE IT BUT...

Correction fluid was invented by Bette Nesmith Graham in California in 1951. Typist Bette thought up the idea of correction fluid to cover her mistakes and make her job easier. She made the first batch out of paint, using her kitchen blender.

GUT FEELING

This would certainly make your birthday party go with a bang – the very first balloons weren't made from rubber, but from the entrails of dead animals. Bladders, intestines and stomachs would be pumped full of air or water and used by clowns or given as gifts to children.

THE INVENTOR OF VELCRO GOT THE IDEA FROM PULLING THISTLES OUT OF HIS DOG'S FUR

INVENTIVE EDISON

When famous inventor Thomas Edison died in 1931, he held over 1,000 patents. His most famous creation was the modern light bulb, but he also invented versions of the record player and movie projector.

PLAY IT SAFE

Ohio businessman Garrett Morgan was a man with safety on his mind. In 1916, he hit the national news when his new 'gas mask' helped to save 32 men trapped underground. He was subsequently inundated with orders from fire crews around the country. Morgan went on to invent another life-saving device – the traffic signal.

WIRED

The coat hanger was invented by Albert J Parkhouse in 1903. He worked at the Timberlake Wire and Novelty Company in Michigan, and arrived for work one day to find that all the coathooks were taken. Annoyed, he picked up a piece of wire and twisted it into the shape of a coat hanger, then used it to hang up his coat. His boss, John B Timberlake, saw this and evidently thought it was an excellent idea, as he then patented it. As a result, the Timberlake company made a fortune. Alas, Parkhouse made nothing.

VENDING MACHINES WERE FIRST INTRODUCED IN LONDON IN THE 1880S TO SELL POSTCARDS

YOU WON'T BELIEVE IT BUT...

Chelsea Lanmon of Texas was just eight when she patented her first invention – a diaper with a pocket for a baby wipe.

CALL WAITING

The first cordless mobile phone, made in 1973, weighed more than a bag of flour and could only be used for 35 minutes before it had to be recharged... for 10 hours. Its creator, Dr Martin Cooper, later said he had been inspired by the communicators on *Star Trek*.

ZIP IT UP
The modern zipper was patented in 1917 by Gideon Sundback. He called it his 'separable fastener', but when it was used on a new range of rubber galoshes, it became known as the zipper, and the name stuck.

YOU WON'T BELIEVE IT BUT...
Several inventors have patented their own designs for flying saucers – but none have ever gotten off the ground.

IN SCOTLAND, JOHN DUNLOP MADE THE WORLD'S FIRST PNEUMATIC TIRE IN 1887 – TO MAKE THE RIDE SMOOTHER ON HIS SON'S TRICYCLE

ROYAL FLUSH
In the late 16th century, Sir John Harington created the first modern flushing toilet in England. His customer? None other than Queen Elizabeth I herself. However, archeologists have discovered the remains of flushing toilets that may date back over 3,000 years.

FLYING HIGH
In 1984, Canadian inventor Jean St-Germain patented what he called the 'levitationarium'. It's a room with a large fan fitted in the floor that allows people to levitate. Amazingly, the idea works and 'indoor skydiving' rooms can be found in Europe and America.

BARBIE BELT
Barbie was invented in 1959 by Ruth Handler, the co-owner of the Mattel toy company. The doll has sold so successfully that, if you put all the Barbies ever sold in a line, they would stretch around the world more than seven times.

YOU WON'T BELIEVE IT BUT...
Roller skates were invented in Holland in the 18th century as a way of ice skating on dry land.

THE FIRST-EVER TV REMOTE CONTROL WAS INVENTED IN 1950 BY THE ZENITH ELECTRONICS CORPORATION AND CALLED THE 'LAZY BONES'

DREAM JEAN TEAM
Levi Strauss was a traveling salesman during the Californian gold rush. In 1853, he was having no luck selling his rough canvas as a wagon covering, so he made it into pants. Although he would later use less itchy material, he'd just invented blue jeans.

FROZEN FOOD REVOLUTION
You probably don't think there's anything amazing about frozen food, but in 1923 the idea of keeping fresh meat and vegetables in ice revolutionized the food industry. And the inventor? That would be Clarence Birdseye.

IT'S AMAZING

The Amazon rainforest is swamped with 10ft/3m of rain every year. This creates a hot and humid environment in which plants can thrive. Because of this, the Amazon forest contains over 2,500 kinds of tree and 30,000 different plants. Around one-third of all the Earth's vegetation grows here.

HOLIDAY HIDEAWAY

Machu Picchu, an ancient Incan settlement in the mountains of Peru, is believed to have been built some time in the 1400s. Hidden from view for centuries, it is one of the best-preserved ancient sites in the world. The stones used in its construction were cut with such precision that you cannot fit a knife between them.

YOU WON'T BELIEVE IT BUT...

The Atacama Desert in Chile is one of the driest places in the world – in some parts, no rain has ever fallen.

ISLAND LIFE

The Galapagos is a group of islands about 600mi/965km off the coast of Ecuador. The islands are so isolated that almost all the animals, plants and birds found there exist nowhere else on Earth.

AN AMAZON ICON, THE VITÓRIA-RÉGIA, IS ONE OF THE WORLD'S LARGEST FLOWERS AND CAN GROW MORE THAN 6FT/1.8M IN DIAMETER

YOU WON'T BELIEVE IT BUT...

Bolivia is the highest and most isolated country in South America. Its capital city, La Paz, is the highest city in the world.

THE NOTORIOUS FLESH-EATING PIRANHA USUALLY EATS OTHER FISH AND RARELY ATTACKS HUMAN BEINGS

WHAT A SPLASH

The highest waterfall in the world is the spectacular Angel Falls in Venezuela, which has a total drop of 3,212ft/979m, with the longest single drop 2,648ft/807m. Angel Falls is very difficult to reach and was unknown to Venezuelans until the early 1930s.

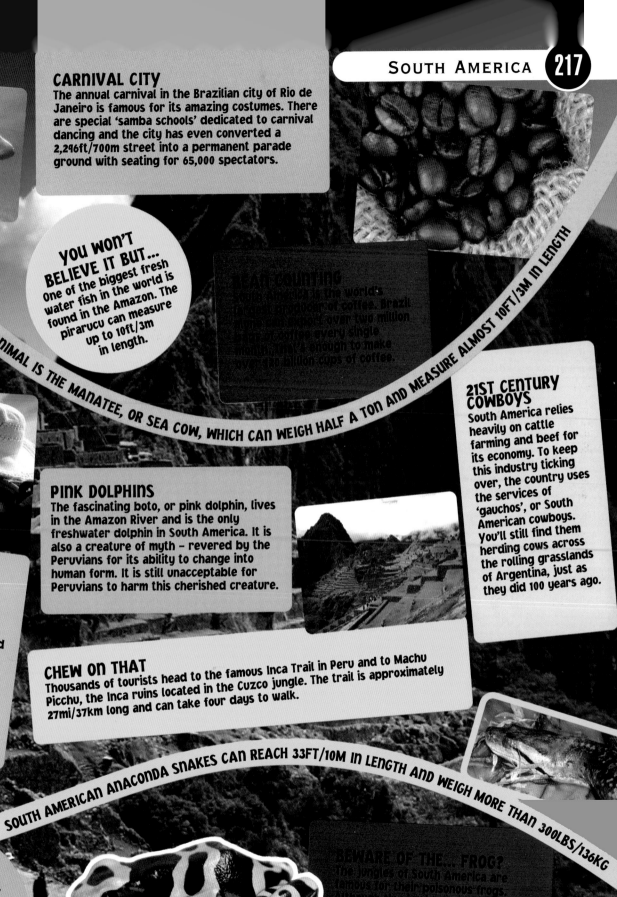

CARNIVAL CITY

The annual carnival in the Brazilian city of Rio de Janeiro is famous for its amazing costumes. There are special 'samba schools' dedicated to carnival dancing and the city has even converted a 2,296ft/700m street into a permanent parade ground with seating for 65,000 spectators.

YOU WON'T BELIEVE IT BUT...

One of the biggest fresh water fish in the world is found in the Amazon. The pirarucu can measure up to 10ft/3m in length.

BEAN COUNTING

South America is the world's largest producer of coffee. Brazil alone can export over two million bags of coffee every single month. That's enough to make over 130 billion cups of coffee.

THE AMAZON'S LARGEST ANIMAL IS THE MANATEE, OR SEA COW, WHICH CAN WEIGH HALF A TON AND MEASURE ALMOST 10FT/3M IN LENGTH

21ST CENTURY COWBOYS

South America relies heavily on cattle farming and beef for its economy. To keep this industry ticking over, the country uses the services of 'gauchos', or South American cowboys. You'll still find them herding cows across the rolling grasslands of Argentina, just as they did 100 years ago.

PINK DOLPHINS

The fascinating boto, or pink dolphin, lives in the Amazon River and is the only freshwater dolphin in South America. It is also a creature of myth – revered by the Peruvians for its ability to change into human form. It is still unacceptable for Peruvians to harm this cherished creature.

BIRDS OF PARADISE

Peru is an absolute haven for birds – and birdwatchers. It boasts 1,800 species of birds, the most found in any country, and this includes 120 that are not found anywhere else.

CHEW ON THAT

Thousands of tourists head to the famous Inca Trail in Peru and to Machu Picchu, the Inca ruins located in the Cuzco jungle. The trail is approximately 27mi/37km long and can take four days to walk.

SOUTH AMERICAN ANACONDA SNAKES CAN REACH 33FT/10M IN LENGTH AND WEIGH MORE THAN 300LBS/136KG

YOU WON'T BELIEVE IT BUT...

The Amazon River discharges around 40,000gal/151,000l of water into the Atlantic Ocean every second.

BEWARE OF THE... FROG?

The jungles of South America are famous for their poisonous frogs. Although tiny in size – often only a couple of inches long – these brightly colored amphibians ooze a deadly poison from their skin. One frog can produce enough poison to kill 100 adult humans.

SMART OCTOPUSES
Octopuses are curious and intelligent creatures. Experiments have shown that they can learn how to do simple tasks, such as taking a cork out of a bottle and unscrewing a jar to reach food. They can also recognize differences between geometrical shapes.

SOME OYSTERS ALTERNATE THEIR GENDER – MALE ONE YEAR, FEMALE THE NEXT

SILENT AND DEADLY
The Funnel Web Spider is widely considered one of the the most dangerous spiders in the world. It gets its name from the shape of the web it spins, it is quite large and is especially notorious because one variety is found in the major Australian city of Sydney.

ONE FINE DAY
Mayflies are small insects, renowned for their short lifespan. A mayfly's life can last from a few hours to just over a day - if they are really lucky. Before they become mayflies the insects spend a year living in water as a naiad - a bit like a caterpillar.

YOU WON'T BELIEVE IT BUT...
More than 95 percent of all animals are invertebrates – that means they don't have a backbone.

YOU WON'T BELIEVE IT BUT...
In Mexico, 1,000 people die from scorpion stings every year. In the United States, that figure drops to four deaths over 11 years.

THERE ARE 52,000 TYPES OF CRUSTACEAN

LOBSTER OVERLOAD
Lobsters used to be so plentiful that Native Americans used them as fertilizer and to bait fishing hooks.

IS IT A STICK?
Just because it looks like a stick, it doesn't mean it is a stick. Stick insects have some of the most remarkable natural camouflage in the animal kingdom. Also, they are the longest insects in the world – sometimes measuring, including legs, over 2ft/0.5m.

BEST DEFENSE
The banana slug found in the Oregon forest releases slime containing anaesthetic as a defense mechanism against predators.

NOT MADE FROM JELLY

Jellyfish have no heart, bones, or brain, and no real eyes. They are more than 95 percent water. The largest kind of jellyfish has a bell (the main body area) that can reach 7.8ft/2.4m across and tentacles that extend over half the length of a soccer field.

OLD-AGE URCHIN

The Red Sea Urchin, a small spiny invertebrate that lives in shallow coastal waters, is among the longest living animals on Earth. They live to be 100 years old, but some lucky creatures will make it to 200 without showing obvious signs of age.

OCTOPUSES HAVE THREE HEARTS

YOU WON'T BELIEVE IT BUT...

The Giant Squid has the biggest eyes of any creature on Earth.

TICK TOCK

Cicadas are large insects with a very good sense of timing. After their eggs hatch, the tiny, ant-like nymphs drop from the trees and burrow underground. After 13 or 17 years, a natural and mysterious 'clock' tells them that it is time to come out – and they all emerge together.

LOTS OF LEGS

The largest kind of centipede lives in the Amazon and Central America – it can reach 12in/30.48cm long and 1in/2.54cm wide. Although most centipedes tend to feed on insects, these giant types have been known to feed on mice, bats and small lizards.

BIG SHELL

The largest snail ever found was nearly 2.5ft/80cm long, with a girth of over 40in/100cm. This trumpet conch was found off the coast of Australia and weighed in at 40lbs/18kg – as much as a small child.

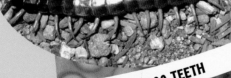

IT'S ESTIMATED THAT A SLUG CAN HAVE UP TO 27,000 TEETH

YOU WON'T BELIEVE IT BUT...

If an octopus is being attacked, it will sometimes detach one of its own arms – this will confuse the predator, allowing the octopus to swim away.

WHAT A BEAUTY

Not all insects are nasty creepy-crawlies. Butterflies are stunningly beautiful and come in all colors, shapes and sizes. By far the biggest is the Queen Alexander Birdwing Butterfly, a native of the rainforests of Papua New Guinea. Its wingspan can be as big as 10in/23cm.

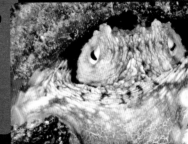

YOU WON'T BELIEVE IT BUT...
The Roman Emperor Heliogabalus once served peas with grains of gold and lentils mixed with precious stones at a banquet.

AS WELL AS MONEY, THE ROMANS USED SALT AND SPICES AS FORMS OF PAYMENT

KEEP OUT
Emperor Hadrian was so worried about the Scottish that he built a wall across the entire width of northern England to stop invasion from the Celts in Scotland. Hadrian's Wall was around 73mi/116km long, 10ft/3m wide and 12ft/3.5m high. Some of it still stands today.

POTTY POWER
During Caligula's four-year reign from 37 to 41 CE, it was a crime to mention a goat in his presence and he also tried to give his horse, Incitatus, one of the most powerful jobs in the Empire.

TWIN TROUBLE
Legend has it that twins Romulus and Remus founded Rome after they were abandoned and raised by a female wolf. Romulus later murdered his brother and named the city after himself.

MOUSE-BRAIN TOOTHPASTE
Having clean teeth was important to the Romans – but instead of minty toothpaste they used powdered mouse-brains, bones and the ashes of dog's teeth mixed with honey.

YOU WON'T BELIEVE IT BUT...
The Circus Maximus stadium seated around 250,000 people, about a quarter of the population of Rome.

TOILET TRADITIONS
The Romans were great engineers and inventors, revolutionizing people's day-to-day life with the invention of aqueducts, sewers, central heating and concrete. They also brought the idea of lavatories that flush to Britain.

PITY THE PIRATES?
Sicilian pirates once captured Julius Caesar, the Roman Emperor, and held him to ransom. Although Caesar charmed his captors by writing poetry for them and playing games, he showed no mercy when he was free. He gathered together some ships, captured the pirates and put them to death.

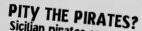

ROMAN REGIONS
The Roman Empire was absolutely huge and spread into Europe, Africa and Asia. At its biggest, the Roman Empire included Britain, France and Spain.

WHAT'S FOR DINNER?
Rich Romans ate extremely well. Meals came in several courses and consisted of boiled meats like mutton, pork and ham, with fruit and pastries for dessert and sweetened wine to drink.

ANCIENT EXTRAVAGANZAS
Roman arenas provided all kinds of spectacular events for the people, from gladiator fighting to floating battleships. Arenas were specially flooded for this watery extravaganza. However, one of the strangest sights was a lion trained to release a live hare from its mouth – unharmed.

YOU WON'T BELIEVE IT BUT...
To cure severe headaches, Roman doctors would drill into your head without any form of painkiller.

FEARSOME FORCE
The Roman Army was extremely ruthless in battles. It numbered around 400,000 men, and soldiers carried daggers, short swords and shields into battle. The equipment weighed up to 60lbs/27kg – about the same as a six-year-old child.

STRONG BELIEFS
The Romans believed in many different gods and goddesses and worshipped them in beautiful temples. They believed that lightning and thunder was Jupiter, the king of the gods, showing his anger.

UP OR DOWN
Romans enjoyed watching gladiator battles in huge stadiums, like the famous Colosseum of Rome. Prisoners and slaves would fight, with the spectators deciding who lived and died with a thumbs up, or a thumbs down.

YOU WON'T BELIEVE IT BUT...
The day before Mount Vesuvius' massive eruption buried Pompeii, the city's inhabitants celebrated the God of Fire's feast day.

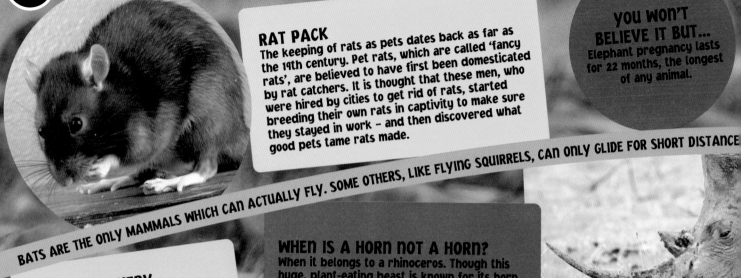

RAT PACK
The keeping of rats as pets dates back as far as the 19th century. Pet rats, which are called 'fancy rats', are believed to have first been domesticated by rat catchers. It is thought that these men, who were hired by cities to get rid of rats, started breeding their own rats in captivity to make sure they stayed in work – and then discovered what good pets tame rats made.

YOU WON'T BELIEVE IT BUT...
Elephant pregnancy lasts for 22 months, the longest of any animal.

BATS ARE THE ONLY MAMMALS WHICH CAN ACTUALLY FLY. SOME OTHERS, LIKE FLYING SQUIRRELS, CAN ONLY GLIDE FOR SHORT DISTANCE

WHEN IS A HORN NOT A HORN?
When it belongs to a rhinoceros. Though this huge, plant-eating beast is known for its horn, it's not made of bone but of thickly matted hair.

BADGER BRAVERY
The African Honey Badger, or Ratel, has been hailed as the 'most fearless' animal in the world. Honey Badgers are so named because of their fondness for breaking into honey bee's nests and eating the honey within. They can withstand the stings of hundreds of bees while doing this.

WANDERING WILDEBEEST
When their grassland home grows dry every May, African Wildebeest migrate to woodlands – all 1.5 million of them at the same time.

NINETY AND COUNTING
There are 40 species of antelope, with the tiniest, the Royal Antelope, only 11in/30cm tall – the same height as a small dog. Found in Africa, the Middle East and Asia, they eat plants and usually have horns which they use like deer – for defense and in battles between males for female antelopes.

TIGERS CAN CONSUME UP TO 90LBS/41KG OF FOOD IN ONE GO – THE EQUIVALENT OF 360 QUARTER-POUNDER BURGERS

YOU WON'T BELIEVE IT BUT...
Deer mark out a territory and stay there all their lives – they have even been known to starve rather than leave.

NO SWEAT
Elephants don't have sweat glands in their skin so the only way they keep cool in the heat is by flapping their big ears. These also make their hearing excellent – they can hear sounds up to 5mi/8km away.

RHINO FAMILY
Rhinoceros mothers are among the most caring in the animal kingdom. The rhino calf is looked after by mum for up to three years. Even after that time, the youngster isn't left to fend for itself – they mix with other youngsters and are looked after by their mothers.

YOU WON'T BELIEVE IT BUT...
'Elephants never forget' isn't just a saying. They have the best memories of any animal.

FLEXIBLE TRUNK
An elephant's trunk is very unusual. It doesn't have any bones in it, but it does have more than 100,000 muscles. Elephants can lift big logs or heavy tree trunks with their trunks. It can serve as a snorkel, a hose, a water bottle or a trumpet.

BIG BILL
The biggest pig ever was Tennessee's 'Big Bill', who weighed 2,551lbs/1,157kg, which is more than a small car – he was so enormous that his belly dragged on the ground. His shoulders were 5ft/1.5m tall and he measured 9ft/2.74m from snout to tail. Bill died in 1933 and his weight has yet to be equaled.

JUMP CRAZY
Springboks, a species of antelope found in southern Africa, like to crazily jump on the spot and can reach heights of up to 13ft/4m. The word comes from the Afrikaans word 'pronk' which means to show off.

TIGONS AND LIGERS
Lions and tigers are so closely related that they can interbreed with each other. When a female lion and a male tiger mate, their offspring is called a Tigon. When a male lion and a female tiger mate, the offspring is called a Liger. Both are very rare and no official figures exist, but Ligers are more common than Tigons.

IN INDIA AND NEPAL, RHINOS CAUSE MORE HUMAN DEATHS THAN ANY OTHER ANIMAL

YOU WON'T BELIEVE IT BUT...
The Bumblebee Bat from Thailand is the smallest mammal in the world. It is 0.4in/11mm long (about the same size as a Bumblebee), weighs about as much as a small coin, and was only discovered in 1973.

COW DELAY
Because cows are regarded as sacred by Hindus, in India cows cause huge hold-ups – if they are sitting on a train track, no one is allowed to shoo the cow away. The train just waits until the cow decides to move on.

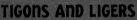

RATS DESTROY AROUND A THIRD OF THE PLANET'S FOOD SUPPLY EVERY YEAR

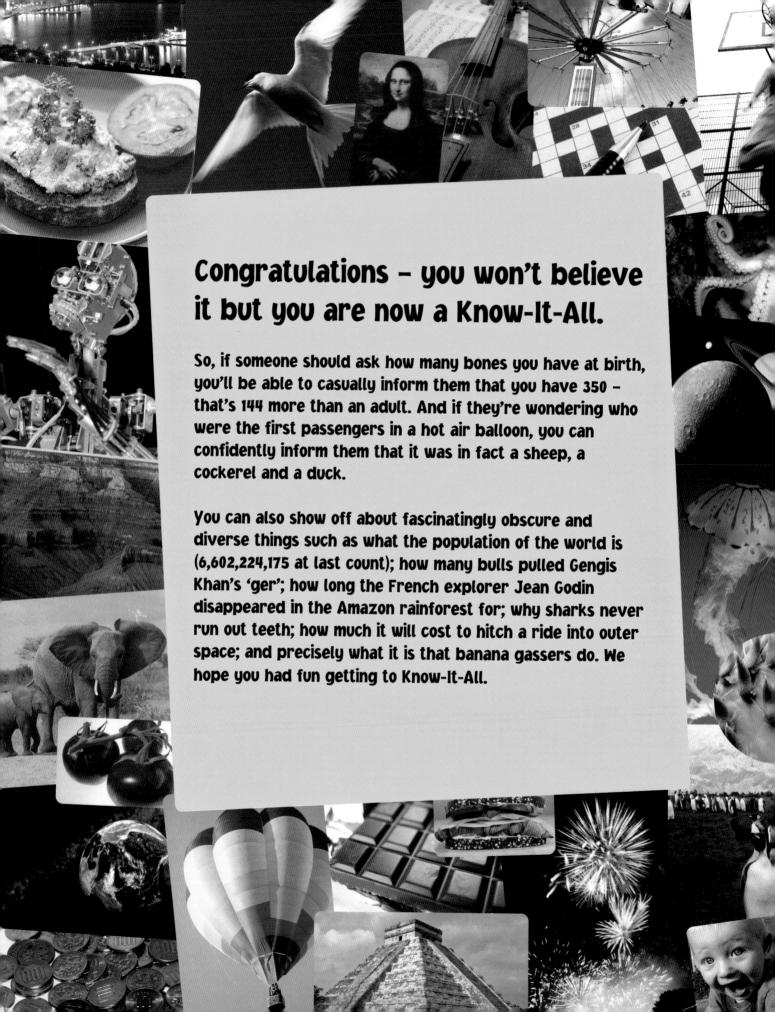

Congratulations – you won't believe it but you are now a Know-It-All.

So, if someone should ask how many bones you have at birth, you'll be able to casually inform them that you have 350 – that's 144 more than an adult. And if they're wondering who were the first passengers in a hot air balloon, you can confidently inform them that it was in fact a sheep, a cockerel and a duck.

You can also show off about fascinatingly obscure and diverse things such as what the population of the world is (6,602,224,175 at last count); how many bulls pulled Gengis Khan's 'ger'; how long the French explorer Jean Godin disappeared in the Amazon rainforest for; why sharks never run out teeth; how much it will cost to hitch a ride into outer space; and precisely what it is that banana gassers do. We hope you had fun getting to Know-It-All.